# A Functional Curriculum for Teaching Students with Disabilities

## THIRD EDITION

# A Functional Curriculum for Teaching Students with Disabilities

## THIRD EDITION

### Volume II
### Nonverbal and Oral Communication

by
Peter J. Valletutti
Michael Bender
Audrey Smith Hoffnung

pro·ed

8700 Shoal Creek Boulevard
Austin, Texas 78757-6897

**pro·ed**

This book is designed in Bookman Light and Serif Gothic.

Production Manager: Alan Grimes
Production Coordinator: Karen Swain
Managing Editor: Tracy Sergo
Art Director: Thomas Barkley
Reprints Buyer: Alicia Woods
Editor: Helen Hyams
Editorial Assistant: Claudette Landry
Editorial Assistant: Martin Wilson

Printed in the United States of America

1  2  3  4  5  6  7  8  9  10    00  99  98  97  96

# Contents

Preface
ix

Acknowledgments
xvii

General Goals
xix

Introduction and Curriculum Overview
1

References
10

 **UNIT 1**
**Nonverbal Communication**
13

General Goals of This Unit
16

Sample Lesson Plan
90

References
93

Suggested Readings
94

Selected Materials/Resources
101

# UNIT 2
## Oral Communication
103

# Preface

*A Functional Curriculum for Teaching Students with Disabilities*, the third edition of *Teaching the Moderately and Severely Handicapped*, is a major revision of the first and second editions. The major alterations made in the present edition have been impelled by several recent phenomena: (a) the changing perceptions of the nature of special education (e.g., inclusion, emphasis on a holistic approach, and the movement toward the development of independent living skills); (b) the identification of new and underserved populations (e.g., infants and toddlers, youth with attention-deficit/hyperactivity disorder); (c) modifications in service delivery (e.g., interagency cooperation and increased parental involvement); (d) recent federal legislation regarding education (e.g., P.L. 99-457, P.L. 101-476, and P.L. 102-119) and the civil and legal rights of persons with disabilities (e.g., Americans with Disabilities Act); and (e) reductions in targeted federal dollars.

The central problem, however, continues to be the nonproductive and, at times, destructive magical thinking engaged in by educators who believe that structural changes alone will automatically result in improvements in education. Unfortunately, many special students continue to receive an education that is not "special" whether they are placed in segregated or inclusive settings. Structural change that does not address the individual and special needs of students with disabilities or attend to the quality of instruction is merely cosmetic, not substantive. We consider this functionally oriented curriculum—if it is implemented by special education teachers, parents, and other trained personnel—to be a critical way of making the education of students with special needs an education that is truly special, regardless of the setting.

The first edition of this text, introduced in the 1970s, coincided with the movement for the educational rights of individuals with disabilities, as mandated by the landmark federal legislation P.L. 94-142. This was also the time when parent and advocacy groups, along with many other professionals, consolidated their efforts based on a collective mission not only to provide special education and related services to all children and youth with handicapping conditions but also to integrate them, whenever appropriate and feasible, in the public schools and the mainstream of society.

Instructional areas and emphases addressed by the first two editions, such as functional academics, interpersonal and social skills, and leisure education, represented a significant departure from the curriculum traditionally being taught in many special education programs. Of equal importance was the attempt to comprehensively and clearly identify appropriate instructional objectives, strategies, and resources that would promote independence, be age appropriate, be suitable for teaching in a natural environment, and be of lifelong functional value.

Much change has occurred since then. Evolving ideological currents have had a significant impact on guiding and determining the content of this new edition of the curriculum series. Several recent developments—the need for interagency cooperation, reduction in targeted federal dollars, emphasis on a holistic approach, the need for a competent core of human service professionals, and the movement toward independent living—have all resulted in major changes in this profession. For example, special education terminology has been modified. The word *handicapped* is no longer used to describe a person who is challenged by a disability. The rejection of the word *handicapped* has come about because the problems experienced by persons with disabilities are viewed as not being within the person him- or herself but rather as arising from social attitudes and perceptions and by society's failure to provide needed programs, services, and resources that will compensate for or minimize the effects of the individual's disability.

This change in terminology has been incorporated in the recent amendments to P.L. 94-142 (the Education for All Handicapped Children Act). These amendments—P.L. 101-476, the Individuals with Disabilities Education Act (IDEA)—reflect the changing concept of disabilities and the role of society in meeting the needs of individuals who have special needs. Of particular importance is the addition of the requirements for transition services, which focus on the successful movement of students from school to community, thus emphasizing the functional skills of independent living and community participation.

Moreover, the preferred descriptor, *disability*, should not be used as a label, as in "He or she is a 'learning disabled' or 'mentally retarded' child." Rather, as a way of accentuating the personhood of the individual, expressions should be used such as "the individual with learning disabilities." In this way, the disability is seen as merely one aspect or part of a total individual, thus minimizing the placement of undue emphasis on the disability by others and by the person him- or herself, while at the same time emphasizing the person in all his or her myriad dimensions.

The concept of the least restrictive environment (LRE) shapes the placement provisions of P.L. 94-142 and its subsequent amendments (P.L. 99-457) as well as P.L. 101-476 and its various state legislative counterparts. LRE led to the implementation of a continuum of educational placements and services—from placement in a regular or mainstreamed class as the least restrictive of possible environments to the most restrictive environment in a nonpublic residential setting. Central to individual placement decisions, however, was the fundamental premise that placement within this continuum should be shaped by the concept central to special education, namely, that the primary determinants are the individualized needs of the students, based on the idiosyncratic nature of their disability.

Although mainstreaming was, at its inception, identified as the least restrictive or the most normalized school environment, it has not always been successfully realized in practice. Too often, needed support services have not been provided to mainstreamed students and their teachers, and inordinate emphasis has been placed on location of service rather than on effective and efficient instructional practices. Teachers assigned to mainstreamed classes, more often than not, were ill-prepared pedagogically and psychologically to teach their students with special educational needs on either an individual or a group basis. Invariably, the curriculum was not modified to reflect the needs of those integrated special students who required instruction in practical knowledge and skills taught from a functional perspective and with a functional purpose. Functional curricular modifications, if they had been assiduously pursued, might have benefited the students without disabilities as well. Typically, the curriculum of the mainstreamed class is test driven and tradition bound, resulting in too much time wasted on the teaching of atomized and irrelevant knowledge.

Recently, however, the concept of mainstreaming has been redefined as part of the inclusion movement or the Regular Education Initiative (REI). The REI maintains that a dual system of regular and special education is unnecessary, inappropriate, and ineffective, and that students with disabilities, regardless of the severity of their disability, can and should be educated in the mainstreamed (regular) setting. This service delivery approach rejects the continuum-of-services concept and views all other alternate placements, except the regular or mainstreamed class, as too restrictive. The collaborative teaching movement emanates from the REI and attempts to respond to some of the problems that resulted from more restrictive placements and misguided mainstreaming. The collaborative approach requires regular and special teachers to work as a team as they plan instruction for and teach all the students (both those with disabilities and those who are not so challenged) in their assigned classes. As the collaborative approach is increasingly being employed, it will be necessary for all teachers, regular and special, to modify the existing regular class curriculum so that it addresses the adaptive behavior needs of all students, whether they have disabilities or not.

This curriculum, although meant primarily for teachers functioning within a special setting, has the additional goal of assisting collaborative teams of teachers as they analyze and modify existing curricula, subsequently design individualized curricula (Individualized Education Programs [IEPs] and Individualized Family Service Plans [IFSPs]), and cooperate with other human service professionals and related human service agencies to meet the life needs of regular as well as special students.

Curricular areas have also changed. For example, vocational education, often associated with skill development and traditional "shop" programs, is now often defined in terms of work readiness, supported employment, and career education. Curricula in the area of leisure education have also gained prominence—a justified development given that free time continues to increase for most people in our culture. The problem of meaningful utilization of leisure time, especially for older people with disabilities, is particularly acute because many are chronically unemployed or underemployed, and therefore not only have expanded free time but also lack the financial resources required for the productive use of that time.

Safety, as a curricular entity, has also gained increasing recognition, especially as more and more programs emphasize community-based education, which entails greater and more numerous threats to safety than the traditional, classroom-based approach. Safety elements should pervade all curricular areas, and therefore have been included in the lesson plans and learning activities of this edition.

Unserved, underserved, and increasing populations of children with disabilities continue to enter educational programs at a rapid rate. Some of this change is a result of recent legislative mandates, such as P.L. 99-457 (Education of the Handicapped Act Amendments). Part H, reauthorized as P.L. 102-119, IDEA Amendments of 1991, mandates the provision of comprehensive early intervention and family services for infants and toddlers and their families (birth through age 2). School programs are also now serving children and youth with disabilities who were not often identified in the 1970s and whose numbers have drastically increased in the 1990s. Examples include children with fetal alcohol syndrome (FAS) and those who have been damaged prenatally (or perinatally) through maternal substance abuse, the AIDS virus, syphilis, or gonorrhea.

Technology continues to play an increasingly important role in educational practice. The instructional use of the personal computer and other instructional technology (including interactive television) is increasing at a rapidly accelerating rate. The use of technology has proven to be of considerable assistance in planning (development of IEPs), in managing teaching (recording of formal and informal assessment data), and in communicating with parents (progress reports and report cards). The personal computer, with its capacity for miniaturization, adaptations, and peripherals, is also moving rapidly to address the habilitative needs of individuals with disabilities. In the near future, as a result of research with neuromuscular feedback and computers, we can expect some individuals who cannot walk—to walk. Other technological advances will make it possible for those who cannot see—to see in some fashion, and those who cannot hear—to hear in some way from implant devices and as yet unknown technologies. The use of assistive technology will also expand as continuing efforts are made to assist students in meeting the demands of an increasingly complex and demanding postindustrial society.

The role of parents (or parent surrogates) is essential to the implementation of this curriculum. Parental participation in decisions regarding placement, IEPs, and needed related services is essential to a holistic approach to educating exceptional children. The parental role in providing pertinent information to teachers should not be minimized, because parents can provide information that is essential for assisting in identifying goals and objectives, establishing educational and programming priorities, and determining areas of interest. Parents have a unique advantage in instructing their children in activities that are best introduced and practiced in the home setting and also in the community. Parents can also serve as effective carryover agents who provide practice sessions and reinforce newly acquired skills as the child performs them within his or her reality contexts.

Because of these various trends and factors, it seems appropriate to now produce a new edition of the curriculum. Teams of teachers, students, parents, clinicians, and other related service staff have been surveyed to find out what needed to be addressed in these three new volumes. Our overriding goal continues to be the presentation of new information and material that will assist teachers, other professionals, and parents in facilitating the functional performance of children and youth with disabilities in the full variety of life situations and contexts. As in past incarnations, the present curriculum assumes that the reader possesses a basic understanding of teaching methods and a fundamental level of expertise in analyzing educational tasks so that they may be used as a framework for evaluating the child's current level of performance and as a means of focusing on specific behaviors requiring remedial or instructional attention. Emphasis continues to be placed on teaching students in reality situations in the home, community, and workplace. Whenever home-based or community-based education is not feasible, teachers must provide realistic classroom simulations that offer students with disabilities opportunities to practice life skills in functional contexts and settings. The past successes of the curriculum have supported our view that reality contexts can be effectively simulated in a classroom setting only if the entire behavior is demonstrated with all its applicable dimensions (psychomotor, affective, and cognitive) expressed as a total, integrated act.

Long-range goals and specific teaching objectives have been identified, in this edition, as "general goals" and "specific objectives" to indicate their relationship to the development and subsequent revisions of the Individualized Education Program (IEP) and the Individualized Family Service Plan (IFSP). Although we have provided readers with suggested activities viewed from an age and grade-level perspective, readers applying the curriculum must appreciate the essential relationship between informal and formal assessment data and the decisions they make as to the relevant goals and objectives to be addressed. Although specific objectives have generally been placed in their developmental sequence, known sequences have been considered only if they make functional sense. Developmental milestones and traditional educational tasks have been deemphasized and eliminated from this curriculum if the identified behavior does not contribute to functional success for the intended population (e.g., drawing a geometric shape or matching wooden blocks of different colors). Furthermore, developmental profiles are less important as children get older, whereas they are central for infants and toddlers.

The curriculum is intended as a guide not only for individuals with disabilities but also for individuals who may be experiencing learning problems but who have not been classified as having a disability. In fact, many high-level goals and suggested activities are included to encourage program implementors not to have restricted or limiting views. There are many nondisabled students and adults, students and adults with mild disabilities, and students and adults with no formally defined disability who are functioning at a lower-than-expected level who would also benefit from the activities in the curriculum. These high-level goals and suggested activities are also meant to guide mainstreamed and collaborating teachers in their modification of regular curricula, which should do much to make inclusion more successful for both the students who have disabilities and those who do not.

As with past editions, this new edition has been designed as a guide to preservice and inservice teachers and other professionals who work directly as service providers to children and adults with disabilities. Parents, surrogates and foster parents, and other family members, as well as service coordinators (case managers), house parents in group homes/apartments or other alternate living arrangements, and counselors in activity centers and workshops should find this curriculum valuable as they interact with and instruct the individuals with whom they work and/or live.

The original curriculum also has had wide acceptance and use as a text for preservice teacher candidates and inservice teachers taking courses in curriculum development and teaching methods in special education at the undergraduate and graduate levels. The current edition has been updated to reflect the present needs of students taking these courses, especially as they interact in diverse practica experiences with previously unserved and underserved populations of individuals with disabilities.

The lists of Selected Materials/Resources attached to each unit is relatively brief because many of the essential materials needed in teaching a functional curriculum are the ordinary materials of life that are invariably found in the home, school, community, and workplace, and because well-designed and well-presented teacher-made materials are usually more appropriate, better focused, and more motivating to students.

The Suggested Readings appended to each unit list not only recent publications but some older, classic materials as well. These classics have been included because they retain their immediacy and appropriateness and thus should not be automatically eliminated from lists of relevant professional literature out of a passion for newness.

This new edition of the curriculum continues to provide information and suggestions that have proven to be of value in the past. The suggested activities provided in this new edition, a direct response to user recommendations and reviews, have been separated into two major categories: Teacher Interventions and Family Interventions. Further, four distinct age/grade levels for each of these interventions have been developed to reflect content deemed appropriate for the following levels: infant and toddler/preschool, primary, intermediate, and secondary. The suggested activities for the infant and toddler/preschool level are meant to meet the functional needs of infants and toddlers (birth through 2 years) and preschool children (3 through 5 years). Additionally, attention needs to be directed to the several alternative settings for teaching children, especially where infants and toddlers are concerned, because they are frequently educated in their own homes and in day-care settings.

Finally, this curriculum does not address all the dimensions of a functional curriculum because to do so is neither practical nor possible. It does not provide all the possible instructional activities that are applicable or would be interesting and motivating to students and adults with disabilities. It does, however, provide a structure and format from which a creative professional can extrapolate additional instructional goals and objectives, design learning activities, and suggest possible responses to the multitude of challenging questions that will arise from the actual implementation of the curriculum.

# Acknowledgments

To all those students, teachers, parents, and support staff who helped us define the objectives of nonverbal and oral communication, and especially to Carol Ann Baglin and Sheréa Makle, who spent unlimited hours on the refinement and editing of this volume.

# General Goals

 ## UNIT 1

I. The student will respond appropriately to the commonly employed gestures of people in his or her environment whether they occur alone or as an integral part of their oral communication.

II. The student will use natural or commonly recognized gestures either alone or in conjunction with speech to communicate his or her needs, wants, interests, and thoughts to others.

III. The student will respond appropriately to the vocal tone and intonational patterns of people in his or her environment whether or not the student comprehends the speaker's verbal message.

IV. The student will use vocal tone patterns (with or without accompanying speech) that communicate his or her feelings to a listener.

V. The student will respond appropriately to the facial expressions of people in his or her environment whether or not the student comprehends the speaker's verbal message.

VI. The student will use facial expressions (with or without accompanying speech) that communicate his or her feelings to a listener.

VII. The student who is unable to communicate through speech or whose speech must be supplemented will use an augmentative or alternative means of communication.

 ## UNIT 2

I. The student will develop the basic visual, motor, auditory, vocal, play, and interactive skills that facilitate the development of oral language during the Preverbal Stage (0–12 months).

II. The student will progress through the One-Word Stage of oral language development (12–18 months).

III. The student will progress through Stages I–V of oral language development (18–48 months).

IV. The student will acquire the oral communication skills that will facilitate successful performance in various learning situations.

V. The student will acquire the oral communication skills that will facilitate successful performance in diverse interpersonal and social interactions.

VI. The student will acquire the oral communication skills that will facilitate successful performance in work situations.

VII. The student will acquire the oral communication skills that will facilitate successful performance in various leisure-time pursuits.

VIII. The student will acquire the oral communication skills that will facilitate successful performance as a member of a household.

IX. The student will acquire the oral communication skills that will facilitate successful performance as a friend and as a member of a family unit.

X. The student will acquire the oral communication skills that will facilitate successful performance as a member of a community.

XI. The student will acquire the oral communication skills that will facilitate successful performance as a consumer of goods and services and as a participant in various financial transactions.

XII. The student will acquire the oral communication skills that will facilitate successful interactions as a traveler within the community.

# Introduction and Curriculum Overview

A primary purpose of special education is to help students with disabilities lead successful and personally fulfilling lives now and in the future. A functional curriculum is designed to prepare students to function as independently as possible in an integrated society (Wheeler, 1987). A broad range of skills, therefore, must be included in the design of a functional curriculum for students with disabilities. It is axiomatic that the more severe the disability, the greater the educational need and challenge, and, thus, the more comprehensive the curriculum.

In addition, the skills needed by individuals with disabilities continue to expand as society becomes more complex. Moreover, with the renewed and increasing emphasis on inclusion and mainstreaming, it is imperative that curricula taught in these settings address the needs of students with disabilities who, given the nature of the traditional curriculum, are less likely to be expected to develop functional skills in these mainstreamed settings. Traditional ways of developing content for students with disabilities, such as through the watering down of the regular curriculum, do not work. If new entrants to the regular education mainstream are to be successfully integrated into the school and community, their programs must be modified in functional, real-life ways. In essence, *life is the curriculum.*

According to Gast and Schuster (1993), "A functional curriculum is a primary *external support* for children with severe disabilities" (p. 471). Gast and Schuster have identified a number of principles that should be observed in the development and implementation of a functional curriculum. These authors believe that the designer/instructor should:

> focus on teaching skills that are chronologically age-appropriate and immediately useful to the learner. Use ecological inventories and compile a community catalog of current and future environments that are important to the students. Define goals based on the prior step. Prioritize goals based on their potential for enhancing independence. Task analyze the skills needed to perform successfully. Conduct a discrepancy analysis to determine what the student can and cannot do. Use principles of applied behavior analysis. Provide instruction in integrated and community settings. (p. 471)

The need for acquiring functional skills has become the cornerstone for most programs involved in teaching special populations. Fortunately, for some mainstreamed students with disabilities, the principles and contents of this approach are increasingly being incorporated into regular educational programs.

# DEFINING THE FUNCTIONAL APPROACH

The functional approach to educating students with or without disabilities is based on a philosophy of education that determines the format and content of a curriculum and that requires an instructional methodology emphasizing the application of knowledge and skills in reality contexts (Bender & Valletutti, 1985; Valletutti & Bender, 1985). Some authorities view this approach as being different from the developmental approach in that its emphasis is on teaching age-appropriate skills that are immediately applicable to diverse life settings (Gast & Schuster, 1993). Patton, Beirne-Smith, and Payne (1990), on the other hand, have posited: "The functional curriculum is a hybrid of the developmental and the behavioral curricula. It attempts to incorporate the best features of the two. Insofar as it emphasizes teaching interrelated classes of behavior and generalization within task classes, it is developmental, but it is behavioral in its emphasis on teaching skills that the infant or child needs now or will need" (p. 298). According to Kirk and Gallagher (1989), "Over the years, from research, common sense, and experience, a philosophy of teaching students with multiple and severe handicaps has evolved. Today our objective is to teach functional age-appropriate skills within the integrated school and nonschool settings, and to base our teaching on the systematic evaluation of students' progress" (p. 467).

Educators using the functional approach identify life skills, specified as instructional goals and objectives, and then seek to facilitate a student's acquisition of these skills. It is adult referenced in that it is a top-down approach, identifying behaviors essential to successful adjustment as a functioning adult rather than having a bottom-up design with its child-oriented focus (Polloway, Patton, Payne, & Payne, 1989). It fosters the development of skills that increase autonomy, as in self-care activities, and encourages constructive codependency, as in cooperative enterprises and mutual problem solving in the home, school, community, and workplace. It endeavors to make the individuals to whom it is applied as successful as possible in meeting their own needs and in satisfying the requirements of living in a community. It also strives to make the individual's life as fulfilling and pleasurable as possible (Cegelka & Greene, 1993).

The functional approach determines the nature of the instructional process. It requires that specified skills be taught in reality contexts. That is, skills are to be taught directly through typical home, school, or community activities, or, if a natural setting is not feasible, indirectly through classroom simulations (Brown, Nietupski, & Hamre-Nietupski, 1976; Polloway et al., 1989).

Conducting an ecological inventory has been suggested as a strategy for generating a functional curriculum that is community referenced. The steps involved in this process include identifying curricular domains (e.g., vocational and leisure), describing present and future environments, prioritizing the activities pertinent to these environments, specifying the skills needed to perform these activities, conducting a discrepancy analysis to determine required skills missing from the student's behavioral repertoire, determining needed adaptations, and, finally, developing a meaningful IEP (Brown et al., 1979).

A functional curriculum identifies *what* is to be taught, whereas the functional approach to instruction determines *how* a skill is to be taught. Whereas a functional curriculum is, in most cases, absolutely essential to instructional programs employed in special classes or special schools, it can also be particularly valuable to teachers of mainstreamed or inclusive classes. These teachers must make functional adaptations to existing curricula if life skills are to be addressed, despite the restrictions imposed by rigid adherence to the subjects traditionally found in school curricula. Teachers, therefore, must analyze the academically driven goals and objectives of traditional curricula and identify their potential practical applications.

# DEVELOPING A FUNCTIONAL CURRICULUM

An analysis of the social roles that people play as children, adolescents, and adults can serve as the foundation for designing a functional curriculum (Bender & Valletutti, 1982; Valletutti & Bender, 1982). Social competency is thus primary in a functional curriculum. "Social competency dimensions are critical to the child's acceptability in the classroom, peer relationships, the efficiency and success of academic efforts, current life adjustment, and future social and vocational success" (Reschly, 1993, p. 232). Closely allied to the concept of a life skills curriculum is the concept of social competence, often referred to as "adaptive behavior." *Adaptive behavior* refers to the individual's effectiveness in meeting the demands and standards of his or her environment based on age and the cultural group to which the individual belongs (Grossman, 1983). According to Drew, Logan, and Hardman (1992), "Adaptive skills are necessary to decrease an individual's dependence on others and increase opportunities for school and community participation" (p. 257). Drew et al. specified that "adaptive skill content areas for school-age retarded children include motor, self-care, social, communication, and functional academic skills" (p. 258).

Curricular models based on the concept of career education emphasize effective participation by the individual in all of life's "occupations." Career education, thus, requires an educational program that starts early in the school career and continues into adulthood (Clark, 1979).

Brolin's (1986) Life-Centered Career Education (LCCE) model identifies 22 major competencies needed for effective functioning in school, family, and community. These skills are divided into three domains: daily living, personal/social, and occupational. Cronin and Patton (1993) have produced a life skills instructional guide for students with special needs. This guide provides information that addresses the importance of life skills instruction and insight as to how to identify major life demands and specific life skills. Professional sources such as these yield a wealth of information on ways of integrating real-life content into the curriculum.

Developers of reality-based curricula, whether identified as functional, life skills, adaptive behavior, or career education, must examine the situations faced by members of society and specify the behaviors expected of them as they function at different stages in their lives. The long-range orientation of education, however, requires that competencies needed by adults be given programming priority.

Functionally oriented curricula must have an adult-outcomes emphasis. This is especially true for those students with disabilities and their nondisabled peers for whom a higher education is neither desired nor appropriate. Adult-outcomes curricula have abandoned their vocational myopia and now deal more comprehensively and realistically with the many elements needed for successful personal and social adjustment in adulthood (Cronin & Gerber, 1982). Students categorized as having diverse learning and behavioral disabilities, as well as students who are at risk for school failure who have not been so classified, are more likely to be stimulated by learning activities that emphasize their present and future problems, needs, and concerns. Regardless of age or grade, students should be prepared for the challenges of life after they graduate or leave school.

If the social-role perspective is accepted, then teachers, parents, counselors, and other trainers must decide which competencies should be included in a curriculum with such a nontraditional approach. This task is not an esoteric or an insurmountable one, however. Through an examination of their own lives and the lives of other adults, educators can easily identify what life skills should be included in a functional curriculum. Moreover, listening and attending to the writings of the students themselves, especially during the adolescent years, will also prove a superb source of functional instructional goals and objectives (Polloway et al., 1989).

The process of selecting the goals and objectives and establishing the functional priorities of a life skills curriculum requires the designer to eliminate those traditional academic tasks that have little or no value. The determinant of inclusion is whether the skill in question is needed or may be needed by the individual now or at some time in the person's future. Patton, Beirne-Smith, and Payne (1990) have suggested that the selection should be governed by an objective's adaptive potential and its direct and frequent application to the individual's environment, the likelihood of its successful acquisition, its potential for improving the quality and level of services available to the individual, and its impact on the reduction of dangerous or harmful behaviors.

Once the functional curriculum has been developed, the student's IEP or IFSP must be formulated based on this general curriculum, with attention devoted to the establishment of instructional priorities. Priorities are determined, in part, on the basis of answers to the following questions:

- Will the acquisition of a skill with less-than-obvious functional relevance lead to the later development of a key functional skill? For example, will it be important to teach an individual to hop and skip because these movements will be incorporated in games, sports, and other leisure activities, such as dancing?

- Is the skill of practical or current value to the individual as he or she functions on a daily basis?

- Will the skill be needed by the individual in the future? A skill that is immediately needed must be assigned greater priority than a skill needed in the future. Age appropriateness is always to be honored whether it applies to the choice of suitable instructional materials or to establishing instructional priorities.

- Has the individual demonstrated an actual need for the development of a particular skill? Teachers, support personnel, and other instructors need to observe the individual to identify the areas in which he or she is experiencing difficulty and utilize these observations in setting programming priorities.

- Has the individual expressed the desire to acquire a specific skill? Students will often ask for needed assistance in acquiring a skill that has psychological importance. These self-identified needs should never be ignored and often will determine educational priorities.

- Do the parents believe that the acquisition of a particular skill will increase their child's adaptive behavior or performance in the home?

- Will the individual's acquisition of a specific skill improve his or her performance in school- and home-related tasks?

- Does the skill have survival value? Clearly, teaching a person how to cross a street safely has greater priority than teaching a youngster to chant or sing a nursery rhyme.

- Will the development of a particular skill facilitate the acquisition of skills pertinent to the goals of other human service professionals who are providing related services? (Valletutti & Dummett, 1992).

On the basis of the responses to these questions, and with essential input from parents and relevant human service professionals, teachers and trainers must develop the student's IFSP or IEP with its stated instructional priorities.

# FUNCTIONALITY AS AN INSTRUCTIONAL PROCESS

In order to teach in a functional way, instructors must ask the questions, "Under what circumstances is this skill applied?" and "Why and when is this skill needed?" The answer to either question determines the functional scenario that structures the instructional plan and process. For example, if the short-term instructional objective is, "The student draws water from the sink," the response to the questions "Under what circumstances . . .?" or "Why and when is this skill needed?" may be, "when washing vegetables in preparing a meal," "when filling ice cube trays," or "when getting water to fill the fish tank." The responses to either of these two questions provide the creative vision out of which the lesson should emerge. The lesson might then involve making a meal for guests in which a salad is prepared and ice cubes are made for the meal's accompanying beverage.

Once the circumstances under which a skill is typically practiced have been identified, teachers, parents, and other instructors, if possible, should provide instructional activities in the skill's usual setting or, at a minimum, in its simulated setting. Whenever the realistic setting for a skill's application is the home, teachers must make the student's parents part of the instructional team by helping them to be effective teachers of their children, assisting them in carrying out functional "homework" assignments, such as doing simple household cleaning and home repairs. Teachers, of course, have primary responsibility for skills that are best developed in the school setting, such as teaching cognitive or academic skills in their functional applications. The community setting is the shared responsibility of both parents and teachers.

Whenever it is not possible to practice a skill in its reality context, learning experiences should be provided in classroom simulations. Instructional materials and equipment in a functional and functioning classroom also must be reality based. Furniture, decorations, appliances, and materials typically found in the home must then be found in the classroom as well. To simulate the community, the school might set up a mock traffic pattern in the gymnasium to practice safely crossing streets, establish a supermarket to practice shopping skills, and assign classroom duties as work tasks that mirror jobs available in the community.

# THE SCOPE OF THE FUNCTIONAL CURRICULUM

A functional curriculum, if it is to meet the needs of students with disabilities, should be formulated in terms of the social roles people are required to play. Suggested instructional activities should be designed to assist students to fill these roles as successfully and productively as possible even when the curriculum is organized around traditional subject areas, and even when it is arranged around skill areas such as vocational, leisure, motor, communication, and interpersonal skills. Included among these roles are the individual as a

- socially competent person who works cooperatively with others for mutually agreed upon goals.
- capable student who learns from others, and, as a helper, assists others to learn.
- contributing member of a family unit.
- successful member of his or her own personal community (e.g., as a neighbor and friend).
- responsible and responsive citizen of the general community.
- skilled consumer of goods and services and participant in financial transactions.
- productive worker.
- skillful participant in diverse leisure-time activities.
- competent traveler who moves about the community while meeting all other social roles.

# DEVELOPING INSTRUCTIONAL PLANS

Instructional plans serve as the blueprint for coordinating and teaching functional skills. In this curriculum, activities are presented in terms of Teacher Interventions and Parent Interventions. Subsumed under these interventions are four age and grade-level designations appropriate to teaching different age groups of children and youth with disabilities: infant and toddler/preschool, primary, intermediate, and secondary.

With its annual goals and their short-term objectives, the curriculum serves as the framework for systematically observing and assessing the student's performance in terms of both process and product. Evaluation occurs as the learner functions on a daily basis in natural settings and as he or she responds to structured and simulated activities. These observations, supplemented by more formally acquired data, aid in selecting what goals and objectives are to be placed, for example, in the student's IEP. Once these decisions are made, lesson planning can commence as follows:

- Lesson planning begins, based on instructional insights acquired from assessment data, with the selection of a priority *annual goal* and its associated *specific objective* from the student's IEP.

- Following this selection, a pertinent *lesson objective* is then constructed. The lesson objective, like the short-term instructional objective, is student oriented and has the dual purpose of structuring the instructional sequence and suggesting the assessment strategy and its performance criterion level. Toward these ends, a lesson objective has three key elements:

  - Clarification of the stimulus situation or conditions: "When given . . ." or "After being shown . . ."

  - Specification of a desired response: "The student will . . ."

  - Establishment of a performance level: "He will do so in four out of five trials" or "She will do so without assistance."

- Next, *materials and equipment* are listed even though a complete list is not really known until the total plan is developed. This segment is placed in the beginning of the plan, however, for ease in reading when the instructor skims the plan immediately prior to its implementation.

- The *motivating activity* is stated. Identifying an appropriate motivating activity may be a challenging task because it is not always easy to identify age-appropriate motivating activities that will capture the attention and encourage the involvement of the different age groups of students with disabilities who are functioning at depressed levels.

- *Instructional procedures* are then enumerated. These are instructor oriented and are sequenced in logical steps arising out of the motivating activity and leading to assessment. The instructional procedure itself is divided into four steps: initiation, guided practice, independent practice, and closure. Evidence that teaching is taking place must be carefully articulated in each of these steps. Demonstrations, assistance, and problem-solving challenges are ways of ensuring that instruction is occurring.

- The *assessment strategy* to be employed is then specified. This procedure should reflect the desired response and performance criteria indicated in the lesson objective. It is instructor oriented and should specify the method to be used in recording observational data.

- At this point, a proposed *follow-up activity or objective* is written to ensure that the sequence of instruction is honored. The hoped-for follow-up activity or objective is composed in positive terms because it can be pursued only if the student successfully meets the plan's lesson objective. If the learner fails to meet the lesson objective, a remedial lesson plan must be written on an ad hoc basis (because it is not possible to predict the reason for failure, especially given that the lesson was designed and taught with the likelihood of instructional success).

- A concluding section, *observations and their instructional insights,* is appended. This section is included in the instructional plan as one means of recording student data and for identifying one's insights as to programming implications for later reference and for use in completing checklists, writing progress reports, and designing and modifying the student's IEP.

Then, introductory information should be provided at the beginning of the instructional plan, such as the following:

- topic area
- name of the designer of the plan
- required time for implementation
- student(s) for whom the plan is intended
- relevant background information on the involved student(s)

Finally, an instructional (lesson) plan should be written in a simple and direct way and be relatively free from jargon so that parents, teacher aides, volunteers, and other appropriate instructors can readily understand it and implement it.

# References

Bender, M., & Valletutti, P. J. (1982). *Teaching functional academics to adolescents and adults with learning problems.* Baltimore: University Park Press.

Bender, M., & Valletutti, P. J. (1985). *Teaching the moderately and severely handicapped: Curriculum objectives, strategies, and activities. Vol. 1: Self-care, motor skills and household management.* Austin, TX: PRO-ED.

Brolin, D. E. (1986). *Life-Centered Career Education: A competency-based approach* (rev. ed.). Reston, VA: Council for Exceptional Children.

Brown, L. F., Branston, M. B., Hamre-Nietupski, S., Johnson, F., Wilcox, B., & Gruenwald, L. (1979). A rationale for comprehensive longitudinal interactions between severely handicapped students and nonhandicapped students and other citizens. *AAESPH Review, 4,* 3–14.

Brown, L. F., Nietupski, J., & Hamre-Nietupski, S. (1976). The criterion of ultimate functioning and public school services for severely handicapped students. In M. A. Thomas (Ed.), *Hey don't forget about me: Education's investment in the severely, profoundly, and multiply handicapped* (pp. 2–15). Reston, VA: Council for Exceptional Children.

Cegelka, P. T., & Greene, G. (1993). Transition to adulthood. In A. E. Blackhurst & W. H. Berdine (Eds.), *An introduction to special education* (3rd ed., pp. 137–175). New York: HarperCollins.

Clark, G. M. (1979). *Career education for the handicapped child in the elementary classroom.* Denver: Love.

Cronin, M. E., & Gerber, P. J. (1982). Preparing the learning disabled adolescent for adulthood. *Topics in Learning & Learning Disabilities, 2,* 55–68.

Cronin, M. E., & Patton, J. R. (1993). *Life skills instruction for all students with special needs: A practical guide for integrating real-life content into the curriculum.* Austin, TX: PRO-ED.

Drew, C. J., Logan, D. R., & Hardman, M. L. (1992). *Mental retardation: A life cycle approach* (5th ed.). New York: Merrill/Macmillan.

Gast, D. L., & Schuster, J. W. (1993). Students with severe developmental disabilities. In A. E. Blackhurst & W. H. Berdine (Eds.), *An introduction to special education* (3rd ed., pp. 455–491). New York: HarperCollins.

Grossman, H. J. (1983). *Classification in mental retardation.* Washington, DC: American Association on Mental Deficiency.

Kirk, S. A., & Gallagher, J. J. (1989). *Educating exceptional children* (6th ed.). Boston: Houghton Mifflin.

Patton, J. R., Beirne-Smith, M., & Payne, J. S. (1990). *Mental retardation* (3rd ed.). Columbus, OH: Merrill.

Polloway, E. A., Patton, J. R., Payne, J. S., & Payne, R. A. (1989). *Strategies for teaching learners with special needs* (4th ed.). New York: Merrill/Macmillan.

Reschly, D. J. (1993). Special education decision making and functional/behavioral assessment. In E. L. Meyen, G. A. Vergason, & R. J. Whelan, *Challenges facing special education* (pp. 227–240). Denver: Love.

Valletutti, P. J., & Bender, M. (1982). *Teaching interpersonal and community living skills: A curriculum model for handicapped adolescents and adults.* Baltimore: University Park Press.

Valletutti, P. J., & Bender, M. (1985). *Teaching the moderately and severely handicapped: Curriculum objectives, strategies, and activities. Vol. 2: Communication and socialization.* Austin, TX: PRO-ED.

Valletutti, P. J., & Dummett, L. (1992). *Cognitive development: A functional approach.* San Diego: Singular Publishing Group.

Wheeler, J. (1987). *Transitioning persons with moderate and severe disabilities from school to adulthood: What makes it work.* Menononie: University of Wisconsin Materials Development Center.

# Nonverbal Communication

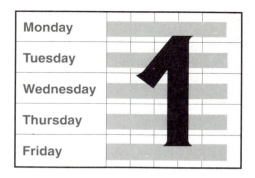

| Monday | |
| Tuesday | |
| Wednesday | |
| Thursday | |
| Friday | |

The nature of human communication cannot be understood nor its development facilitated without viewing it as a total or multimodal communication process consisting of paralinguistic elements (e.g., intonation, rate, and stress) and nonlinguistic elements (e.g., eye contact, distance between speakers, and artifactual clues such as clothing and grooming elements), as well as verbal elements.

When a young child acquires language, gestural, vocal, facial, and other body language elements such as posture are inextricably interwoven with verbal components. For children with disabilities and for those who are not disabled, comprehension and use of gestural language is often more readily acquired than oral language, for which gestural language sometimes serves both as a precursor and as a facilitator. The oral language of many students with significant developmental delay can frequently be stimulated by the earlier development of gestural understandings.

For students with disabilities who require an augmentative or alternative type of communication, a frequently employed programming option is a form of sign language that incorporates representational signs whose physical imagery is a motor abstract of the underlying language concept. The ability to comprehend and express oneself through customary gestures, facial expressions and other body language elements, and vocal intonation patterns is necessary to effective and productive life functioning in the myriad social roles an individual fulfills within the general culture and in personal subcultures.

## AUGMENTATIVE AND ALTERNATIVE COMMUNICATION

Augmentative and alternative communication (AAC) is a set of systems and instructional interventions that assist students who are nonvocal or who have severe speech production problems that profoundly diminish the intelligibility of their speech and, thus, their ability to communicate their needs, thoughts, and feelings to others.

Augmentative approaches are supplemental; they are designed to be utilized in conjunction with whatever intelligible or recognizable vocalizations the individual is able to produce (Kirk, Gallagher, & Anastasiow, 1993). Alternative communication approaches, on the other hand, are designed to provide nonvocal students with a means of communication other than speech (Polloway & Smith, 1992). Frequently employed AAC strategies include the use of communication boards containing letters, words, pictures, pictographs, and/or arbitrary symbols; manual signing systems; computers with synthetic voice output; and keyboards for typing messages and for word processing.

AAC systems can be divided into two categories: *aided* and *unaided* (Lloyd & Kangas, 1994). Unaided systems require no external materials or equipment and the transmission of the message is direct from the student to the viewer or listener. Aided strategies, on the other hand, require external materials or equipment such as communication boards and computers with synthetic voice output.

The best example of unaided communication is the use of manual signing. Finger spelling and American Sign Language (ASL) are the most commonly used forms of manual signing. Finger spelling involves the use of standardized hand positions that correspond with alphabetic symbols. ASL, the preferred sign language of most prelinguistically deaf individuals, is a distinct language that uses English vocabulary within its own grammatical structure. Less frequently employed gesture systems include Signed English, Pidgin Signed English, Seeing Essential English, and Signing Exact English (Gearheart, Mullen, & Gearheart, 1993; Kirk et al., 1993).

The determination of what an effective and efficient communication system should be is influenced by both the student's motor functioning (which suggests specific modes of response) and his or her level of intellectual functioning (which determines whether photographs, pictures, letters, words, pictographs, or arbitrary and abstract symbols are to be used on communication boards and computer displays) (Lloyd & Kangas, 1994).

A commercially available checklist, *INCH: INteraction CHecklist for Augmentative Communication* (Bolton & Dashiell, 1989), provides a systematic strategy for observing and evaluating the interaction between users of communication aids and augmentative systems. In establishing a suitable response mode, a teacher or trainer (with the advice of an AAC communication specialist, when available) decides whether the student has sufficient motor skills and range of motion to utilize direct selection. Direct-selection strategies include using eye movements and eye gaze, pointing to a display or typing on a keyboard with the unaided hand, using an adapted hand or head-piece with an attached pointer, utilizing a flashlight or a light beam attached to the head, and using pointing sticks held in the mouth (Hunt & Marshall, 1994; Lloyd & Kangas, 1994).

If the student does not have sufficient motor skills to utilize a direct-response system, then a scanning selection response mode can be employed. In a scanning system, messages are presented in a prearranged sequence (for example, on a computer screen or flash cards), and the student responds to the intended message with a previously established signal, depending on motoric factors. Commonly used signals include eye movements, primitive vocalizations, and head shakes and nods (Hunt & Marshall, 1994; Lloyd & Kangas, 1994).

Electronic scanning is also possible. In electronic visual scanning, the choice of a desired message is accomplished by using a switch-operated light, while an auditory scanning procedure requires a teacher or trainer to say what he or she perceives the student's selection to be, with the student indicating the correctness of the choice. A wide variety of switches can be used with most electronic communication aids, including those activated by the hand or foot and sip and puff pneumatic switches (Lloyd & Kangas, 1994).

With ever-increasing advances in assistive technology, computerized speech is increasing in popularity. Words or phrases can be recorded, stored, and then retrieved, when desired, by the student. For greater flexibility and for students with higher intellects, a conventional alphabet system or phonetic spelling alphabet can be recorded and stored and then retrieved by the student, when needed, using a sound-by-sound process (Hunt & Marshall, 1994).[1]

## FACILITATED COMMUNICATION

Facilitated communication is a highly controversial alternative means of communication that has been used with purported success by students with severe mental retardation and with autism (Beirne-Smith, Patton, & Ittenbach, 1994). Basically, this strategy requires teachers and trainers to hold the arm or wrist of a person with autism as he or she communicates with a keyboard or communication board. We have many years of experience in the field and have witnessed many enthusiastic demonstrations by teachers, therapists, and parents who are convinced of its efficacy; however, we have never witnessed its successful application.

---

[1]For a detailed and informative discussion of symbol sets and systems that have been produced specifically for communication boards and other picture-based communication aids (e.g., the Oakland Picture Dictionary, PCS, and Communicaid), highly pictographic symbol sets (e.g., Picsyms and Picture Communication Symbols), abstract representational sets (e.g., Lexigrams), symbol sets that contain ideograms and pictographs (e.g., Picsyms and Pictogram Ideogram Communication symbols), and rule-based systems (e.g., Blissymbolics and Sigsymbols), see Lloyd and Kangas (1994). For a list of commercially available augmentative communication aids, see Polloway and Smith (1992, pp. 170–171), and for a discussion of language code systems such as Morse code and Morse WSKE II, a commercially available computerized communication system that utilizes extended Morse codes, see Polloway and Smith (1992, p. 176).

# General Goals of This Unit

I. The student will respond appropriately to the commonly employed gestures of people in his or her environment whether they occur alone or as an integral part of their oral communication.

II. The student will use natural or commonly recognized gestures either alone or in conjunction with speech to communicate his or her needs, wants, interests, and thoughts to others.

III. The student will respond appropriately to the vocal tone and intonational patterns of people in his or her environment whether or not the student comprehends the speaker's verbal message.

IV. The student will use vocal tone patterns (with or without accompanying speech) that communicate his or her feelings to a listener.

V. The student will respond appropriately to the facial expressions of people in his or her environment whether or not the student comprehends the speaker's verbal message.

VI. The student will use facial expressions (with or without accompanying speech) that communicate his or her feelings to a listener.

VII. The student who is unable to communicate through speech or whose speech must be supplemented will use an augmentative or alternative means of communication.

## GOAL I.

The student will respond appropriately to the commonly employed gestures of people in his or her environment whether they occur alone or as an integral part of their oral communication.

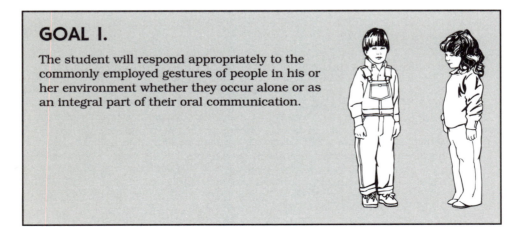

Goal I has been developed based on several key assumptions:

1. The student is able to control the movements of his or her arms and hands.

2. The student has the ability to interact with people, that is, has eye contact and maintains attention.

3. The student is able to demonstrate his or her intentions.

4. The student is able to inhibit behaviors and to continue desired behaviors.

5. There is a universality of some gestures within the general culture.

6. The person or persons providing the instruction or training will be skilled in using gestures without verbalizing whenever there is a need to focus the student's attention on the gesture alone.

## SPECIFIC OBJECTIVES

The student:

❒ A. Looks at and pays attention to a person who is waving his or her hand or arm.

❒ B. Looks at an object or person to whom someone is pointing.

❒ C. Stops an ongoing behavior in response to the "No" headshake, with or without the accompanying warning signal of a shaking index finger.

❒ D. Continues a behavior in response to an approving nod of the head.

❒ E. Gives a person an object in response to the "Give me" gesture (an extended hand or the alternating flexion and extension of the hand).

❒ F. Responds to the "Goodbye" wave of someone by waving "Goodbye" in return. (Note: This is likely to be purely imitation during the initial stages.)

❒ G. Responds to the "Hi" or "Hello" gesture by gesturing "Hi" in return. (Note: This is likely to be purely imitation during the initial stages.)

❒ H. Becomes quiet in response to the "Sh" gesture (with or without an accompanying sound) and stops an ongoing behavior in response to the warning signal of a shaking finger.

❏ I. Responds to a caregiver's gestural question (with or without verbalization), "Are you hungry?" or its equivalent, "Do you want something to eat?" (caregiver moves fingers of one hand to the mouth).

❏ J. Responds to a caregiver's gestural question (with or without verbalization), "Are you thirsty?" or its equivalent, "Do you want something to drink?" (caregiver forms a circle with index finger and thumb and moves circle toward the mouth while tilting the head back).

❏ K. Responds to a caregiver's gestural question (with or without verbalization), "Do you feel sick?" or "Does something hurt you?" (caregiver touches child's forehead, rubs child's stomach, or gently touches the area of the child's body where pain is suspected).

❏ L. Responds to a caregiver's gestural question (with or without verbalization), "Do you have to go to the bathroom?" (caregiver uses an appropriate gesture, perhaps the manual alphabet letter "T").

❏ M. Responds to a caregiver's gestural question (with or without verbalization), "Are you tired (or sleepy)?" (caregiver holds hands together at cheek while tilting head to one side).

❏ N. Responds to a caregiver's gestural question (with or without verbalization), "Are you cold?" (caregiver folds arms together, hands on elbows, while shivering slightly).

❏ O. Responds to a caregiver's gestural question (with or without verbalization), "Are you warm (or hot)?" (caregiver uses a waving hand to fan himself or herself while releasing a stream of air through the lips to make a "Whew!" sound).

❏ P. Goes to a caregiver who signals, "Come here!"

❏ Q. Stands up when signaled to do so (with or without verbalization) (caregiver extends an arm with palm up, then slowly elevates the extended arm toward the ceiling).

❏ R. Sits down when signaled to do so (with or without verbalization) (caregiver extends an arm with palm down and slowly moves the extended arm toward the floor).

❏ S. Selects a requested object by its size in response to a person's use of the "Size" gesture (hands or fingers held parallel to each other at differing distances, with close = little and far apart = big), which indicates the desired size of an object. (Note: This objective assumes that the student has the concept of size.)

☐ T. Selects a requested number of objects when a person indicates the quantity desired by holding up the appropriate number of fingers. (Note: This objective assumes that the student has the ability to give, to select one object, to understand the identifying gesture, and to comply with the request.)

☐ U. The male student shakes hands in response to an adult male extending his hand when greeting and saying, "Goodbye." (Note: This skill requires an understanding of cultural expectations.)

# SUGGESTED ACTIVITIES

## Specific Objective A

The student looks at and pays attention to a person who is waving his or her hand or arm.

## Teacher Interventions

**Infant and Toddler/Preschool Level.** Wait for the student to be engrossed in an activity. Wave your hand directly in the student's line of vision until his or her eyes fix on either your hand or your eyes. If the student looks in your eyes, give him or her a favorite toy or snack item. If the student looks at your hand, take his or her face by the chin with your other hand, and move his or her face with that hand as the hand being looked at finds and picks up a colorful *new* toy.

If the student then looks at the toy, bring it up to your eyes, smile, and verbalize your excitement. Join the student in playing with the toy while you periodically talk to him or her, all the while encouraging a gaze shift from the toy to your eyes whenever you speak to the student.

**Primary Level.** Engage in a play activity that includes puppets. Move one puppet in an attempt to gain the attention of another puppet, and say, "When I wave my arm and talk to you, I want to get your attention because I have something important to say to you. So please look at me!" When the second puppet looks at the first puppet, manipulate both puppets so that they engage in a game such as beanbag toss with each other.

Follow up by telling the student to manipulate one puppet while you or a classmate manipulate the other. Demonstrate your enjoyment with appropriate verbalizations and laughter.

## Family Interventions

**Infant and Toddler/Preschool Level.**  Ask the parents to wait until their child is engrossed in an activity and they wish to gain his or her attention for feeding, play, or some other interesting or stimulating activity. Tell them to use the hand-wave gesture and to say, "It's time for ___. Stop what you are doing and let me have your attention." Encourage them not to start the activity until the child establishes eye contact.

**Primary Level.**  Ask the parents to role-play scenes with dolls or stuffed animals. Encourage them to (a) look into the doll's or animal's eyes and engage in a conversation, (b) stop talking and engage the doll or stuffed animal in a motor activity (for example, playing with a toy car), and (c) resume the conversation.

---

### Specific Objective B

The student looks at an object or person to whom someone is pointing.

---

## Teacher Interventions

**Infant and Toddler/Preschool Level.**   Place various interesting objects on the student's desk. Point to an object. If the student looks at the object to which you have pointed, tell the student that he or she may pick it up and play with it. Follow up by placing objects at a distance from the student's desk, and reward him or her for looking at the object. Be sure to say such things as "I pointed to that new toy because I thought you would like to play with it."

**Primary Level.**  Play a game in which everyone is expected to do something when he or she is pointed to (e.g., clapping hands, doing a dance step, hopping in place, or sounding a rhythm instrument). Say such things as "Did you all see (classmate's name) clap her hands when she was pointed to?"

Follow up with a "Point, Give, and Then Everybody Play" game in which the student is given an object that he or she must then give to a classmate you have pointed to. Use as many different objects as there are students in the class,

## Family Interventions

**Infant and Toddler/Preschool Level.** Ask the parents to place toys and objects that interest their child around the house. Tell them to join the child in a "Where Does It Belong?" game in which they point to an object and the child picks it up and then returns it to its proper storage area (e.g., a spoon is washed and returned to the kitchen drawer, a doll is returned to a doll carriage, or a ball is returned to a toy chest). (See Figure 1.1.)

**Primary Level.** Ask the parents to show their child several photographs of different family members and to play a "Guess Who" game. Tell the parents to identify an element in the photograph at the start of the activity, for example, "The person I am thinking of is wearing a shirt and tie."

Tell the parents to praise the child if he or she points to the correct photograph. However, remind the parents that if the child doesn't respond or points to the wrong photograph, they should point to the correct one and point out any features to which they had referred.

Tell the parents to then conclude the activity by providing the child with a question whose answer cannot be found in the photograph, for example, "Which one is a picture of Cousin Helen's father?"

| Item | Storage Area |
|---|---|
| Fresh produce | Refrigerator |
| Canned goods | Pantry |
| Frozen foods | Freezer |
| Toys | Toy chest |
| Dresses and suits | Bedroom closet |
| Socks and underwear | Bureau drawer |
| Knives, forks, and spoons | Kitchen drawer |
| Umbrella | Umbrella stand |

**FIGURE 1.1.** Household items and their storage areas.

---

> ### Specific Objective C
>
> The student stops an ongoing behavior in response to the "No" headshake, with or without the accompanying warning signal of a shaking index finger.

---

## Teacher Interventions

**Infant and Toddler/Preschool Level.** Whenever the student is engaging in a noisy or destructive activity, approach him or her while shaking your head vigorously and saying, "No!" Immediately stop the student from continuing the activity by either gently covering the student's mouth or physically restraining him or her from continuing the activity. Explain why you are stopping the student, and either suggest that he or she engage in a constructive activity more quietly or suggest a different activity. Release the student.

If the student either engages in the former activity less noisily or engages in the new activity, reward him or her. If the student fails to behave appropriately, repeat the "No" headshake and say, "No!" until the behavior is modified.

**Primary and Intermediate Levels.** Take the student for walks in the community. If the student behaves in a socially unacceptable way, warn him or her verbally with an accompanying headshake. Stop the student from continuing the behavior, explaining why it is unacceptable.

## Family Interventions

**Infant and Toddler/Preschool Level.** Ask the parents to play a game of house in which they model reprimanding a doll or stuffed animal for inappropriate behavior. Encourage them to then give the role of "parent" to the child, who must reprove the doll or stuffed animal for unacceptable behavior by using the "No" headshake and other behaviors such as shaking a finger, vocalizing (with the appropriate intonation) a negative "Uh-Uh," and/or saying, "No!"

Remind the parents to carry over this role play into situations involving the child, by stopping the child in a fashion similar to that demonstrated in the role play.

**Primary and Intermediate Levels.** Urge the parents to use the "No" headshake when their child misbehaves in the home or on trips in the community.

---

> ### Specific Objective D
> The student continues a behavior in response to an approving nod of the head.

---

## Teacher Interventions

**Infant and Toddler/Preschool Level.**   Whenever the student is engaging appropriately in a suitable activity, indicate your pleasure by nodding your approval while praising him or her at regular or intermittent intervals (depending on your management strategy).

Also, play the "Guess Which Hand" game, in which a small toy is placed in one of your hands while your hands are behind your back. When you place your closed hands in front of the student, tell him or her to pick the hand with the toy. If the student selects the correct hand, nod your approval and vocalize the positive "Mmm-Mmm."

**Primary and Intermediate Levels.**   Role-play situations in which you interact with a busy person by asking that person to confirm information or to provide directions (e.g., to a salesperson, say, "Is this where I can exchange this defective ___?" and to an usher in a sports stadium, say, "Is this the stairway to the bleachers?"). Involve the student in the role play as the one asking for confirmation of information or directions, with you acting as the busy person who gives either the "No" headshake or the "Yes" nod.

## Family Interventions

**Infant and Toddler/Preschool Level.**   Tell the parents to indicate their approval when their child is involved in a constructive activity by vocalizing along with an approving smile and nod of the head.

**Primary and Intermediate Levels.**   Ask the parents to assign their child household chores and to periodically demonstrate their approval both while the child is performing the task and after the task has been successfully completed. Remind the parents to keep indicating disapproval as well, so that the message of the "No" headshake and the "Yes" nod is clear.

---

### Specific Objective E

The student gives a person an object in response to the "Give me" gesture (an extended hand or the alternating flexion and extension of the hand).

---

(See the Sample Lesson Plan at the end of Unit 1.)

## Teacher Interventions

**Infant and Toddler/Preschool Level.**  Place several objects and toys in front of the student. After he or she has had sufficient opportunity to examine and/or play with them, point to one of the toys and gesture "Give me." Thank the student for giving you the item and explain that you want to put it back in its storage area (see Figure 1.1). Repeat for each of the toys and objects. Involve the student in returning each item to its storage area.

**Primary Level.**  Engage the student in several construction and collaborative activities, such as planting a garden, carrying out a recipe, or engaging in a woodworking project, in which he or she plays the part of the assistant or apprentice and must respond correctly and quickly to the "Give me" gesture.

**Intermediate Level.**  Role-play "The Operating Room," in which you play the part of the surgeon and the student plays the part of the nurse. Engage in other work-related role plays in which an assistant must pass materials and equipment to the person in charge (e.g., passing tools and nails to a carpenter).

## Family Interventions

**Infant and Toddler/Preschool Level.**  Ask the parents to require their child to give them various items found in the home (e.g., asking the child to hand them the meat to put in the freezer and the cans to put on a shelf in the pantry when unpacking the groceries).

**Primary Level.**  Encourage the parents to involve the child in a variety of multistep activities in which the child must respond in an established sequence to the "Give me" gesture (e.g., when putting up shelves, the parent gestures "Give me" for the bracket, then the screwdriver, and next the screws).

**Intermediate Level.** Ask the parents to point out examples of people working in the community who, in the course of their work, pass things to each other and signal "Give me." For example, they might observe workers putting up billboard displays, paramedics providing emergency treatment, and salespeople in a department store working together to enter charges on a cash register and to wrap, bag, and staple a receipt on a package.

---

## Specific Objective F

The student responds to the "Goodbye" wave of someone by waving "Goodbye" in return. (Note: This is likely to be purely imitation during the initial stages.)

---

## Teacher Interventions

**Infant and Toddler/Preschool Level.** Introduce the "Goodbye" wave by singing the song, "So Long, It's Been Good to Know You." Wave "Goodbye" in time to the music. Explain that, when people leave each other for more than a short time, they often say and wave "Goodbye." On a number of occasions leave the room for a little while when a volunteer, an aide, a fellow human service professional, or a collaborating teacher is in the learning area.

Be sure to say such things as "See you in just a little while. I'm only going to the supply closet to pick up some arts-and-crafts supplies." Contrast these situations with saying "Goodbye" at the end of the school day or week. Be sure to explain that you are saying and waving "Goodbye" because you will be separated for a long time. Also explain that people should wave "Goodbye" in response to a "Goodbye" wave of a departing person.

**Primary Level.** Invite guest speakers to the classroom. Ask these speakers to wave "Goodbye" as they depart. Also take the student for trips into the community to visit community helpers and human service professionals at their place of employment. Model thanking and waving "Goodbye" to these individuals after a visit. Remember also to thank and wave "Goodbye" to the bus driver.

## Family Interventions

**Infant and Toddler/Preschool Level.** Ask the parents to wave "Goodbye" to their child whenever they are leaving the child for an extended period of time and when they send the child off to school or to a relative or friend who is taking the child on an outing.

**Primary Level.** Encourage the parents to point out that they say and wave "Goodbye" whenever they leave someone's house after a visit. Tell them to refrain from saying or waving "Goodbye" in response to the host's "Goodbye" wave until the child has first done so.

---

### Specific Objective G

The student responds to the "Hi" or "Hello" gesture by gesturing "Hi" in return. (Note: This is likely to be purely imitation during the initial stages.)

---

## Teacher Interventions

**Infant and Toddler/Preschool Level.** Greet the student each day with the "Hi" gesture. Sometimes accompany it with verbalization and at other times use the gesture alone. Encourage the student to wave "Hi" in return. Use physical prompts if necessary.

**Primary Level.** Arrange for a "surprise" visit to the student's home. Greet the family members who are home. Discuss the possible dangers of greeting people who are strangers and who are acting in a threatening or peculiar manner.

Be certain not to make the student unduly wary of strangers, since returning a stranger's greeting when, for example, the student is in the company of an adult may be appropriate, especially in small communities where greeting others is customary behavior.

## Family Interventions

**Infant and Toddler/Preschool Level.** Ask the parents to take their child along on visits to the homes of relatives and friends. Encourage them to greet the person who answers the door and to tell the child to join in the greeting, providing physical assistance as needed.

**Primary Level.** Ask the parents to take the child for walks in the neighborhood and greet crossing guards, storekeepers, and other people familiar to the child. Remind the parents to emphasize greeting people whom they know and avoiding responding to strangers in a dimly lit area or who are acting in a bizarre way.

---

 ## Specific Objective H

The student becomes quiet in response to the "Sh" gesture (with or without an accompanying sound) and stops an ongoing behavior in response to the warning signal of a shaking finger.

---

## Teacher Interventions

**Infant and Toddler/Preschool Level.** Whenever the student is unduly noisy, indicate "Sh." Gesture "Sh" with the accompanying sound to a noisy peer. Explain that the sound and the movement of your index finger in front of your pursed lips is a special way of saying "Be quiet" when someone is being too noisy.

**Primary and Intermediate Levels.** Take the student to places in the community where being quiet is the appropriate behavior, for example, a public library, a movie theater (during the movie), and, when possible, a clinic or hospital setting (see Unit 2, "Oral Communication," Goal X, Specific Objective C, Figure 2.48). Discuss why it is important to be quiet in these settings. Contrast these situations by taking the student to a noisy place, for example, a Little League game.

## Family Interventions

**Infant and Toddler/Preschool Level.** If there are other children in the home, ask the parents to remember to silence them with the "Sh" gesture whenever the noise level becomes uncomfortable. Tell them to do the same with the child. Remind them to explain the meaning of this gesture, for example, following the gesture by saying such things as "You were playing nicely with your toys and then you got so loud that I couldn't hear what your brother was saying to me."

**Primary and Intermediate Levels.** Ask the parents to take the child to different locations in the community where different noise levels are appropriate, that is, silence while watching a movie (except for appropriate laughter) or listening to a sermon, low-level sound or talking while visiting someone who is ill, and higher sound levels while being a spectator at a sports event or the circus.

---

### Specific Objective I

The student responds to a caregiver's gestural question (with or without verbalization), "Are you hungry?" or its equivalent, "Do you want something to eat?" (caregiver moves fingers of one hand to the mouth).

---

## Teacher Interventions

**Infant and Toddler/Preschool Level.** Before lunch and snack times, signal to the student the gestural question, "Are you hungry?" (sometimes with and sometimes without verbalization). If the student indicates in some way that he or she is hungry, say, "Wonderful! We are going to have our snack (or lunch) in just a few minutes."

**Primary Level.** Take the student for a trip in the community to a fast-food restaurant or cafeteria. Ask the gestural question (sometimes with and sometimes without verbalization), and say, for example, "I am just checking to see whether or not you are hungry before we order lunch."

## Family Interventions

**Infant and Toddler/Preschool Level.** Ask the parents to use the gestural question, "Are you hungry?" as early as possible during infancy whether they believe their child understands it or not. Tell them that if they believe the child wants to eat, even if he or she does not give any response, they should pretend that the child has given a positive response by saying, "Yes, I think you are hungry!" and then giving the child the food.

**Primary and Intermediate Levels.** Ask the parents to take the child to a variety of eating places: fast-food restaurants, cafeterias, buffet-style restaurants, and more formal restaurants. Encourage them to check with the child before ordering, by using the gestural question, "Are you hungry?"

## Specific Objective J

The student responds to a caregiver's gestural question (with or without verbalization), "Are you thirsty?" or its equivalent, "Do you want something to drink?" (caregiver forms a circle with index finger and thumb and moves circle toward the mouth while tilting the head back).

## Teacher Interventions

**Infant and Toddler/Preschool Level.**   After a salty snack or a physical activity, ask the student the gestural question (sometimes with and sometimes without verbalization), "Are you thirsty?" If the student indicates in some way that he or she is thirsty, provide water or a healthy beverage.

**Primary Level.**   Provide the student with a daily snack that usually includes a beverage. On some occasions do not serve a beverage and say, "We are out of orange juice." Then ask the gestural question (with or without verbalization), "Are you thirsty?" or the gestural question's other possible meaning, "Do you want something to drink?" Continue by saying, "If you are thirsty (or want something to drink), we have ___ juice instead." If the student indicates "Yes" in some way, give him or her the drink.

## Family Interventions

**Infant and Toddler/Preschool Level.**   Ask the parents to use the gestural question, "Are you thirsty?" as early as possible during infancy whether they believe their child understands it or not. Tell them that if they believe the child is thirsty, even if he or she does not give any response, they should pretend that the child has given a positive response by saying, "Yes, I see that you are thirsty!" and then giving the child a drink.

**Primary and Intermediate Levels.**   Ask the parents to take the child to a variety of eating places: fast-food restaurants, cafeterias, buffet-style restaurants, and more formal restaurants. Encourage them to check with the child, by using the gestural question, "Are you thirsty?" before ordering a beverage as part of the meal or snack.

---

> ## Specific Objective K
>
> The student responds to a caregiver's gestural question (with or without verbalization), "Do you feel sick?" or "Does something hurt you?" (caregiver touches child's forehead, rubs child's stomach, or gently touches the area of the child's body where pain is suspected).

---

## Teacher Interventions

**Infant and Toddler/Preschool Level.** Play "Doctor" with dolls, stuffed animals, or puppets. In your play, use the question gesture (sometimes with and sometimes without verbalization), "Do you feel sick?" or "Does something hurt you?" Moreover, be alert to the possibility that the student might be ill.

Observe the student's facial expressions and other body language to determine whether he or she is in some discomfort or is having pain. If so, ask the gestural question (with or without verbalization), "Do you feel sick?" or "Does something hurt you?" (touch the student's forehead, rub his or her stomach, or gently touch the area of the body where you suspect the pain or discomfort might be).

**Primary Level.** At all times, be alert to the possibility that the student might be ill. Observe the student's facial expressions and other body language to determine whether he or she is in some discomfort or is having pain. If so, ask the gestural question (with or without verbalization), "Do you feel sick?" or "Does something hurt you?" (touch the student's forehead, rub his or her stomach, or gently touch the area of the body where you suspect the pain or discomfort might be).

## Family Interventions

**Infant and Toddler/Preschool Level.** Remind the parents that they must be alert to any signs shown by their child that might indicate that he or she is not feeling well or is in pain. Speak about the need to differentiate between cries of hunger and those that might indicate pain.

Ask the parents to use the gestural question, "Do you feel sick?" or "Does something hurt you?" as early as possible during infancy whether they believe the child understands it or not. Caution them to discourage any malingering on the part of the child.

**Primary Level.**  Tell the parents to be alert to the possibility that the child might be ill. Explain that, if a communication deficit exists, it is especially important to be alert.

Remind the parents to observe the child's facial expressions and other body language to determine whether he or she is in some discomfort or is having pain. If so, remind the parents to ask the gestural question (with or without verbalization), "Do you feel sick?" or "Does something hurt you?" (the parents touch the child's forehead, rub his or her stomach, or gently touch the area of the body where they suspect the pain or discomfort might be).

---

 ## Specific Objective L

The student responds to a caregiver's gestural question (with or without verbalization), "Do you have to go to the bathroom?" (caregiver uses an appropriate gesture, perhaps the manual alphabet letter "T").

---

## Teacher and Family Interventions

**Infant and Toddler/Preschool and Primary Levels.**  If no time has already been established, set aside specific times during the school day (e.g., before recess or during free time) when the student is free to go to the bathroom. At these times, use a consistent gesture to ask the student whether he or she needs to go to the bathroom. Reward the student for indicating "Yes" or "No" correctly and in an appropriate way.

Also, be alert to any behaviors of the student that indicate a need to go to the bathroom. Very often the student will become very quiet, begin to fidget, stare into space, make facial grimaces, or exhibit some other consistent behavior just before he or she begins to void. When these body language signals occur, ask the gestural question and take the student to the bathroom.

**Intermediate Level.**  Take the student for a walk through his or her community or go to a community event (e.g., a ball game, movies, or a puppet show). At an appropriate time, ask the gestural question, with or without verbalization. Reward the student for indicating "Yes" or "No" correctly and in an appropriate way.

> ### Specific Objective M
>
> The student responds to a caregiver's gestural question (with or without verbalization), "Are you tired (or sleepy)?" (caregiver holds hands together at cheek while tilting head to one side).

## Teacher Interventions

**Infant and Toddler/Preschool Level.**   Be alert to any behavior of the student that indicates that he or she might be sleepy or tired. Ask the student the gestural question (sometimes with and sometimes without verbalization), "Are you tired (or sleepy)?" If the student indicates in some way that he or she is tired (depending on his or her age), place him or her in a carriage, crib, cot, or bed.

**Primary Level.**   Act out the story "Goldilocks and the Three Bears," with the student acting out all the parts. When a character in the story becomes tired, ask the student, using the gestural question, whether he or she is tired (or sleepy). Praise the student for pantomiming fatigue. Check out other children's stories in which a character becomes tired and goes to sleep, such as "The Shoemaker and the Elves."

## Family Interventions

**Infant and Toddler/Preschool Level.**   Ask the parents to demonstrate the tired (sleepy) gesture while simultaneously yawning and saying that they are tired. Remind them that the child does not have to understand the verbal message. Tell them to then ask the child whether he or she is tired (or sleepy). Encourage the parents to have a rest period if the child indicates "Yes" in some way.

**Primary and Intermediate Levels.**   Ask the parents to take their child on trips in the community that are likely to result in the need for a short rest period. Tell them to indicate their own fatigue and to use the gestural question to determine whether their child is also tired (or sleepy). Ask the parents to discuss the need for rest.

> ### Specific Objective N
>
> The student responds to a caregiver's gestural question (with or without verbalization), "Are you cold?" (caregiver folds arms together, hands on elbows, while shivering slightly).

## Teacher Interventions

**Infant and Toddler/Preschool Level.**  On a cool or cold day, turn the thermostat to a lower-than-usual temperature. When you start to feel cold, use the "I am cold" gesture, and explain that you are cold.

(Note: This is the same gesture as in the gestural question but with different body language, basically involving pointing—that is, it is a question when pointing to someone else after the gesture, and it is a statement when pointing to oneself before the gesture.) Follow up by asking the gestural question of the student.

**Primary and Intermediate Levels.**  Take the student to a neighborhood swimming pool (e.g., the Department of Parks and Recreation, the YMCA, the YWCA, or a community high school), preferably one that is out-of-doors. When the student comes out of the water, use the gestural question (with or without verbalization) to determine whether he or she is cold.

## Family Interventions

**Infant and Toddler/Preschool Level.**  Encourage the parents to use the "I am cold" gesture to indicate that they are cold when they are at home or moving about the community. Tell them to follow up by asking their child whether he or she is cold as well.

**Primary and Intermediate Levels.**  Remind the parents to ask their child, at appropriate times, whether he or she is cold, for example, at a family picnic when there has been a sudden change in the weather (a cool wind has arisen) or at home when the electricity has gone out (because of an ice or snow storm). Encourage the parents, at times such as these, to identify steps that can be taken to become warmer and to prevent illness.

```
┌─────────────────────────────────────────────────────────┐
│  ╔═══════════════════════════════════════════════════╗  │
│  ║  ♨    Specific Objective O                         ║  │
│  ║                                                     ║  │
│  ║  The student responds to a caregiver's gestural    ║  │
│  ║  question (with or without verbalization), "Are    ║  │
│  ║  you warm (or hot)?" (caregiver uses a waving      ║  │
│  ║  hand to fan himself or herself while releasing    ║  │
│  ║  a stream of air through the lips to make a        ║  │
│  ║  "Whew!" sound).                                    ║  │
│  ╚═══════════════════════════════════════════════════╝  │
└─────────────────────────────────────────────────────────┘
```

## Teacher Interventions

**Infant and Toddler/Preschool Level.**   On a hot day, show the student that you are hot by wiping your brow and making the "I am hot!" gesture.

(Note: This is the same gesture as in the gestural question but with different body language, basically involving pointing—that is, it is a question when pointing to someone else after the gesture, and it is a statement when pointing to oneself before the gesture.)

Follow up by asking the gestural question of the student. Show the student how a hand fan is used, and explain that using your hand as if it were a fan is a way of telling someone you are hot.

**Primary and Intermediate Levels.**   On a hot day, take the student for a trip into the community. Arrange to take him or her to places with and without air conditioning. When in an air-conditioned place, indicate in some way that you are comfortable. When in a non-air-conditioned place, use the "I am hot!" gesture to indicate your discomfort. Follow up by asking the student the gestural question.

## Family Interventions

**Infant and Toddler/Preschool Level.**   Tell the parents to make the "I am hot!" gesture whenever the house becomes unusually warm, requiring some action to be taken, such as turning down the heat during cold weather or opening the windows or turning on a fan or air conditioner during warm or hot weather.

**Primary and Intermediate Levels.**   Ask the parents to take their child for trips in the community. When they are in a warm or hot place (e.g., in a crowded or poorly ventilated area or near a restaurant window that is flooded with afternoon sunlight), the parents should use the gestural question (with or without verbalization) to determine whether the child is hot. Encourage them to take steps, such as moving to new seats away from the restaurant window, to become more comfortable.

---

### Specific Objective P

The student goes to a caregiver who signals, "Come here!"

---

## Teacher Interventions

**Infant and Toddler/Preschool Level.**   Engage in a task that requires the student's participation (e.g., say, "Come here, please. I need you to hold the other side of this chart while I staple it to the bulletin board" or "Come here, please. I need you to hold the other end of this rope while your classmates jump over it"). Get the student's attention, and use the "Come here" gesture to get him or her to join you. Explain why waving your hand is a good way to show how the student must move.

**Primary and Intermediate Levels.**   Take the student for trips in the community. Signal "Come here!" (sometimes with and sometimes without verbalization) when you see something interesting that you want to share with him or her (e.g., a cute puppy, an interesting sign or billboard, or an interesting exhibit or artwork at a museum).

## Family Interventions

**Infant and Toddler/Preschool Level.**   Ask the parents to require the participation of their child in different activities (e.g., asking the child to join them in preparing a simple snack, in carrying materials from one room to another, or in setting the table). Encourage them to demonstrate the relationship between the nature of the gesture and the requested movement pattern.

**Primary and Intermediate Levels.**   Encourage the parents to take the child for trips in the community and to signal "Come here!" (sometimes with and sometimes without verbalization) when they see something interesting that they wish to share with the child (e.g., Aunt Mildred's new car, a new building or shopping center, or some pretty flowers, trees, or shrubbery).

---

### Specific Objective Q

The student stands up when signaled to do so (with or without verbalization) (caregiver extends an arm with palm up, then slowly elevates the extended arm toward the ceiling).

---

(Note: This gesture is included because it is often used in classroom settings and may be used by family members in play and behavioral management activities.)

## Teacher Interventions

**Infant and Toddler/Preschool Level.** Play the game "Simple Simon." Include the "Stand up" command, using both the gesture and the words. After the student understands the nature of the game and this specific command, modify the game by making it a pantomime game in which each of the commands is given by using gestures alone.

**Primary Level.** Play the Hap Palmer record, "Parade of Colors." Assign a color to each child and signal the child to stand when his or her assigned color is called. Involve the student in school-based activities that require standing at designated times (e.g., to pledge allegiance to the flag, to engage in physical fitness activities, or to go to another area of the school or learning area). Signal the required action with the "Stand up" gesture.

## Family Interventions

**Infant and Toddler/Preschool Level.** Ask the parents to play "School" with the child, with one of them playing the part of the teacher. Encourage them to give the child activities that involve getting up from a sitting position.

**Primary Level.** Ask the parents to review with their child, role-play, and then actually experience those situations that arise in the community when it may be necessary to stand (e.g., at a church or temple service, at a movie theater to allow someone to pass comfortably, or at a sports event in response to the playing or singing of "The Star Spangled Banner").

> ## Specific Objective R
>
> The student sits down when signaled to do so (with or without verbalization) (caregiver extends an arm with palm down and slowly moves the extended arm toward the floor).

(Note: This gesture is included because it is often used in classroom settings and may be used by family members in play and behavioral management activities.)

## Teacher Interventions

**Infant and Toddler/Preschool Level.** Play the game "Simple Simon." Include the "Sit down" command, using both the gesture and the words. After the student understands the nature of the game and this specific command, modify the game by making it a pantomime game in which each of the commands is given by using gestures alone.

**Primary Level.** Involve the student in school-based activities that require him or her to sit at designated times (e.g., on returning to the learning area after lunch or recess or after a visit to the bathroom). Signal the required action by using the "Sit down" gesture.

## Family Interventions

**Infant and Toddler/Preschool Level.** Tell the parents to use the "Sit down" gesture when reprimanding the child and asking him or her to sit down because he or she has been too active or boisterous. Also, ask the parents to play a modification of the game of "Musical Chairs" in which each of the participants has a chair available, and to use the "Sit down" gesture every time the music stops. Tell them that, once the child understands the gesture, they should proceed by playing the actual game of "Musical Chairs."

**Primary and Intermediate Levels.** Ask the parents to take the child on public transportation and to indicate when there is an empty seat by pointing to the seat and gesturing "Sit down." Encourage the parents to go to community events in auditoriums and stadiums where they have reserved seats. Tell them to involve the child in finding their seats and then saying, "Sit down," using the appropriate gesture.

> ### Specific Objective S
>
> The student selects a requested object by its size in response to a person's use of the "Size" gesture (hands or fingers held parallel to each other at differing distances, with close = little and far apart = big), which indicates the desired size of an object. (Note: This objective assumes that the student has the concept of size.)

## Teacher Interventions

**Infant and Toddler/Preschool Level.**   Give the student a selection of different sizes of the same toy (cars, balls, or blocks) that he or she may play with. Ask the student which *one* he or she would like to play with or look at by using the "Size" gesture (sometimes with and sometimes without verbalization). Repeat the activity with objects such as pencils, crayons, and books.

**Primary and Intermediate Levels.**   Ask the student to help you in sorting different sizes of an item such as canned goods (for a classroom store or for cooking activities), nuts and bolts (for a work-assembly task), and envelopes (for a mailing task). Indicate the size item you want the student to pick up or retrieve by using the "Size" gesture.

## Family Interventions

**Infant and Toddler/Preschool Level.**   Ask the parents to obtain two sizes of a high-interest toy (e.g., a toy car) and to place them in front of their child. Tell them to say and gesture "Give me" and to follow up by making one of the "Size" gestures. Tell them to explain, through speech and pantomime, that the size of the object corresponds to the size indicated by the hands or fingers.

**Primary and Intermediate Levels.**   Ask the parents to involve their child in various household tasks and to bring them different sizes of an item in response to the "Size" gesture (e.g., either a bath towel or a face towel, an economy-size or small box of detergent, or a large or small suitcase).

> ### Specific Objective T
>
> The student selects a requested number of objects when a person indicates the quantity desired by holding up the appropriate number of fingers. (Note: This objective assumes that the student has the ability to give, to select one object, to understand the identifying gesture, and to comply with the request.)

## Teacher Interventions

**Infant and Toddler/Preschool Level.**   Sing and chant finger plays and counting songs (e.g., "Ten Little Indian Boys and Girls" or "One, Two, Buckle My Shoe").

**Primary and Intermediate Levels.**   Pick up one of a number of objects that are all the same in terms of size, shape, and color, and take the index finger of the student's preferred hand and tap a first object with that finger. Then hold up one of your fingers and assist the student in picking up the object and matching it to your raised finger.

Continue this way until the student is able to select the correct number of items, starting with one and progressing to higher numbers when the student demonstrates the skill of counting with meaning.

**Secondary Level.**   Involve the student in work assignments in which he or she assists you by giving you the asked-for (gestured) number of items (two eggs, three nuts and bolts, four nails, etc.).

## Family Interventions

**Infant and Toddler/Preschool Level.**   Ask the parents to sing number songs such as "This Old Man" to their child and to show the child picture books that provide an opportunity to count (e.g., the number of chickens, the number of toys, and the number of houses appearing in the illustrations).

**Primary Level.**   Ask the parents to ask the child to get a designated number of cups and plates out of the cabinet and utensils from the drawer in response to the number of fingers they hold up.

**Intermediate and Secondary Levels.** Encourage the parents to involve the youngster in work assignments in which the child assists them by giving the asked-for (gestured) number of items (two light bulbs, three paper clips, four napkins, etc.).

 ## Specific Objective U

The male student shakes hands in response to an adult male extending his hand when greeting and saying, "Goodbye." (Note: This skill requires an understanding of cultural expectations.)

## Teacher Interventions

**Infant and Toddler/Preschool Level.** Modify the song "If You're Happy and You Know It" to include the action of shaking hands. Sing the song "How Do You Do, My Partner?" and extend your hand for the student to shake.

**Primary and Intermediate Levels.** Discuss with the male student the customary practice of shaking the hand of a male relative or friend when greeting him. Show the student photographs of adult relatives and family friends, and ask him to point out the males in the photographs. Explain that when he meets his male friends and relatives, they might extend their hand to be shaken in a firm way.

## Family Interventions

**Infant and Toddler/Preschool Level.** Ask the father or another male relative to sing the song "How Do You Do, My Partner?" and to extend his hand for the child to shake.

**Primary and Intermediate Levels.** Ask the child's parents to discuss with him the various times when he might be expected to shake the hand of a male relative or friend. Encourage the parents to take the child on trips in the community in which the opportunity arises to shake the hand of an adult male relative, a family friend, or a neighbor.

## GOAL II.

The student will use natural or commonly recognized gestures either alone or in conjunction with speech to communicate his or her needs, wants, interests, and thoughts to others.

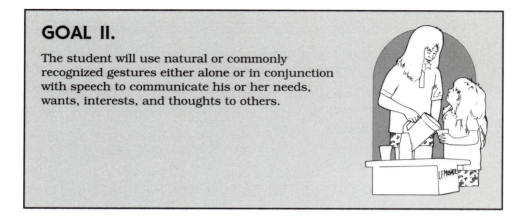

Goal II has been developed based on several key assumptions:

1. The student is able to control the movements of his or her arms and hands.

2. The student has the ability to interact with people (e.g., has eye contact and maintains attention).

3. The student is able to demonstrate his or her intentions.

4. The student is able to inhibit behaviors and to continue desired behaviors.

5. There is a universality of some gestures within the general culture.

6. The person or persons providing the instruction or training will be skilled in using gestures without verbalizing whenever there is a need to focus the student's attention on the gesture alone.

7. The student who is expected to develop expressive gestural skills has already acquired the parallel receptive skills.

Most specific objectives in Goal II have a receptive counterpart in Goal I.

## SPECIFIC OBJECTIVES

The student:

❑ A. Gains a person's attention (with or without vocalization) by waving his or her hand or arm.

❑ B. Points to a desired object (if he or she is unable to name it).

❏ C. Shakes his or her head "No" when he or she does not want an object or does not want something to occur.

❏ D. Nods his or her head to indicate that he or she wants an object or approves a suggested activity.

❏ E. Who wishes a desired object indicates "Give me" by extending a hand or alternately flexing and extending the fingers.

❏ F. Waves "Goodbye" when leaving someone to go to a new location.

❏ G. Gestures "Hi" or "Hello" on greeting a person.

❏ H. Indicates "Be quiet" by using the "Sh" gesture with or without sound.

❏ I. Who is hungry and unable to obtain food without assistance indicates through gesture (moving the fingers of one hand toward the mouth) that he or she is hungry.

❏ J. Who is unable to speak and is thirsty and unable to obtain a beverage without assistance indicates through gesture (forming a circle with the index finger and thumb and moving the circle toward the mouth while tilting the head back) that he or she is thirsty.

❏ K. Who is unable to speak and is feeling ill or is in pain indicates the location of the pain or discomfort by rubbing or touching the location and showing a pained expression.

❏ L. Who is unable to speak and cannot take care of his or her toileting needs unassisted indicates the need to be taken to the bathroom by using a socially acceptable gesture, established by the caregiver (e.g., the manual alphabet letter "T").

❏ M. Who is unable to speak, is tired or sleepy, and is unable to get to a resting place without assistance indicates through gesture (holding the hands together at the cheek while tilting the head to one side) that he or she is tired or sleepy.

❏ N. Who is unable to speak and is too cold indicates that he or she is uncomfortable by folding the arms together, hands on elbows, while shivering slightly.

❏ O. Who is unable to speak and is too warm or hot indicates that he or she is uncomfortable by waving his or her hand like a fan while releasing a stream of air through the lips in a "Whew" sound.

❐ P.  Who is unable to speak and wants someone to join him or her indicates "Come here" by waving the flexed fingers of one hand toward his or her body several times.

❐ Q.  Who is unable to speak and is unable to obtain an object of a desired size indicates his or her wishes by using the "Size" gesture (hands or fingers held parallel to each other at differing distances, with close = little and far apart = big). (Note: This objective assumes that the student has the concept of size.)

❐ R.  Who is unable to speak and is unable to obtain a desired number of objects indicates his or her wishes by using the fingers to indicate the desired amount. (Note: This objective assumes that the student has basic number concepts.)

# SUGGESTED ACTIVITIES

---

## Specific Objective A

The student gains a person's attention (with or without vocalization) by waving his or her hand or arm.

---

## Teacher Interventions

**Infant and Toddler/Preschool Level.**  Stand or sit in front of a mirror with the student. Make the "Attention-getting" wave. Assist the student in imitating your movements. When the student has approximated the movement, tell him or her that the gesture will help him or her get the attention of others. (Note: If the student is able to vocalize or verbalize to get a person's attention, indicate that the gesture will help, especially if the place is noisy and the person is unable to hear the student.)

Play the part of a preoccupied person who is playing with one of the student's favorite toys. If the student waves for your attention, with or without vocalization or verbalization, give him or her your attention, and join the student in playing with the toy.

**Primary Level.**  Demonstrate how to gain a classmate's attention without interrupting the individual unnecessarily or in a rude way. Wait for a noisy activity and ask the student to take some interesting materials to a student who is busy.

## Family Interventions

**Infant and Toddler/Preschool Level.** Ask the parents to pretend to be preoccupied at important times (e.g., when their child is likely to be hungry or to want attention because of having soiled himself or herself). Tell them to respond only if the child indicates in a socially acceptable manner that he or she needs their attention.

**Primary Level.** Remind the parents that they must not respond to their child if he or she grabs or touches them to gain attention. Tell them they should remove the hand or push it away, explain that the child should have gotten their attention in a better way, and then resume their previous activity.

---

### Specific Objective B

The student points to a desired object (if he or she is unable to name it).

---

## Teacher Interventions

**Infant and Toddler/Preschool Level.** Place several objects, such as toys, that interest the student on a table or desk in front of him or her. Tell the student that there is only enough time for him or her to play with one of them. If the student is unable to name the desired object, ask him or her to point to the one he or she wishes to play with.

**Primary Level.** Tell the student he or she can choose a game to play with, or a magazine or picture book to show to one or more of his or her classmates or family members, from several placed in front of him or her. Tell the student to choose the game, magazine, or book by pointing to the one of his or her choice.

## Family Interventions

**Infant and Toddler/Preschool Level.** Ask the parents to place several snack food items in front of their child. Tell them to give the child a choice of only one and to encourage him or her to point to his or her selection.

**Primary Level.** Ask the parents to take their child on a shopping trip during which he or she can select one article of clothing (e.g., "Point to which of these two shirts you would like!") or a snack item (e.g., "Point to the picture of the flavor of frozen yogurt you would like us to buy for you!").

---

 ## Specific Objective C

The student shakes his or her head "No" when he or she does not want an object or does not want something to occur.

---

## Teacher Interventions

**Infant and Toddler/Preschool Level.** Identify a food item or a toy that the student does not like or enjoy. Place that item and a more preferred item in the student's view, pick up the item that he or she does not particularly care for, and offer it to the student while saying, "I thought you would like this one rather than the other one." Encourage the student to shake his or her head "No" with or without vocalization or verbalization.

**Primary and Intermediate Levels.** Suggest several different activities to the student. Among these activities should be a favorite one as well as some that are less favored. Tell the student that you will say each possible activity over again and that he or she should listen carefully and indicate whether he or she chooses the activity named. Name the preferred activity last.

## Family Interventions

**Infant and Toddler/Preschool Level.** Ask the parents to give their child choices of objects to play with and food items to eat. Tell them to include in the choices items that the child does not like and that he or she will decline by shaking his or her head "No!"

**Primary and Intermediate Levels.** Ask the parents to repeat the activity from the infant/toddler and preschool level, but this time to offer the child a choice of activities.

---

 ## Specific Objective D

The student nods his or her head to indicate that he or she wants an object or approves a suggested activity.

---

## Teacher and Family Interventions

Repeat the Suggested Activities in Specific Objective C for both Teacher and Family Interventions. This time, however, have the student select the preferred item or activity with a nod of his or her head.

---

### Specific Objective E

The student who wishes a desired object indicates "Give me" by extending a hand or alternately flexing and extending the fingers.

---

## Teacher Interventions

**Infant and Toddler/Preschool Level.** Place several objects or snack items in front of the student. Tell the student that you will point to each item in turn and that he or she should tell you which one he or she would like by signaling "Give me" with his or her hand.

**Primary and Intermediate Levels.** Place clothing items of different colors (e.g., socks) in front of the student. Show him or her a shirt or blouse that is the same color as one of the items. Tell the student that you will point to each of the items (socks) and that he or she should gesture "Give me" when the item pointed to is the same color as the shirt or blouse.

## Family Interventions

**Infant and Toddler/Preschool Level.** Ask the parents to place a desired object on a shelf out of the reach of their child. Tell them to ask the child to indicate whether he or she wants the object by signaling "Give me."

**Primary Level.** Ask the parents to take their child on a family outing, such as a picnic, where toys and play equipment are part of the recreational possibilities. Tell them to point out that the toys and play equipment are for everyone and that the child must select the one he or she wishes by gesturing "Give me" when the toys and play equipment are passed out to everyone.

---

**Specific Objective F**

The student waves "Goodbye" when leaving someone to go to a new location.

---

## Teacher Interventions

**Infant and Toddler/Preschool Level.**   When the student leaves the learning area for the day or when you are leaving the student's home, say, "Goodbye," and remind the student to wave "Goodbye" to you with or without verbalization.

**Primary Level.**   Engage the student in play with hand puppets, where the puppets engage in various play and speech exchanges and interactions that are appropriate to the student's level of functioning. Remind the student that the puppets should say and wave "Goodbye" to each other before they are put away.

## Family Interventions

**Infant and Toddler/Preschool Level.**   Ask the parents to encourage their child to wave "Goodbye" when he or she is leaving them to go to school (e.g., at the school bus) or when he or she is departing the home in the company of a responsible family member.

**Primary Level.**   Tell the parents to take their child for visits to the homes of relatives, friends, and neighbors and to encourage the child to wave and say "Goodbye" when leaving.

---

**Specific Objective G**

The student gestures "Hi" or "Hello" on greeting a person.

---

## Teacher Interventions

**Infant and Toddler/Preschool Level.**   When the student arrives at the learning area for the day or when you arrive at the student's home, say "Hi" or "Hello," and remind the student to greet you with the "Hi" gesture, with or without verbalization.

**Primary and Intermediate Levels.**  Role-play various situations in which the student is expected to greet a person to whom he or she is introduced. Follow up by inviting a guest to the classroom or learning area and introducing the individual to the student, who is expected to initiate the greeting by using the appropriate gesture, with or without verbalization.

## Family Interventions

**Infant and Toddler/Preschool Level.**  Ask the parents to encourage the student to gesture "Hi" when he or she returns home from school or from an outing in the community.

**Primary and Intermediate Levels.**  Ask the parents to introduce their child to new acquaintances and to encourage him or her to greet the person, with or without verbalization.

---

### Specific Objective H

The student indicates "Be quiet" by using the "Sh" gesture with or without sound.

---

## Teacher Interventions

**Infant and Toddler/Preschool Level.**  When a noisy situation arises because of the behavior of someone else, ask the student to join you in using the "Sh" gesture to ask the person to be quiet. Also, play "House," where a doll or stuffed animal is put to bed. Join the student in singing or humming a simple lullaby (a created one will do nicely) and saying, "Sh, it's time to go to sleep."

**Primary and Intermediate Levels.**  Play a record, audiocassette, or CD at too high a volume. Ask the student if it is disturbing him or her. Remind the student to indicate that the noise is annoying by gently gesturing "Sh." Explain that when we wish to make someone quiet, we can ask that person, "Please be quiet," or we can gesture and make the "Sh" sound.

## Family Interventions

**Infant and Toddler/Preschool Level.**  Ask the parents to sing "Rock-a-Bye Baby" or some other lullaby (an ethnic lullaby also is appropriate). Tell them to pretend that a doll has fallen asleep or, if there is a younger child in the home who is being put to sleep, to gesture "Sh," so as not to wake the doll or the younger child. Remind them that this activity can be done when anyone in the household is sleeping.

**Primary and Intermediate Levels.**  Ask the parents to take their child to a public place where noise is inappropriate, such as a theater, concert hall, library, or hospital. Tell them to point out how quiet the place is, and also when someone is being noisy.

Encourage the parents to engage the child in role plays in which he or she asks another person to be quiet, for example, while looking at a magazine in a public library.

---

## Specific Objective 1

The student who is hungry and unable to obtain food without assistance indicates through gesture (moving the fingers of one hand toward the mouth) that he or she is hungry.

---

## Teacher Interventions

**Infant and Toddler/Preschool Level.**  Deliberately forget to give the student a snack while providing a snack to others. If the student gestures appropriately, apologize for forgetting him or her, praise him or her for reminding you, and provide the snack. Make certain that the student is not using this gesture to gain attention or out of gluttony.

**Primary and Intermediate Levels.**  Take the student for a walk in the community, and do not break for lunch at the usual time. Before going on the trip, tell the student that he or she should let you know when to stop for lunch.

## Family Interventions

**Infant and Toddler/Preschool Level.**  Ask the parents to give the child less than his or her usual portion of food at a family meal. Tell them to ask the child, when he or she has finished eating, whether he or she is still hungry. Remind them not to give the child additional food until the child has indicated that he or she is still hungry or would like more.

**Primary and Intermediate Levels.**   Encourage the parents to take their child on trips that involve packing a lunch (e.g., a picnic, a trip to the beach, or a long car trip). Tell them that they should ask the child to let them know when he or she is hungry. Caution them not to serve the food or allow the child to eat if it is not an appropriate time.

---

### Specific Objective J

The student who is unable to speak and is thirsty and unable to obtain a beverage without assistance indicates through gesture (forming a circle with the index finger and thumb and moving the circle toward the mouth while tilting the head back) that he or she is thirsty.

---

## Teacher Interventions

**Infant and Toddler/Preschool Level.**   Demonstrate to the student how to make the "I am thirsty" gesture. Use a cup to help with the hand position. Serve a snack that includes a beverage, and expect the student to ask for the beverage by signaling with the "I am thirsty" gesture. Occasionally, forget to serve the beverage.

**Primary and Intermediate Levels.**   Engage the student in an active game or other strenuous physical activity. After the activity, ask the student whether he or she has become thirsty as a result of all the "work." Encourage the student to gesture "I am thirsty" whenever he or she is thirsty (e.g., after lunch or a salty snack).

## Family Interventions

**Infant and Toddler/Preschool Level.**   Tell the parents not to respond if their child points to the sink when he or she wants some water. Ask them to demonstrate the "I am thirsty" gesture and to encourage their child to use the gesture whenever he or she is thirsty and would like a beverage. If the child takes some oral medication, ask the parents to omit the water and to encourage the child to use the "I am thirsty" sign to indicate that he or she needs water or juice to take the pills.

**Primary and Intermediate Levels.**   Ask the parents to take their child for walks in the community where there are public drinking fountains (e.g., parks, playgrounds, or shopping malls). Tell them to encourage the child to ask (gesture) for water when he or she is thirsty.

---

### Specific Objective K

The student who is unable to speak and is feeling ill or is in pain indicates the location of the pain or discomfort by rubbing or touching the location and showing a pained expression.

---

## Teacher Interventions

**Infant and Toddler/Preschool Level.**  Play a "Let's Pretend" game. Ask the student to pretend that his or her head hurts. Demonstrate how to show someone else that you have a pain in your head by placing the palm of your hand on your head or by rubbing it. Then ask the student to pretend and gesture that he or she has (a) a toothache, (b) a sore finger, (c) a backache, or (d) a pain in the stomach.

**Primary and Intermediate Levels.**  Role-play going to the "Doctor's Office" or "Clinic." Tell the student to show the doctor or nurse where he or she has a pain by using the appropriate gesture. Name the part of the body that hurts in this pretend game so that the student can use the gesture to tell someone else what pains him or her.

## Family Interventions

**Infant and Toddler/Preschool Level.**  Ask the parents to engage in a role play in which they pretend that they have been hurt. Encourage them to use props like bandages and Band-Aids on different parts of the body and to demonstrate communicating pain or discomfort. Tell them to continue by reversing roles.

**Primary and Intermediate Levels.**  Encourage the parents to have the child accompany them when they visit a dentist or doctor. Before the visit, remind the parents to use the appropriate gesture and to explain: "When some part of my body hurts, I sometimes rub it to ease the pain. Doing that also is a good way of letting someone else know that you are in pain."

## Specific Objective L

The student who is unable to speak and cannot take care of his or her toileting needs unassisted indicates the need to be taken to the bathroom by using a socially acceptable gesture, established by the caregiver (e.g., the manual alphabet letter "T").

## Teacher Interventions

**Infant and Toddler/Preschool Level.**  After consultation with the parents, determine a suitable gesture for the student to use when he or she needs to go to the bathroom. Reward the student for using it appropriately, and remind the student that he or she should have used it whenever he or she fails to do so.

**Primary and Intermediate Levels.**  Take the student to a shopping center, a park, or a playground. Remind the student to let you know when he or she needs to go or be taken to the restroom.

## Family Interventions

**Infant and Toddler/Preschool Level.**  Make certain that the parents consistently use and require the child to use the established gesture during toilet training activities.

**Primary and Intermediate Levels.**  Encourage the parents to show their child the locations of restrooms in the community. When these restrooms are located, remind the parents to review the appropriate gesture with their child and to expect the child to use the gesture at appropriate times.

## Specific Objective M

The student who is unable to speak, is tired or sleepy, and is unable to get to a resting place without assistance indicates through gesture (holding the hands together at the cheek while tilting the head to one side) that he or she is tired or sleepy.

## Teacher Interventions

**Infant and Toddler/Preschool Level.**  Pretend that you are tired at the end of the school day. Yawn, cover your mouth, and then say, "I am tired." As you say the word "tired," simultaneously use the "I am sleepy" gesture. Immediately after, tell the student that you cannot wait to go home to lie down and rest. Follow up by asking the student to show you what he or she should do to let you know that he or she is tired.

**Primary and Intermediate Levels.**  Take the student on an all-day field trip or a long nature walk or hike. Tell the student to let you know if he or she becomes tired so that you can stop to rest.

## Family Interventions

**Infant and Toddler/Preschool Level.**  Ask the parents to observe their child to determine when he or she is growing tired. Tell them at these times to demonstrate and discuss the "I am tired (sleepy)" gesture and then to say such things as "I see that your eyes are beginning to close and that you are rubbing them. That seems to be telling me that you are tired or sleepy. If that is so, show me that you are tired."

**Primary and Intermediate Levels.**  Ask the parents to involve their child in a variety of all-day leisure activities that are likely to require the expenditure of a great deal of energy (e.g., going to an amusement park, playing at a playground, or swimming at a pool or beach).

Tell the parents, at the start of the trip, to say such things as "During the day you may get hungry, feel thirsty, and get tired. It is your responsibility to let me know how you feel." Remind the parents that it may be necessary to review these gestures at this point.

 ## Specific Objective N

The student who is unable to speak and is too cold indicates that he or she is uncomfortable by folding the arms together, hands on elbows, while shivering slightly.

## Teacher Interventions

**Infant and Toddler/Preschool Level.**  After you have demonstrated the "I am cold" gesture and asked the student the gestural question, "Are you cold?"

on a number of occasions, tell the student that it is his or her responsibility to let you know when he or she is cold. Make it clear that if the student lets you know rather than waiting for you to suspect that he or she might be cold, you will do something *right away* to help him or her. Engage the student in a role play in which you are busy (e.g., marking papers, reading the newspaper, or doing a crafts project) and he or she must first get your attention and then indicate that he or she is cold.

**Primary and Intermediate Levels.**   On a cool or cold day, tell the student to show you the garments he or she should wear to go out to the play area for recess. If the student does not select warm clothing (e.g., mittens, a scarf, and a hat), say, "If you don't put on your ___ and ___ and ___, you are likely to become cold. If you become cold, show me how you would let someone know." Repeat this activity for a variety of weather conditions and for a variety of destinations. (See Figure 1.2.)

## Family Interventions

**Infant and Toddler/Preschool Level.**   Ask the parents to engage their child in play with dolls and stuffed animals in which they manipulate the toy so that it makes the "I am cold" gesture, then, with the child's participation, dress the doll or stuffed animal to go out in cold weather. Tell the parents to manipulate the doll or stuffed animal so that it "says," "I am cold." Encourage them to remind their child to let them know when he or she is cold.

| Weather Conditions | Appropriate Articles of Clothing |
| --- | --- |
| Cold | Gloves or mittens, hat, scarf, overcoat, heavy jacket, snowsuit, and heavy sweater |
| Hot | Sleeveless shirt or blouse, light pants or slacks, and shorts |
| Cool | Long-sleeved shirt or blouse, light jacket, medium-weight slacks or pants, and light sweater |
| Warm | Sleeveless shirt or blouse and lightweight slacks or pants |
| Rain | Raincoat, slicker, rain hat, rubbers, and umbrella |

**FIGURE 1.2.**   Weather conditions and appropriate articles of clothing.

**Primary and Intermediate Levels.** Encourage the parents to involve their child in making decisions about garments to be worn and about the use of heating, air-conditioning, and ventilating systems. Ask them to model resetting the thermostat, turning on an air conditioner or fan, and wearing different clothing both indoors and out during different weather conditions and seasons. Urge the parents to especially do these things in response to the child's indication of his or her state relative to being too cold or too hot.

---

 ## Specific Objective O

The student who is unable to speak and is too warm or hot indicates that he or she is uncomfortable by waving his or her hand like a fan while releasing a stream of air through the lips in a "Whew" sound.

---

## Teacher Interventions

**Infant and Toddler/Preschool Level.** See the suggested activity in Specific Objective N, at the infant and toddler/preschool level, and modify it, as needed, to work on the "I am hot" gesture.

(Note: It might be wise to work on objectives N and O together so that the relationship between the two different contexts may be made more clear to the student.)

**Primary and Intermediate Levels.** See the suggested activity in Specific Objective N, at the primary and intermediate levels, and modify it, as needed, to work on the "I am hot" gesture.

(Note: It might be wise to work on objectives N and O together so that the relationship between the two different contexts may become more clear.)

## Family Interventions

**Infant and Toddler/Preschool Level.** Review the suggested activity in Specific Objective N with the parents. Ask them to modify it for the "I am hot" gesture.

**Primary and Intermediate Levels.** Ask the parents to practice the suggested activity in Specific Objective N.

---

### Specific Objective P

The student who is unable to speak and wants someone to join him or her indicates "Come here" by waving the flexed fingers of one hand toward his or her body several times.

---

## Teacher Interventions

**Infant and Toddler/Preschool Level.** Give the student a simple fine motor task with which he or she is likely to experience difficulty. Before you give the student the task, say that you are available to help, if needed. Show the student the "Come here" gesture, and remind him or her to use it if your assistance is needed.

(Note: Only provide help if it is needed, to help the student differentiate between times when he or she can do something independently and times when help is truly needed.)

**Primary and Intermediate Levels.** Take the student on a trip in the community. Tell the student that there will be times during the day when he or she might wish to share something with someone else or to request someone to join him or her. Demonstrate using the "Come here" gesture to ask someone to sit next to you on the school bus, join you to look at something in a store window display, and help you make a decision on an item to be purchased.

After your demonstrations, tell the student to tell you or a classmate to join him or her on several different occasions during the remaining part of the trip.

## Family Interventions

**Infant and Toddler/Preschool Level.** Ask the parents to use the "Come here" gesture whenever their child must be attended to (e.g., when he or she must be dressed or fed) or is expected to assist in a household chore (e.g., clearing the dinner dishes).

Tell the parents to assist the child in determining when he or she needs help and in making the "Come here, I need your help" gesture.

**Primary and Intermediate Levels.** Ask the parents to encourage their child to use the "Come here" gesture when he or she wishes another person to join him or her for a specific activity.

## Specific Objective Q

The student who is unable to speak and is unable to obtain an object of a desired size indicates his or her wishes by using the "Size" gesture (hands or fingers held parallel to each other at differing distances, with close = little and far apart = big). (Note: This objective assumes that the student has the concept of size.)

## Teacher Interventions

**Infant and Toddler/Preschool Level.**   Give the student various objects to measure with his or her hands. Ask the student to show you how big the item is by demonstrating the size with his or her hands held away from the measured object.

Show the student photographs of different-sized animals (e.g., a puppy and a fully grown dog), and ask him or her to show you the size of each one by using his or her hands.

**Primary and Intermediate Levels.**   Give the student a choice of several different-sized samples of the same object. Ask the student to indicate the item he or she would like *without pointing to it*. Be sure to include items that might require the student to request the smaller or smallest sample (e.g., a baseball rather than a basketball to play baseball or a small portion of a nonpreferred food) as well as the bigger or biggest (e.g., a favorite snack item or stuffed animal).

## Family Interventions

**Infant and Toddler/Preschool Level.**   Ask the parents to show their child various items found in the home that differ in size (e.g., glassware, chinaware, and eating and cooking utensils). Encourage them to indicate the size of the item being looked at by using the "Size" gesture. Tell them to require the child to indicate the size of a desire utensil, glass, or cup by using the "Size" gesture.

**Primary and Intermediate Levels.**   Encourage the parents to involve their child in making decisions about items to be purchased whenever a decision about size is part of the judgment (e.g., "Both these pictures are nice but we must pick something that is the right size to hang on the kitchen wall. Show me with your hands which one we should pick," or "I like both these radios. Which one do you think I should buy?").

---

## Specific Objective R

The student who is unable to speak and is unable to obtain a desired number of objects indicates his or her wishes by using the fingers to indicate the desired amount. (Note: This objective assumes that the student has basic number concepts.)

---

## Teacher Interventions

**Infant and Toddler/Preschool Level.**  Show the student a number of items and ask him or her to show you, by holding up fingers, the number of items desired or needed. Make certain that the student's fingers have a one-to-one correspondence with the number of items.

(Note: It is essential to deal with both the number needed and the number desired, because the number desired of a preferred item is likely to be all that are available. For the number needed, you may wish to use, for example, the number of napkins needed for all the individuals having a snack or lunch or the number of toothbrushes needed for everyone in the class.)

**Primary and Intermediate Levels.**  Give the student a variety of tasks that require him or her to indicate the number of an item needed to carry out the tasks satisfactorily (e.g., spools of thread needed for the students doing a clothing repair task, scissors needed for a crafts project, pieces of sandpaper for a woodworking project, or playing pieces for a board game).

## Family Interventions

**Infant and Toddler/Preschool Level.**  Encourage the parents to involve their child in joining them in counting the number of a particular item found in the home (e.g., plants, fish in the fish tank, doors and windows, or lamps).

**Primary and Intermediate Levels.**  Encourage the parents to expect their child to indicate the number of items needed for a particular household activity (e.g., number of eggs for a recipe, number of hooks needed to hang pictures, number of clean pillowcases needed to remake the beds after a change of linens, or number of dust cloths needed for everyone in the family to join in dusting the furniture).

## GOAL III.

The student will respond appropriately to the vocal tone and intonational patterns of people in his or her environment whether or not the student comprehends the speaker's verbal message.

# SPECIFIC OBJECTIVES

The student:

☐ A. Responds to the vocal utterance of approval, praise, contentment, or happiness (with or without speech) by smiling and/or by continuing an ongoing activity.

☐ B. Ceases a behavior in response to a vocal utterance that indicates annoyance or disapproval (with or without words).

☐ C. Responds to the rising vocal intonation pattern that indicates that a person is asking a "Yes" or "No" question or a question in which the student, as the responder, is expected to indicate a choice (as contrasted with the vocal pattern that accompanies a simple statement or a "Wh" question).

☐ D. Leaves the area or moves away from a person who is expressing anger (with or without words).

☐ E. Responds to the vocal utterance of disappointment or sadness (with or without words) by comforting the individual.

# SUGGESTED ACTIVITIES

## Specific Objective A

The student responds to the vocal utterance of approval, praise, contentment, or happiness (with or without speech) by smiling and/or by continuing an ongoing activity.

## Teacher Interventions

**Infant and Toddler/Preschool Level.**  When greeting the student, when making eye contact, and when interacting positively with the student, smile to show that you are pleased with him or her. Explain that when people are happy and content, their voice and face usually show it.

Sing some happy melodies, and comment on the way your voice sounds happy when you sing a happy song (e.g., "If You're Happy and You Know It"). Next, say, "Listen to me and look at me as I say something happy: 'I am so happy to see you.'" (You may wish to do this in front of a wall mirror as well as face-to-face.) Do this for a number of different joyful messages (e.g., "Isn't it a lovely day, today!" "I'm glad to see that you are feeling better," or "I like the way you are sitting there playing quietly with your toy").

After you have said each of these messages, tell the student that you are going to say it once again, but this time you are going to leave out the words. Tell the student to listen to the sound of your voice when you are sending someone a happy message. Ask him or her to practice smiling in response to a happy voice.

Follow up by telling the student that if someone uses a happy voice while the student is doing something, he or she should continue the activity if he or she wants to.

**Primary and Intermediate Levels.**  At these levels, concentrate on using a pleasant, approving voice as a way of regulating the student's behavior, in effect saying, "I like what you're doing so it's okay with me if you want to continue doing it!"

## Family Interventions

**Infant and Toddler/Preschool Level.**  Ask the parents to sing happy songs to their child and to encourage the child to hum or sing along (whether or not the child understands the words). Encourage the parents to make happy or pleased comments by saying such things as "I am so happy that you are making progress and are not spilling your pudding when you feed yourself."

Tell the parents to comment favorably when the child smiles on hearing these words of praise. Tell them that, if the child does not respond, they should say such things as "I praised you, so I'd sure like a smile in return."

**Primary and Intermediate Levels.**  Encourage the parents to emphasize the regulating function of the voice by using a happy voice and a positive message whenever their child is behaving in a suitable, appropriate, and productive way.

---

| | Specific Objective B |
|---|---|
| | The student ceases a behavior in response to a vocal utterance that indicates annoyance or disapproval (with or without words). |

---

## Teacher Interventions

**Infant and Toddler/Preschool Level.**   Explain that when people are annoyed or disapproving, their voice and face usually show it. Then say, "Listen to me and look at me as I say something that shows that I do not like what you are doing: 'Stop playing with your food!'" (You may wish to do this in front of a wall mirror as well as face-to-face.)

Do this for a number of different messages of reprimand (e.g., I want you to stop wiping your nose on the back of your hand. Use a tissue!" or "Don't make that awful-sounding noise! It is really annoying").

After you have communicated each of these messages, tell the student that you are going to say it once again, but this time you are going to leave out the words. Tell the student to listen to the sound of your voice when you are sending someone a message of disapproval or reprimand.

Follow up by telling the student that if someone uses a voice like that while the student is doing something, he or she should stop doing it.

**Primary and Intermediate Levels.**   Whenever the student is engaged in a behavior that is distracting or disturbing to others, reprimand the student and explain why you are annoyed or disapprove of the behavior. Contrast these vocal tones with the approving vocal tones you use when the student *ceases* an inappropriate behavior.

## Family Interventions

**Infant and Toddler/Preschool Level.**   Urge the parents to use words of reprimand whenever their child is engaged in a disturbing, inappropriate, or annoying activity, especially one that will interfere in the future with interpersonal relationships.

**Primary and Intermediate Levels.**   Encourage the parents to discuss situation-specific behaviors and to role-play these situations. Tell them to voice their approval or disapproval of the behavior portrayed by their child as part of the role play. Remind them to continue using their voice to indicate their disapproval whenever their child is behaving in an inappropriate, nonproductive, or disturbing way.

---

### Specific Objective C

The student responds to the rising vocal intonation pattern that indicates that a person is asking a "Yes" or "No" question or a question in which the student, as the responder, is expected to indicate a choice (as contrasted with the vocal pattern that accompanies a simple statement or a "Wh" question).

---

(Note: A "Wh" question, when a choice of responses is given by the questioner, also involves a rising intonation pattern. A rhetorical question may have a rising intonation pattern, but it is not considered in this curriculum because of its complexity.)

## Teacher Interventions

**Infant and Toddler/Preschool Level.** Begin by dealing with the "Yes" or "No" question as it relates to the student's possessions. Place several possessions in front of the student and say, "This is your shirt," "This is your lunch box," and "This is your toothbrush." Follow up by asking the question form of these statements. Point out that when you want the student to respond in some way to something you have said, your voice goes up at the end. (Illustrate the rising intonation at this point.)

**Primary and Intermediate Levels.** Once the student responds to the "Yes" or "No" question about his or her possessions, proceed to dealing with "Yes" or "No" questions that concern wants, desires, and feelings (e.g., "Do you want a drink?" "Would you like to listen to some music now?" or "Are you feeling better today?").

**Secondary Level.** Introduce a question in which the student must make a choice between possible responses (i.e., either a preference or a correct response) (e.g., "Would you like to go swimming or bowling?" "Which would you prefer, milk or orange juice?" or "Who is older, you or your brother?").

## Family Interventions

**Infant and Toddler/Preschool Level.**  Ask the parents to ask their child a number of "Yes" or "No" questions about his or her possessions and the possessions of other members of the household to obtain both positive and negative responses (e.g., "Is this your hat?" "Is this your sister's hairbrush?" or "Is this my watch?").

**Primary and Intermediate Levels.**  Tell the parents that once their child responds to the "Yes" or "No" questions about his or her possessions, they should proceed to dealing with "Yes" or "No" questions that concern wants, desires, and feelings (e.g., "Do you want to go shopping with us?" "Would you like to visit Grandma and Grandpa?" or "Are you tired and do you need to rest?").

**Secondary Level.**  Ask the parents to practice asking questions of their youngster that require the child to select a preferred response or the correct response as recommended in the Teacher Interventions for the secondary level.

---

 ## Specific Objective D

The student leaves the area or moves away from a person who is expressing anger (with or without words).

---

## Teacher Interventions

**Infant and Toddler/Preschool Level.**  Review with the student the difference in the voice pattern of an approving comment and a disapproving comment or reprimand. Once the student differentiates between these two vocal patterns, introduce the vocal pattern that indicates anger. Explain that when someone talks to the student in an angry voice, it is usually wise either to leave the area or to move away from that person, if at all possible.

**Primary and Intermediate Levels.**  Read newspaper and magazine stories in which someone who was enraged harmed another person. Continue to assist the student in distinguishing the difference in vocal patterns between a reprimand and rage.

## Family Interventions

**Infant and Toddler/Preschool Level.**  Ask the parents, when they make statements of approval or reprimand, to draw their child's attention to the difference in vocal tone in addition to pointing out the reason for the statement.

**Primary and Intermediate Levels.**  Ask the parents to tape several scenes from television programs that depict an angry individual who threatens and/or harms someone else. (Note: Taping of individual scenes is recommended, since parents should be advised to restrict the viewing of violent television programming.)

Encourage the parents to discuss what actions can be taken when someone is expressing uncontrolled anger, for example, leaving the area or apologizing if the anger resulted from discourteous or inappropriate behavior.

---

### Specific Objective E

The student responds to the vocal utterance of disappointment or sadness (with or without words) by comforting the individual.

---

## Teacher Interventions

**Infant and Toddler/Preschool Level.**  If you have been disappointed or saddened by something that has happened in your life (and it is not too personal), share it with the student. Make certain that you vocally communicate your disappointment ("I was hoping to visit my friend, Florence, on our winter recess, but I won't be able to") or sadness ("My dog was hit by a car and is at the vet's"). If you have no experiences to communicate, role-play disappointing or sad occurrences.

**Primary and Intermediate Levels.**  Engage the student in a discussion of what he or she might do when a friend or relative is expressing disappointment or sadness. Explain what is meant by comforting someone, and discuss possible acceptable ways to do so.

As a follow-up to your discussion, engage the student in creative dramatics with puppets in which the student comforts the "saddened" or "disappointed" puppet.

## Family Interventions

**Infant and Toddler/Preschool Level.**  Tell the parents that when they have been disappointed or saddened and when it is appropriate to do so, they should share the information and their feelings (with or without words) with their child. Tell them to also demonstrate comforting a family member who is expressing sadness or disappointment.

**Primary and Intermediate Levels.**  Encourage the parents to join their child in watching television talk shows that present people who have experienced sorrow or disappointment. Tell them to ask the child to identify the person who is expressing sorrow or disappointment and any people (the host or audience members) who are trying to provide comfort.

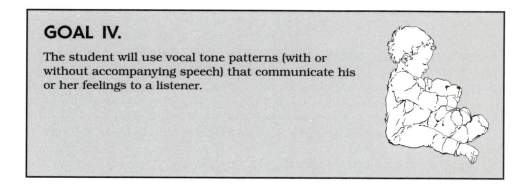

### GOAL IV.

The student will use vocal tone patterns (with or without accompanying speech) that communicate his or her feelings to a listener.

(Note: While vocal tone patterns are acquired to a large extent through imitation, some students may have little or monotonous vocal affect or stereotyped intonational patterns.)

## SPECIFIC OBJECTIVES

The student:

&#10065; A.  Expresses happiness or pleasure vocally (with or without words) whenever something pleasurable or desirable occurs.

&#10065; B.  Vocalizes disappointment or sadness (with or without words) when denied participation in a desired activity and when something occurs that makes him or her sad.

&#10065; C.  Expresses anger in a controlled way (with or without words) whenever appropriate.

&#10065; D.  Expresses fear (with or without words) when confronted with a fearful situation.

❑ E. Uses a rising vocal intonation pattern when asking a "Yes" or "No" question or a question that asks the listener to select either the correct or the preferred response.

# SUGGESTED ACTIVITIES

---

### Specific Objective A

The student expresses happiness or pleasure vocally (with or without words) whenever something pleasurable or desirable occurs.

---

## Teacher Interventions

**Infant and Toddler/Preschool Level.** Identify a toy or a food item that the student enjoys. Show the student the preferred item and ask him or her to indicate whether he or she would like to have it. Make certain that the student uses an appropriate vocal tone pattern (with or without words).

**Primary and Intermediate Levels.** Explain to the student that he or she must provide you with feedback whenever you suggest an activity or when he or she is engaged in an activity. Demonstrate how you behave and how your voice sounds when you approve of an activity as well as when you are contentedly engaged in a pleasurable activity.

Communicate, for example, the basic feelings incorporated in a statement such as "I am really enjoying building with these differently shaped pieces of wood." Make certain that the student demonstrates the appropriate vocal affect.

## Family Interventions

**Infant and Toddler/Preschool Level.** Ask the parents to determine their child's repertoire of desired objects, toys, foods, games, and activities. When the child is involved with these items and activities, encourage the parents to ask the child how he or she is feeling. Remind the parents to expect the child to vocally express happiness or pleasure.

**Primary and Intermediate Levels.** Encourage the parents to expect their child to indicate his or her preferences by using a vocal tone that communicates happiness or pleasure. Tell the parents to explain that they need to know the child's feelings in order to provide experiences that he or she enjoys whenever possible.

> ### Specific Objective B
>
> The student vocalizes disappointment or sadness (with or without words) when denied participation in a desired activity and when something occurs that makes him or her sad.

## Teacher Interventions

**Infant and Toddler/Preschool Level.**   Ask the parents if there have been real situations that have disappointed or saddened the student and that you can use in classroom activities. If so, ask the student to recall these situations and review his or her feelings and the way he or she might sound when expressing them.

If the parents cannot supply any examples, read or tell the student stories or anecdotes about individuals who have been disappointed (the ice storm prevented them from going to a friend's birthday party) or were made sad (Uncle Tony lost his job). Ask the student to show disappointment or sadness in his or her voice.

**Primary and Intermediate Levels.**   Give the student hypothetical situations, and ask the student to demonstrate with his or her voice (with or without speech) how he or she feels. Mix happy and sad experiences.

## Family Interventions

**Infant and Toddler/Preschool Level.**   Encourage the parents to share their feelings with the child and to comment on the way different feelings make their voice sound different. Tell them to contrast the opposite emotions of happiness and sadness.

**Primary and Intermediate Levels.**   Ask the parents to ascertain whether their child is using the appropriate vocal affect in expressing his or her feelings whenever actual situations arise. Tell them to talk about recent incidents and to recall incidents from the past that have caused pleasure and/or happiness or disappointment and/or sadness.

> ### Specific Objective C
>
> The student expresses anger in a controlled way (with or without words) whenever appropriate.

## Teacher Interventions

**Infant and Toddler/Preschool Level.** Discuss the difference between anger and disappointment. Also explore the difference between controlled anger and rage or temper tantrums. Show the student videotaped sequences of someone who is having a temper tantrum or is otherwise enraged. Explain that *uncontrolled* anger is not acceptable behavior.

**Primary and Intermediate Levels.** Review with the student situations that may cause people to become angry. Review the difference between anger and disappointment. Explore the difference between controlled anger and rage or temper tantrums. Model disappointment and anger in specific situations (e.g., *disappointment* at not being able to go somewhere we would like and *anger* when someone has stolen or deliberately damaged our property).

Ask the student to demonstrate disappointment and controlled anger (with or without words) when given specific situations that may occur in the school and at home in which these feelings are appropriate. Make certain that the student demonstrates the appropriate vocal affect.

**Secondary Level.** Review situations that might occur in the community and in the workplace that may cause someone to become angry. Role-play these situations and make certain that the student demonstrates the appropriate vocal affect.

## Family Interventions

**Infant and Toddler/Preschool Level.** Provide the parents with strategies that they can apply if and when their child has a temper tantrum (ignoring the behavior is usually the best strategy). Ask the parents to wait for the child to become angry.

Tell them that if the child expresses anger in a controlled manner, with the appropriate vocal affect, and if the anger is appropriate to the situation, they should say such things as "You are angry because Tommy took your toy without asking permission. That *is* a reason for getting angry. I *like* the way you showed your anger without losing your temper."

**Primary and Intermediate Levels.** Ask the parents to review situations that may cause people to become angry. Tell them to clarify the difference between controlled anger and rage. Encourage them to identify situations that may occur in their home and in their travels in the community that may make them angry. Remind them to model being angry in a controlled way whenever these situations occur in their lives.

**Secondary Level.** Ask the parents to talk about situations they have faced in the past, especially those that deal with the world of work and interactions with relatives and friends. Tell them to communicate that, while it may be appropriate to voice anger in a controlled way, it is also important for the child to resolve the problem or issue after the anger has been expressed.

---

### Specific Objective D

The student expresses fear (with or without words) when confronted with a fearful situation.

---

## Teacher Interventions

**Infant and Toddler/Preschool Level.** If a situation arises in which the student voices or in some other way expresses fear, indicate that you understand that the student is afraid and are glad he or she let you know so that you can offer comfort or protection. If possible, assist the student in identifying situations that he or she should not fear (e.g., when the lights have gone out temporarily or during a thunderstorm when he or she is safe in the home).

**Primary Level.** Explain that there are times when people should be fearful (e.g., when facing an emergency situation such as being in a house that is on fire or during an earthquake, tornado, flood, or other natural disaster). Model how your voice might sound during such times. Ask the student to do so. Observe the student to see whether he or she has a particular fear that may not be rational. Help to desensitize the student by introducing the feared object at a distance and gradually bringing it closer to him or her.

(Note: Some students may have an inordinate fear of objects that are benign, such as feathers or stuffed animals. Use the desensitization technique whenever this occurs.)

**Intermediate and Secondary Levels.** Help the student to differentiate between situations that he or she should fear and those that are not fearful. Make certain that the student demonstrates fear vocally (with or without words) when appropriate. (See Figure 1.3.)

## Family Interventions

**Infant and Toddler/Preschool Level.** Tell the parents that if a frightening situation arises, they should demonstrate controlled fear and comfort their child. Encourage them to explain that if the child is frightened, he or she should communicate it to get help from somebody. At this level, ask the parents to concentrate on communicating fear, whether it is rational or not.

**Primary and Intermediate Levels.** Ask the parents, at these levels, to assist the child in differentiating situations that occur in the life of the family that are fearful from those that should not be feared.

Tell the parents to help the child differentiate between situations that may cause concern or worry but that are not to be feared (e.g., "I am concerned because the wind is very strong, but we should not be afraid because I have closed the shutters and the new front door is made of steel" or "I am concerned that I have cut myself and bled from my cut, but I am not afraid since the bleeding has stopped and first aid has been applied"). Ask the parents to role-play similar situations and to make certain that the child demonstrates controlled fear during fearful situations.

| Benign Situation | Fearful Situation |
| --- | --- |
| Being safely in an automobile during a lightning storm | Being in an open area during a lightning storm |
| A barking dog on a leash and under the control of its owner | A barking dog not on a leash and with no owner nearby |
| A horror or science-fiction movie or video | A threatening person with a weapon such as a gun or knife |
| A wild animal at a zoo who is in an enclosed or protected area | A wild animal in a wooded area |
| A fire drill | An actual fire |
| A noon siren | An emergency alarm |

**FIGURE 1.3.** Benign and fearful situations.

**Secondary Level.**   At this level, encourage the parents to help their youngster identify fearful situations that may occur as they move about the community and when they are alone in a home setting. Review communicating one's fear vocally (but not inordinately so to avoid confusion and misunderstandings) when seeking the help of others, such as when calling 911 or telephoning a physician.

---

### Specific Objective E

The student uses a rising vocal intonation pattern when asking a "Yes" or "No" question or a question that asks the listener to select either the correct or the preferred response.

---

## Teacher Interventions

**Infant and Toddler/Preschool Level.**   Whenever the student asks a question that calls for a "Yes" or "No" response, as in requesting an object (e.g., "May I play with the large wooden blocks?"), whether it is syntactically complete or correct, respond only if the student uses a rising intonation pattern. Provide assistance, when needed, by demonstrating the rising intonation pattern.

**Primary Level.**   Set up a learning situation in which the student must ask whether something belongs to you or not. Make certain that the student asks the "Yes" or "No" question with a rising inflection.

**Intermediate Level.**   Implement an instructional plan in which the student must determine what a classmate's feelings, wants, and behaviors are in response to "Yes" or "No" questions (e.g., "Do you like to watch baseball on television?" "Would you like to take a trip this summer to an amusement park?" "Did you give the note to your parents?" or "Have you finished your lunch?").

**Secondary Level.**   Ask the student to conduct an interview in which he or she must determine a classmate's or your preferences (e.g., "Do you prefer frankfurters or hamburgers?" "Would you rather play basketball or volleyball?" or "Would you prefer working in a fast-food restaurant or in a factory setting?").

## Family Interventions

**Infant and Toddler/Preschool Level.**  Ask the parents to set up situations in which their child needs to ask for something specific to happen (e.g., "May I have a glass of chocolate milk?" "May I give Rover his food?" or "Will you help me tie my shoe?"). Tell them to make certain that the child uses a rising inflection.

**Primary and Intermediate Levels.**  Ask the parents to engage the child in simple conversations that involve a series of questions and responses. (See Figure 1.4.)

**Secondary Level.**  Ask the parents to set up situations in which their youngster seeks information (e.g., "Should I wear this dress when I go on the job interview?") or wishes to determine someone's preference (e.g., when asking on a date, "Would you prefer going to a movie on Friday night or going to see the school team play in the football tournament?").

## GOAL V.

The student will respond appropriately to the facial expressions of people in his or her environment whether or not the student comprehends the speaker's verbal message.

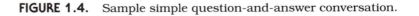

CHILD:  "Can we go swimming tomorrow?"

PARENT:  "Yes, I have a day off and the weather should be fine."

CHILD:  "Is it all right if my friend, Mary, comes with us?"

PARENT:  "That would be fine."

CHILD:  "What time shall I tell her to be ready?"

PARENT:  "At 9:30 in the morning."

**FIGURE 1.4.**   Sample simple question-and-answer conversation.

# SPECIFIC OBJECTIVES

The student:

❏ A. Responds to a person who is smiling by smiling in return.

❏ B. Responds to a smile of approval (with or without speech) by continuing an activity.

❏ C. Responds to a facial expression of disappointment or sadness (with or without speech) by comforting the person who is unhappy.

❏ D. Ceases an activity or removes himself or herself from a situation in response to the facial expression (with or without words) of a person who is angry.

❏ E. Identifies when a person is frightened and removes the frightening stimulus and/or comforts the person (with or without speech).

# SUGGESTED ACTIVITIES

## Specific Objective A

The student responds to a person who is smiling by smiling in return.

## Teacher Interventions

**Infant and Toddler/Preschool Level.** Present the student with activities that usually evoke a pleasurable response, such as participating in a game, listening or dancing to music, and playing with toys. Tell the student that you are having a wonderful time as you smile broadly and say, "See how I smile when I am happy!"

Then ask the student to show his or her happiness by smiling in turn. If the student has difficulty, place him or her in front of a mirror and, if necessary, use your fingers to help the student retract his or her lips.

**Primary Level.** Show the student several photographs of people who are smiling and several of people who are not smiling. Tell the student to point to the smiling faces and to smile in turn.

## Family Interventions

**Infant and Toddler/Preschool Level.** Ask the parents to play a variation of "Simon Says" in which the child is expected to imitate facial expressions (e.g., "Simon says, 'Make a face just like mine!'").

**Primary Level.** Encourage the parents to take their child for visits to the homes of friends, relatives, and neighbors. Prior to the visit tell them to explain that people smile when greeting each other. Ask them to practice greetings with a smile prior to the visit and then to praise the child for smiling when doing the actual greeting.

---

### Specific Objective B

The student responds to a smile of approval (with or without speech) by continuing an activity.

---

## Teacher Interventions

**Infant and Toddler/Preschool Level.** Wait until the student is engaged in an appropriate activity and demonstrate your approval by smiling and saying such things as "I like the way you are playing quietly with your new toy!" Intermittently reward the student with just a smile.

**Primary Level.** Give the student a "smiley-face" sticker for engaging in a cooperative class activity. Paste it on the personal behavior chart or notebook that is sent home for parents to review and on which they send notes of their own to school.

## Family Interventions

**Infant and Toddler/Preschool Level.** Ask the parents to demonstrate their approval both verbally and with a smile, explaining that positive reinforcement is a powerful management tool that usually will result in improved behavior and learning.

**Primary Level.** Ask the parents to take their child for trips into the community and to reward him or her for behaving appropriately on these trips (e.g., "I like the way you waited your turn on the line to see Santa Claus!").

---

> **Specific Objective C**
>
> The student responds to a facial expression of disappointment or sadness (with or without speech) by comforting the person who is unhappy.

---

## Teacher Interventions

**Infant and Toddler/Preschool Level.**  Wait for a situation to occur that evokes disappointment or sadness, such as a broken toy or a spilled dessert. Say words of comfort such as "I'm sorry that the toy is broken, and I know how you must feel," while reflecting your chagrin in your facial expression and gently rubbing the back of the student's hand. When a similar incident occurs, express your sorrow, and ask the student to comfort you by placing his or her hand on the back of yours and joining you in looking sad.

**Primary Level.**  Role-play sad or disappointing situations and ask the student to show how the actor playing the part is feeling. Follow up a correct response by asking the student to express words of comfort, if possible, or to gently place his or her hand on the actor's hand. Reward the student for independently comforting a classmate who is experiencing sadness or disappointment.

**Intermediate Level.**  Repeat the primary-level activity. Be sure, at this level, to indicate in some way that not every person wants to be comforted when he or she is disappointed or sad and may prefer to be alone. Help the student identify body language that says, "Stay away from me until I get over this feeling!"

## Family Interventions

**Infant and Toddler/Preschool Level.**  Ask the parents to purchase a crying doll. Tell them to role-play comforting the doll and to encourage their child to do the same.

**Primary Level.**  Ask the parents to share their own moments of sadness with their child and to say such things as "I heard that my friend, Barbara, is sick and in the hospital. I am sad and worried about her. Come over here and sit by me."

---

**Specific Objective D**

The student ceases an activity or removes himself or herself from a situation in response to the facial expression (with or without words) of a person who is angry.

---

## Teacher Interventions

**Infant and Toddler/Preschool Level.** If the student comes into direct contact with an angry peer who is acting out his or her anger, move the student away from that peer. Explain why you have moved the student.

**Primary Level.** Show the student photographs of people who are angry and several of people who are not angry. Ask the student to identify who the angry people are and to explain what the student would do if he or she were confronted by an angry person.

## Family Interventions

**Infant and Toddler/Preschool Level.** Tell the parents that if their child engages in a destructive or inappropriate activity, they should show their disapproval by facially demonstrating their anger. Remind the parents to engage the child in an appropriate activity when the destructive activity has stopped.

(Note: Make certain that the parents differentiate between controlled anger and rage and that they understand that controlled anger, appropriately expressed and legitimately aroused, is acceptable.)

**Primary Level.** Ask the parents to take photographs of themselves and other family members in which sadness, happiness, and anger are depicted. Tell them to present their child with hypothetical situations taken from previously demonstrated real experiences and to ask the child to respond to the photograph presented (e.g., "You are helping Mommy dust the furniture. Show me how I would look," "Your brother is sick. Show me how Daddy would look," or "You threw your dinner plate on the floor. Show me how I would look").

## Specific Objective E

The student identifies when a person is frightened and removes the frightening stimulus and/or comforts the person (with or without speech).

## Teacher Interventions

**Infant and Toddler/Preschool Level.**   If a classmate expresses fear in a nonemergency situation, approach the frightened peer and reassure him or her by holding his or her hand. Encourage the student to join you in comforting the classmate.

**Primary and Intermediate Levels.**   Reward the student for independently comforting a frightened peer at appropriate times and in an appropriate way. Give the student a collection of photographs and pictures from magazines and newspapers and ask him or her to separate them into happy, sad, angry, and frightened faces. Ask the student to explain what he or she would do if the person were a close friend or relative.

## Family Interventions

**Infant and Toddler/Preschool Level.**   Tell the parents to demonstrate how they deal with occasions when the child has become frightened. If there is a younger sibling in the home, ask the parents to involve the child in their efforts to calm the sibling down and to restore the sibling to a more comfortable state.

**Primary Level.**   Ask the parents to explain the difference between being concerned about something and being frightened. Tell them to involve their child in role plays in which the child must comfort an actor who appears to be frightened while in a nonemergency situation (e.g., when seeing a harmless insect).

## GOAL VI.

The student will use facial expressions (with or without accompanying speech) that communicate his or her feelings to a listener.

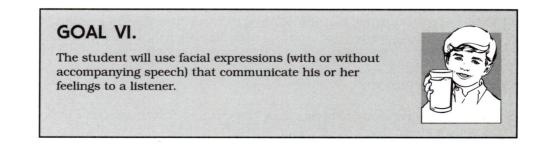

# SPECIFIC OBJECTIVES

The student:

❐ A. Smiles when receiving a favored object or when seeing a favorite person.

❐ B. Smiles when praised or rewarded.

❐ C. Smiles when told good news.

❐ D. Makes a sad face when disappointed, sad, or unhappy.

❐ E. Expresses fear facially (with or without speech) when confronted with a stimulus that he or she fears.

❐ F. Expresses anger facially (with or without speech) when interfered with or threatened.

# SUGGESTED ACTIVITIES

## Specific Objective A

The student smiles when receiving a favored object or when seeing a favorite person.

## Teacher Interventions

**Infant and Toddler/Preschool Level.** Ask the parents to tell you what their child's favorite toys and playthings are. Then collect a variety of objects. Tell the student that he or she may choose only one to play with and that the student must let you know his or her choice by smiling when you hold up the one he or she would like.

**Primary Level.** Arrange for the student's parent, sibling, or other friend or family member to visit the classroom. Ask the student if he or she is happy to see the visitor. Tell the student to show pleasure by smiling while greeting the visitor.

## Family Interventions

**Infant and Toddler/Preschool Level.** Ask the parents to demonstrate their happiness to their child when he or she helps them or gives them a gift made in school. Remind the parents to tell the child that a smile is a nice way to show one's appreciation.

**Primary Level.** Tell the parents to take their child on shopping trips whose purpose is to buy something for the child. Encourage them to show the item before making the purchase and to ask the child to approve the purchase with a smile.

---

 **Specific Objective B**

The student smiles when praised or rewarded.

---

## Teacher Interventions

**Infant and Toddler/Preschool Level.** Praise and reward the student for attempts and successes and for behaving appropriately. Encourage the student to smile to show that he or she is pleased to be praised and rewarded.

**Primary Level.** Vary your rewards and your words of praise for a "job" well done. View rewards developmentally with the goal of progressing from tangible rewards to social reinforcers. Do not forget to reward the student for smiling his or her "Thank you" when rewarded.

## Family Interventions

**Infant and Toddler/Preschool Level.** Make certain that the parents understand the power of rewards as a motivation for continuing efforts on the part of their child and as a way of encouraging appropriate behavior.

**Primary Level.** Tell the parents to explain to their child that a smile is one way of saying "Thank you" to someone who has been kind.

---

 **Specific Objective C**

The student smiles when told good news.

---

## Teacher Interventions

**Infant and Toddler/Preschool Level.** Tell the student a happy story or anecdote. Smile broadly at the happy ending and encourage the student to show that he or she liked the story or anecdote by smiling as well.

**Primary Level.** Read news stories from newspapers and magazines and encourage the student to express his or her reaction to the "good news." If you have arranged an enjoyable field trip (e.g., to the zoo), ask the student to indicate with just facial expressions whether he or she wishes to go on the trip.

**Intermediate and Secondary Levels.** If the student has favorite sports teams, share the result of the most recent game and ask the student to show you with facial expressions how he or she feels.

## Family Interventions

**Infant and Toddler/Preschool Level.** Ask the parents to share any good news received by the family (e.g., "Aunt Lucy just called and said she is coming to visit us. We know you like to play with Aunt Lucy. Show me by smiling if you are looking forward to her visit").

**Primary Level.** Ask the parents to suggest to their child one of his or her favorite activities (e.g., "Would you like to go to the playground to play on the merry-go-round?"). Remind them to tell the child to indicate "Yes" by smiling.

---

### Specific Objective D

The student makes a sad face when disappointed, sad, or unhappy.

---

## Teacher Interventions

**Infant and Toddler/Preschool Level.** When an actual situation arises that is likely to disappoint a student or make him or her sad (e.g., "We can't go to the school playground after lunch because it is raining"), ask the student how he or she feels. Demonstrate your agreement by also looking sad or disappointed.

**Primary Level.** Read stories or tell anecdotes that have happy endings and others that have sad endings. Ask the student to show you with facial expressions how he or she feels at the end of each story.

**Intermediate and Secondary Levels.** Ask the parents to share information with you about actual family incidents and occurrences that have caused the family to be disappointed or saddened. (Be sure not to invade the family's or student's privacy in carrying out this activity!)

Discuss these situations with the student and ask him or her to express his or her feelings, with or without words.

## Family Interventions

**Infant and Toddler/Preschool Level.** Encourage the parents to demonstrate their disappointment or sadness to their child whenever they are saddened. At this level, make certain that the parents express the emotion and state the reason in simple terms without elaboration (e.g., "I am sad because our dog is sick").

**Primary Level.** Ask the parents, at this level, to discuss in greater detail family situations that have caused them to be sad or disappointed (e.g., "I was hoping to get the new job I applied for but I didn't get it. It would have meant more income for the family").

**Intermediate and Secondary Levels.** At these levels, ask the parents to share news with their youngster that is of a more serious nature such as news about accidents, serious illnesses, and death.

---

 ## Specific Objective E

The student expresses fear facially (with or without speech) when confronted with a stimulus that he or she fears.

---

## Teacher Interventions

**Infant and Toddler/Preschool Level.** Sit the student in front of a mirror and practice making happy, sad, and fearful faces. After the student has successfully made these faces, present him or her with a simple situation to respond to by showing the appropriate face.

**Primary and Intermediate Levels.** If the student expresses fear of an object or situation that is not truly fearful, desensitize it. Discuss the situations that we all should fear and how to successfully deal with them (e.g., a natural disaster, a fire, or a threatening person).

## Family Interventions

**Infant and Toddler/Preschool Level.** Ask the parents to become aware of any inordinate fears they have, such as a fear of insects, to make certain that they do not communicate these fears to their child.

**Primary and Intermediate Levels.** Tell the parents to help their child distinguish between situations that are truly fearful and those that are not to be feared. Encourage them to identify strategies for dealing with both types of situations.

---

### Specific Objective F

The student expresses anger facially (with or without speech) when interfered with or threatened.

---

## Teacher Interventions

**Infant and Toddler/Preschool Level.** Demonstrate controlled anger when a student aggressively interferes with or attacks another student. Say, "I am responsible for all the students in this class, and I will not allow anyone to hurt any of my students."

**Primary Level.** Tell the student that, while you will help protect him or her from being interfered with or attacked by others, the student must protect himself or herself whenever you or other adults are not present. Explain that by showing controlled anger facially and with words, it is possible to make an attacker or abuser stop.

**Intermediate and Secondary Levels.** Role-play or discuss situations in which the student should show his or her anger (e.g., someone is touching the student in a private place or someone has taken something belonging to him or her). Be sure to help the student differentiate between these situations and those when anger will result in greater danger, for example, when the person has a gun.

## Family Interventions

**Infant and Toddler/Preschool Level.**  Ask the parents to demonstrate controlled anger when a situation occurs in the home that should arouse anger (e.g., a sibling has used a toy to injure another sibling).

**Primary Level.**  Ask the parents to help their child express legitimate anger in a controlled way when the child is interfered with, is taken undue advantage of by a sibling during household play, or is in the community and is attacked or taken advantage of.

**Intermediate and Secondary Levels.**  Encourage the parents to review with their youngster situations that may occur in the child's life when he or she should express anger (e.g., when someone is physically abusive), when the child should refrain from expressing anger (e.g., when threatened with a gun or other weapon), and when expressing anger may cause greater problems than dealing with the matter at a more opportune and less emotional time (e.g., when dealing with a work supervisor who the youngster thinks has been unfair).

## GOAL VII.

The student who is unable to communicate through speech or whose speech must be supplemented will use an augmentative or alternative means of communication.

# SPECIFIC OBJECTIVES

Employing *one* of the following, the student:

❒ A.  Uses a sign language to communicate his or her needs, wants, interests, and thoughts.

❒ B.  Uses a communication board with pictures, letters, words, pictographs, and representational, abstract, and arbitrary symbols to communicate his or her needs, wants, interests, and thoughts.

❒ C.  Uses a keyboard to type messages and for word processing.

❐ D. Uses a personal computer system, including a voice synthesizer and graphics and other video displays with pictures, letters, words, pictographs, and representational, abstract, and arbitrary symbols, to communicate his or her needs, wants, interests, and thoughts.

# SUGGESTED ACTIVITIES

---

### Specific Objective A

The student uses a sign language to communicate his or her needs, wants, interests, and thoughts.

---

## Teacher Interventions

**Infant and Toddler/Preschool Level.** When working with a student who it has been determined is unlikely to be able to communicate sufficiently or at all through speech and natural gestures and for whom it has been determined that a sign language system is the most appropriate augmentative or alternative means of communication, instruct the student in a commonly used sign language, preferably a combination of finger spelling and ASL or, perhaps, Signed English.

Observe the young student to determine the words for which signs should be introduced and taught. Always speak while you are signing. (See Figures 1.5 and 1.6.)

**Primary, Intermediate, and Secondary Levels.** Once it has been determined by the multidisciplinary team, the parents, an augmentative communication specialist (if available), and the student (when appropriate) that the use of a sign language system is the most appropriate augmentative or alternative means of communication, instruct the student in the system in an organized and structured way, gradually increasing his or her skill in self-expression.

Be certain that the important others (especially family members and teachers) in the life of the student possess the necessary skills to communicate with him or her.

## Family Interventions

**Infant and Toddler/Preschool Level.** Check with the parents to determine whether they agree that a sign language system is the most appropriate means

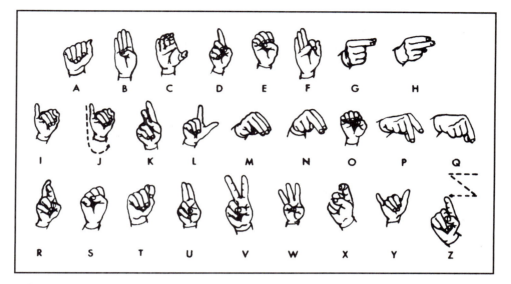

**FIGURE 1.5.** The manual alphabet as seen by the receiver. Courtesy of the National Association of the Deaf.

of communication for their child. Also determine whether they have the desire and the time and will put in the needed effort to learn the system along with the child. Involve them in selecting the signs to be taught.

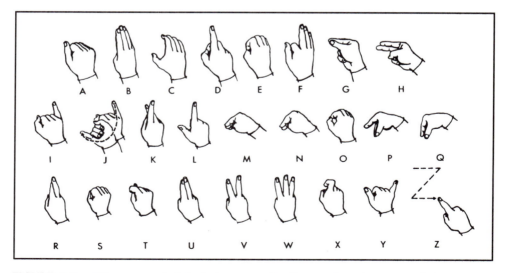

**FIGURE 1.6.** The manual alphabet as seen by the sender. Courtesy of the National Association of the Deaf.

**Primary, Intermediate, and Secondary Levels.** Once a sign language system has been selected as the most appropriate augmentative or alternative means of communication for the specific child, work closely with the parents to make certain that everyone who is part of the communication system works cooperatively together.

Make sure that the parents use the system in an organized and structured way, gradually increasing their own skill and the youngster's skill in self-expression.

---

### Specific Objective B

The student uses a communication board with pictures, letters, words, pictographs, and representational, abstract, and arbitrary symbols to communicate his or her needs, wants, interests, and thoughts.

---

## Teacher Interventions

**Infant and Toddler/Preschool Level.** When working with a student who it has been determined is unlikely to be able to communicate sufficiently or at all through speech and natural gestures and for whom the use of a picture, letter, or word communication board has been determined to be the most appropriate augmentative or alternative means of communication, take an inventory of the vocabulary needed by the student. Begin with a picture communication board at this level, using photographs, pictures from magazines, or simple drawings.

**Primary Level.** If the student is using his or her picture communication board successfully, begin the development of letter and word communication boards. Both these boards should be considered for development: the letter board for its portability when the student is functioning out of the school or home setting and the word board for its greater speed.

**Intermediate and Secondary Levels.** Gradually increase the scope of the communication boards, proceeding in an organized fashion to allow the student to express more complex ideas and to engage in more detailed and elaborate conversations and discussions. Depending on the student's intellectual level, utilize other symbol sets and systems such as pictographs and representational, abstract, and arbitrary symbols, whether they are made by the teacher or commercially available.

(See the introduction to Unit 1, Suggested Readings, and Selected Materials/Resources for further information.)

## Family Interventions

**Infant and Toddler/Preschool Level.** Ask the parents to assist you in identifying the key vocabulary for their child's picture communication board. Make certain that the child has a duplicate of the school's communication board for use in the home setting when the expanding picture board is no longer readily portable.

   Determine the range of physical and vocal skills of the child who it has been determined is unlikely to be able to communicate through speech. Incorporate these vocalizations and movements (e.g., eyes up for "Yes" and down for "No" to answer your questions about the exact location of a word, a tap of the child's foot a certain number of times to indicate the number of the panel on the communication board where the word is found, or a specific vocal sound to signal the location of a word on the board).

**Primary Level.** Ask the parents to participate in deciding whether to develop letter and word communication boards as a replacement for the picture communication board for the child who can progress to this level. Impress upon the parents the need to practice communicating with their child on a daily basis.

**Intermediate and Secondary Levels.** Inform the parents that they should gradually increase the scope of the communication boards and proceed, in an organized fashion, to increase the ability of their youngster to express more complex ideas and to engage in more detailed and elaborate conversations and discussions. (See Teacher Interventions, intermediate and secondary levels, for further suggestions.)

---

 ## Specific Objective C

The student uses a keyboard to type messages and for word processing.

---

## Teacher Interventions

**Primary Level.** If the student is able, instruct him or her in the use of a keyboard on a typewriter or a computer, either unaided or aided (e.g., using a stick attached to a headband or held in the student's mouth), depending on the student's motor skills, including range of motion.

**Intermediate and Secondary Levels.** At these levels, decide on a word-processing program and assist the student who is developmentally capable in acquiring word-processing skills.

## Family Interventions

**Primary Level.** Ask the parents to practice typing skills with their child and to use any aids that they have identified in conjunction with the teacher and other professionals, including an augmentative communication specialist, if available.

**Intermediate and Secondary Levels.** Inform the parents that they should attempt, at these levels, to assist their youngster in acquiring word-processing skills.

---

### Specific Objective D

The student uses a personal computer system, including a voice synthesizer and graphics and other video displays with pictures, letters, words, pictographs, and representational, abstract, and arbitrary symbols, to communicate his or her needs, wants, interests, and thoughts.

---

## Teacher Interventions

**Infant and Toddler/Preschool Level.** Show the student a personal computer and some interesting graphics displayed on the computer. Print out a colorful display using computer graphics.

**Primary Level.** Begin with letter and word communication boards and show the student, using one or two fingers, how he or she can type the letters on the monitor.

(Note: Special equipment such as guard plates and hand-held pointers may be necessary. Check with a computer consultant or an occupational therapist to determine the adaptations needed by the student.)

**Intermediate and Secondary Levels.** Use computer games as reinforcement and as a way of motivating the student to use the computer. Based on the student's motor functioning and intellectual level, determine the most effective and efficient communication system to establish an appropriate and comfortable mode of response as well as the symbols to be used in computer displays.

Become acquainted with the variety of commercial materials available, and determine which one is appropriate for the student and his or her family.

## Family Interventions

Review the Teacher Interventions for each of the levels with the parents. Make certain that the parents are fully involved in identifying their child's communication needs, skills, needed assistive devices, and required technology. Be sure that both school personnel and family members are working cooperatively to develop the best possible communication system for the youngster.

# Sample Lesson Plan

**Topic Area:**   Nonverbal Communication

**Designed by:**   Sandra Whitewater

**Time Recommended:**   30 minutes

**Student Involved:**   Anna (Primary Special Class)

## Background Information:

The student has limited oral receptive language. She does appear to comprehend some spoken words, for example, she looks at the ceiling light fixture when someone says, "Light." She also appears to comprehend some gestural language; for example, (a) she looks at a person who is waving his or her hand for attention, (b) when an object is pointed to she will look at that object, and (c) she responds appropriately to a headshake or nod. She has yet to demonstrate an understanding of any other gesture by responding appropriately. (Note: I have checked to determine that Anna has no known food allergies!)

## General Goal *(Nonverbal Communication I):*

The student will respond appropriately to the commonly employed gestures of people in his or her environment whether they occur alone or as an integral part of their oral communication.

## Specific Objective *(Nonverbal Communication I-E):*

The student gives a person an object in response to the "Give me" gesture (an extended hand or the alternating flexion and extension of the hand).

## Lesson Objective:

When the student is asked to assist you in carrying out several construction and collaborative tasks, she will respond correctly and quickly to the "Give me" gesture by giving you the item pointed to.

## Materials and Equipment:

- a package of seeds
- a trowel and several flowerpots containing soil
- salt and pepper shakers
- a large wooden spoon
- a hammer and nails and a wooden birdhouse
- sliced bread, peanut butter, and grape jelly
- a butter knife, a teaspoon, and two sandwich plates
- two glasses and a container of milk
- two placemats and napkins

## Motivating Activity:

Make a simple snack with the cooperation of one of the student's class-mates (e.g., peanut butter-and-jelly sandwiches). As you are preparing the snack, point out how the classmate is assisting by responding quickly when signaled "Give me." When you are finished, give the student and the classmate the sandwich and a glass of milk as a late-afternoon snack. Explain that you were able to make the snack with the help of someone else who gave you the items requested.

## Instructional Procedures:

**Initiation**—Tell the student that when she finishes her snack, she will help you complete some tasks just as her classmate did. Explain that you will be pointing to the objects you have placed on your desk and then sig-naling "Give me." At this point show the gesture, and explain that when the student sees you make the gesture she is to give you the object to which you previously pointed. Demonstrate with the seeds, the hammer and nails, the wooden spoon, and the salt and pepper shakers.

**Guided Practice**—Then say, "Let's start by fixing this wooden birdhouse that is falling apart. When I am ready, I will point to the items I need and signal you to give me the items." Point first to the hammer and then to the nails.

**Independent Practice**—Ask the student to help a classmate plant some seeds in the flowerpots on the windowsill and to give the classmate the seeds and the trowel when signaled to do so.

**Closure**—Ask the student to help you prepare a recipe for tomorrow's snack and to assist you when you need the salt, the pepper, and the wooden spoon.

## Assessment Strategy:

Observe the student to determine whether she correctly and quickly responded to the "Give me" gesture.

## Follow-Up Activity or Objective:

If the student achieves the lesson objective, proceed to a lesson requiring the student to respond appropriately to the "Goodbye" wave.

## Observations and Their Instructional Insights:

# References

Beirne-Smith, M., Patton, J. R., & Ittenbach, R. (1994). *Mental retardation* (4th ed.). New York: Merrill/Macmillan.

Bolton, S., & Dashiell, S. (1989). *INCH: INteraction CHecklist for Augmentative Communication.* Wauconda, IL: Don Johnston Developmental Equipment.

Gearheart, B., Mullen, R. C., & Gearheart, V. (1993). *Exceptional individuals: An introduction.* Pacific Grove, CA: Brooks/Cole.

Hunt, N., & Marshall, K. (1994). *Exceptional children and youth: An introduction to special education.* Boston: Houghton Mifflin.

Kirk, S. A., Gallagher, J. J., & Anastasiow, N. J. (1993). *Educating exceptional children* (7th ed.). Boston: Houghton Mifflin.

Lloyd, L. L., & Kangas, K. A. (1994). Alternative and augmentative communication. In G. H. Shames, E. H. Wiig, & W. A. Secord (Eds.), *Human communication disorders: An introduction* (4th ed., pp. 606–657). New York: Merrill/Macmillan.

Polloway, E. A., & Smith, T.E.C. (1992). *Language instruction for students with disabilities* (2nd ed.). Denver, CO: Love.

# Suggested Readings

Abrahamsen, A., Cavallo, M., & McCluer, A. (1985). Is the sign advantage a robust phenomenon? From gesture to language in two modalities. *Merrill-Palmer Quarterly, 31,* 177–209.

Acredalo, L., & Goodwyn, S. (1985). Symbolic gesturing in language development: A case study. *Human Development, 28,* 40–49.

Alberto, P., Garrett, E., Briggs, T., & Unberger, F. (1983). Selection and initiation of a nonverbal communication program for severely handicapped students. *Focus on Exceptional Children, 15*(7), 1–15.

Baker, C., & Padden, C. (1978). *American Sign Language: A book of its history, structure, and community.* Silver Spring, MD: T.J. Publishers.

Baumgart, D., Johnson, J., & Helmstetter, E. (1990). *Augmentative and alternative communication systems for persons with moderate and severe disabilities.* Baltimore: Paul H. Brookes.

Bernstein, D. K., & Tiegerman, E. (1989). *Language and communication disorders in children* (2nd ed.). New York: Merrill/Macmillan.

Beukelman, D. R., & Yorkston, K. M. (1989). Augmentative and alternative communication application for persons with severe acquired communication disorders: An introduction. *Augmentative and Alternative Communication, 5,* 42–48.

Biklen, D. (1992). Typing to talk: Facilitative communication. *American Journal of Speech-Language Pathology, 1,* 15–17.

Biklen, D. (1994). *Communication unbound: How facilitated communication is challenging traditional views of autism and ability/disability.* New York: Teachers College Press.

Blackstone, S. W., & Bruskin, D. M. (Eds.). (1986). *Augmentative communication: An introduction.* Rockville, MD: American Speech-Language-Hearing Association.

Bleck, E. E. (1982). Nonoral communication. In E. E. Bleck & D. A. Nagel (Eds.), *Physically handicapped children: A medical atlas for teachers* (pp. 145–169). Philadelphia: Grune & Stratton.

Boone, D. R., & McFarlane, S. C. (1988). *The voice and voice therapy* (4th ed.). Englewood Cliffs, NJ: Prentice-Hall.

Bornstein, H. (Ed.). (1990). *Manual communication: Implications for education.* Washington, DC: Gallaudet University Press.

Bornstein, H., Saulnier, K., & Hamilton, L. (1983). *The comprehensive Signed English dictionary.* Washington, DC: Gallaudet College Press.

Bower, T.G.R. (1989). *The rational infant.* New York: W. H. Freeman.

Bricker, D. D. (1972). Imitative sign training as a facilitator of word-object association with low-functioning children. *American Journal of Mental Deficiency, 76,* 509–516.

Bryan, T. (1977). Learning disabled children's comprehension of nonverbal communication. *Journal of Learning Disabilities, 10,* 501–506.

Bryen, D. N., Goldman, A. S., & Quinlisk-Gill, S. (1988). Sign language with students with severe/profound mental retardation: How effective is it? *Education and Training of the Mentally Retarded, 23,* 129–137.

Bryen, D. N., & McGinley, V. (1991). Sign language input to community residents with mental retardation. *Education and Training of the Mentally Retarded, 26,* 207–213.

Burkhart, L. J. (1987). *Using computers and speech synthesis to facilitate communication interaction with young and/or severely handicapped children.* Santa Barbara, CA: Special Needs Project.

Buzolich, M. J., & Wiemann, J. M. (1988). Turn taking in atypical conversations: The case of the speaker/augmented-communicator dyad. *Journal of Speech and Hearing Disorders, 55,* 118–123.

Calculator, S., & Dollaghan, C. (1982). The use of communication boards in a residential setting: An evaluation. *Journal of Speech and Hearing Disorders, 47,* 281–287.

Carlson, F. (1981). A format for selecting vocabulary for the non-speaking child. *Language, Speech and Hearing Services in Schools, 12,* 240–245.

Cipani, E. C., & Spooner, F. (Eds.). (1994). *Curricular and instructional approaches for persons with severe disabilities.* Des Moines, IA: Longwood.

Clark, C. (1984). A close look at the standard rebus system and Blissymbolics. *Journal of the Association for Persons with Severe Handicaps, 9,* 37–48.

Clement, M. (1961). Morse code method of communication for the severely handicapped cerebral palsied child. *Cerebral Palsy Review, 22,* 15–16.

Coleman, C. L., Cook, A. M., & Meyers, L. S. (1980). Assessing non-oral clients for assistive communication devices. *Journal of Speech and Hearing Disorders, 45,* 515–526.

Crossley, R. (1989). *Communication for training facilitated communications.* Melbourne, Australia: DEAL Communication Center.

Crossley, R. (1994). *Facilitated communication training.* New York: Teachers College Press.

Deich, R. E., & Hodges, P. M. (1977). *Language without speech.* New York: Brunner/Mazel.

Dennis, R., Reichle, S., Williams, W., & Vogelsberg, R. T. (1982). Motoric factors influencing the selection of vocabulary for sign-production programs. *Journal of the Association for the Severely Handicapped, 7,* 20–32.

Detamore, K., & Lippke, B. (1980). Handicapped students learn language skills with communication boards. *Teaching Exceptional Children, 12,* 104–106.

DeVito, J. A. (1978). *Communicology: An introduction to the study of communication.* New York: HarperCollins.

DuBose, R. F. (1978). Development of communication in nonverbal children. *Education and Training of the Mentally Retarded, 13,* 37–41.

Dunst, C. J., & Lowe, L. W. (1986). From reflex to symbol: Describing, explaining, and fostering communication competence. *Augmentative and Alternative Communication, 2,* 11–18.

Egolf, D., & Chester, S. (1973). Nonverbal communication and the disorders of speech and language. *ASHA, 15,* 511–518.

Ekman, P., & Friesen, M. V. (1969). The repertoire of nonverbal behavior: Categories, origins, usage, and coding. *Semiotica, 1,* 31–39.

Fischer, S. (1982). Sign language and manual communication. In D. G. Sims, G. G. Walter, & R. L. Whitehead (Eds.), *Deafness and communication: Assessment and training* (pp. 90–106). Baltimore: Williams & Wilkins.

Fristoe, J., & Lloyd, L. (1980). Planning an initial expressive sign lexicon for persons with severe communication impairment. *Journal of Speech and Hearing Disorders, 45,* 170–180.

Funnell, E., & Allpert, A. (1989). Symbolically speaking: Communicating with Blissymbols in aphasia. *Aphasiology, 3,* 279–300.

Gallender, D. (1980). *Symbol communication for the severely handicapped.* Springfield, IL: Charles C Thomas.

Geers, A., Moog, J., & Schick, B. (1984). Acquisition of spoken and signed English by profoundly deaf children. *Journal of Speech and Hearing Disorders, 49,* 378–388.

Goosens, C. A., & Crain, S. S. (1985). *Augmentative communication: Intervention resource.* Birmingham: Sparks Center for Developmental and Learning Disabilities, University of Alabama.

Goosens, C. A., & Crain, S. S. (1987). Overview of nonelectric eye-gaze communication techniques. *Augmentative and Alternative Communication, 3,* 77–89.

Gustason, G., Pfetzing, D., & Zawolkow, E. (1986). *Signed Exact English: The system that matches signs to English words.* Los Alamitos, CA: Modern Signs Press.

Hamre-Nietupski, S., Nietupski, S., & Rathe, T. (1986). Letting the data do the talking: Selecting the appropriate nonverbal communication system for severely handicapped students. *Teaching Exceptional Children, 52,* 130–134.

Harris, D. (1982). Communicative interaction process involving nonvocal physically handicapped children. *Topics in Language Disorders, 2,* 21–37.

Horner, R., & Budd, C. (1985). Acquisition of manual sign use: Collateral reduction of maladaptive behavior and factors limiting generalization. *Education and Training of the Mentally Retarded, 20,* 39–47.

Huer, M. B., & Lloyd, L. L. (1990). AAC users' perspective on augmentative and alternative communication. *Augmentative and Alternative Communication, 4,* 242–249.

Hurlbut, B., Iwata, B., & Green, J. (1982). Nonvocal language acquisition in adolescents with severe physical disabilities: Blissymbol versus iconic stimulus formats. *Journal of Applied Behavior Analysis, 15,* 241–258.

Jewell, K. H. (1989). A custom-made head pointer for children. *American Journal of Occupational Therapy, 43,* 456–460.

Jones, T. (1980). Is it necessary to decide whether to use a non-oral communication system with retarded children? *Education and Training of the Mentally Retarded, 15,* 157–160.

Kangas, K. A., & Lloyd, L. L. (1988). Early cognitive prerequisites to augmentative and alternative communication use: What are we waiting for? *Augmentative and Alternative Communication, 4,* 211–221.

Kannenberg, P., Marquardt, T. P., & Larson, J. (1988). Speech intelligibility and two voice output communication aids. *Journal of Communication Disorders, 21,* 11–20.

Knapp, M. (1980). *Essentials of nonverbal communication.* Troy, MO: Holt, Rinehart & Winston.

Krauss, R. M., Apple, W., Morency, N., Wenzel, C., & Winton, W. (1981). Verbal, vocal, and visible factors in judgments of another's affect. *Journal of Personality and Social Psychology, 14,* 15–19.

Lewis, R. (1993). *Special education technology: Classroom applications.* Pacific Grove, CA: Brooks/Cole.

Light, J. (1989). Toward a definition of communicative competence for individuals using augmentative and alternative communication systems. *Augmentative and Alternative Communication, 5,* 137–144.

Lloyd, L. L., Quist, R. W., & Windsor, J. (1990). A proposed augmentative and alternative communication model. *Augmentative and Alternative Communication, 6,* 172–183.

Marshall, P. (1980). Augmentative communication: The call of one's life. *Communicating Together, 8*(2), 5–6.

McAnally, P. L., Rose, S., & Quigley, S. P. (1994). *Language learning practices with deaf children* (2nd ed.). Austin, TX: PRO-ED.

McEwen, I. R., & Karlan, G. (1989). Assessment of effects of position on communication board access by individuals with cerebral palsy. *Augmentative and Alternative Communication, 5,* 235–242.

McEwen, I. R., & Lloyd, L. L. (1990). Some considerations about the motor requirements for manual signs. *Augmentative and Alternative Communication, 6,* 207–216.

McNaughton, S. (1985). *Communicating with Blissymbolics.* Toronto, Canada: Blissymbolics Communication Institute.

Meltzoff, A., & Moore, M. (1977). Imitation of facial expressions and manual gestures by human neonates. *Science, 198,* 75–78.

Meyer, L. H., Peck, C. A., & Brown, L. (1991). *Critical issues in the lives of people with severe disabilities.* Baltimore: Paul H. Brookes.

Miller, J., & Allaire, J. (1987). Augmentative communication. In M. E. Snell (Ed.), *Systematic instruction of persons with severe handicaps* (pp. 273–297). Columbus, OH: Merrill.

Mills, J., & Higgins, J. (1984). *The assessment for non-speech communication.* San Diego, CA: California Publications.

Minskoff, E. H. (1980). Teaching approach for developing nonverbal communication skills in students with social perception deficits. Part 1. *Journal of Learning Disabilities, 13,* 118–124.

Minskoff, E. H. (1980). Teaching approach for developing nonverbal communication skills in students with social perception deficits. Part 2. *Journal of Learning Disabilities, 13,* 203–208.

Mirenda, P., & Iacono, T. (1990). Communication options for persons with severe and profound disabilities: State of the art and future directions. *Journal of the Association for Persons with Severe Handicaps, 15,* 3–21.

Mirenda, P., & Mathy-Laikko, P. (1989). Augmentative and alternative communication for persons with severe congenital communication disorders. *Augmentative and Alternative Communication, 5,* 3–13.

Mithaug, D., & Liberty, S. (1980). Word discrimination training to improve the communication skills of a severely retarded, non-vocal woman: A case study. *Education and Treatment of Children, 3,* 1–12.

Mizuko, M. (1987). Transparency and ease of learning of symbols represented by Blissymbols, PCS, and PICSYMS. *Augmentative and Alternative Communication, 3,* 129–136.

Moncur, J. P., & Brackett, I. P. (1974). *Modifying vocal behavior.* New York: HarperCollins.

Munson, J. H., Nordquist, C. L., & Thuma-Rew, S. L. (1987). *Communication systems for persons with severe neuromotor impairment.* Iowa City: Division of Developmental Disabilities, University of Iowa.

Musselwhite, C. R., & St. Louis, K. W. (1988). *Communication programming for the severely handicapped: Vocal and non-vocal strategies* (2nd ed.). Boston: Little, Brown.

Mysak, E. D. (Ed.). (1987). *Communication disorders of the cerebral palsied: Assessment and treatment.* New York: Thieme Medical.

Orlansky, M. D., & Borvillian, J. D. (1984). The role of iconicity in early sign language acquisition. *Journal of Speech and Hearing Disorders, 49,* 287–292.

Owens, R. E., & House, L. (1984). Decision-making processes in augmentative communication. *Journal of Speech and Hearing Disorders, 49,* 18–25.

Paul, P. V. (1994). *Language and deafness.* San Diego: Singular.

Pecyna, P. (1988). Rebus symbol communication training with a severely handicapped preschool child: A case study. *Language, Speech and Hearing Services in Schools, 19,* 128–143.

Polloway, E. A., & Smith, T.E.C. (1992). *Language instruction for students with disabilities* (2nd ed.). Denver, CO: Love.

Reich, R. (1978). Gestural facilitation of expressive language in moderately/severely retarded preschoolers. *Mental Retardation, 16,* 113–117.

Reichle, J., & Karlan, G. (1985). The selection of an augmentative system in communication intervention: A critique of decision rules. *Journal of the Association for Persons with Severe Handicaps, 10,* 146–156.

Reichle, J., & Keogh, W. J. (1986). Communication instruction for learners with severe handicaps: Some unresolved issues. In R. H. Horner, L. H. Meyer, & H.D.B. Fredricks (Eds.), *Education of learners with severe handicaps: Exemplary service strategies* (2nd ed., pp. 189–219). Baltimore: Paul H. Brookes.

Reichle, J., Williams, W., & Ryan, S. (1981). Selecting signs for the formulation of an augmentative communicative modality. *Journal of the Association for the Severely Handicapped, 6,* 48–56.

Reichle, J., York, J., & Sigafoos, J. (1991). *Implementing augmentative and alternative communication: Strategies for learners with severe disabilities.* Baltimore: Paul H. Brookes.

Rittenhouse, R., & Myers, J. (1985). Teaching functional sign language to severely delayed children. *Teaching Exceptional Children, 17,* 62–67.

Romski, M., Sevick, R., & Pate, J. (1988). Establishment of symbolic communication in persons with severe retardation. *Journal of Speech and Hearing Disorders, 53,* 94–107.

Rotholz, D., Berkowitz, S., & Burberry, J. (1989). Functionality of two modes of communication in the community by students with developmental disabilities: A comparison of signing and communication book. *Journal of the Association for Persons with Severe Handicaps, 14,* 227–232.

Rourke, B. P. (1989). *Nonverbal learning disabilities: The syndrome and the model.* New York: Guilford Press.

Salisbury, C., Walmbold, C., & Walter, O. (1978). Manual communication for the severely handicapped: An assessment and instructional strategy. *Education and Training of the Mentally Retarded, 13,* 393–397.

Schaeffer, B., Musil, A., & Kollinzas, G. (1980). *Total communication: A signed speech program for nonverbal children.* Champaign, IL: Research Press.

Schiefelbusch, R. L. (Ed.). (1980). *Nonspeech language and communication analysis and intervention.* Baltimore: University Park Press.

Shane, H. C. (Ed.). (1994). *Facilitated communication: The clinical and social phenomenon.* San Diego, CA: Singular.

Shane, H. C., & Bashir, A. (1980). Election criteria for the adoption of an augmentative communication system: Preliminary considerations. *Journal of Speech and Hearing Disorders, 45,* 408–414.

Siegel-Causey, E., & Guess, D. (1989). *Enhancing nonsymbolic communication interaction among learners with severe disabilities.* Baltimore: Paul H. Brookes.

Sienkiewiecz-Mercer, R., & Kaplan, S. B. (1989). *I raise my eyes to say yes.* Boston: Houghton Mifflin.

Silverman, F. (1989). *Communication for the speechless* (2nd ed.). Englewood Cliffs, NJ: Prentice-Hall.

Skelly, M. (1979). *Amer-Ind gestural code based on universal American Indian hand talk.* New York: Elsevier.

Smith-Lewis, M., & Ford, A. (1987). A user's perspective on augmentative communication. *Augmentative and Alternative Communication, 3,* 12–17.

Spignesi, A., & Shor, R. E. (1981). The judgment of facial expressions, contexts, and their combination. *Journal of General Psychology, 104,* 41–58.

Sternberg, L., McNerney, C., & Pegnatore, L. (1987). Developing primitive signaling behavior of students with profound mental retardation. *Mental Retardation, 25,* 13–20.

Thal, D., & Tobias, S. (1992). Communicative gestures in children with delayed onset of oral expressive vocabulary. *Journal of Speech and Hearing Research, 35,* 1281–1289.

Thal, D., Tobias, S., & Morrison, D. (1991). Language and gestures in late talkers: A one-year follow-up. *Journal of Speech and Hearing Disorders, 34*, 604–612.

Traynor, C. D., & Beukelman, D. R. (1984). Nonvocal communication augmentation using microcomputers. *Exceptional Education Quarterly, 4*(4), 90–103.

Valletutti, P. J. (1989). The nature and development of nonverbal communication. In P. J. Valletutti, M. McKnight Taylor, & A. S. Hoffnung, *Facilitating communication in young children with handicapping conditions: A guide for special educators* (pp. 117–122). Austin, TX: PRO-ED.

Vanderheiden, G. C. (1984). High and low technology approaches in the development of communication systems for severely physically handicapped persons. *Exceptional Education Quarterly, 4*(4), 40–56.

Vanderheiden, G. C., & Lloyd, L. L. (1986). Non-speech modes and systems. In S. W. Blackstone (Ed.), *Augmentative communication* (pp. 49–161). Rockville, MD: American Speech-Language-Hearing Association.

Van Dijk, J. (1986). An educational curriculum for deaf-blind multiply handicapped persons. In D. Ellis (Ed.), *Sensory impairments in mentally retarded people* (pp. 375–382). Austin, TX: PRO-ED.

von Tetzchner, S., & Martinsen, H. (1992). *Introduction to symbolic and augmentative communication.* San Diego, CA: Singular.

Weller, E. L., & Mahoney, G. J. (1983). A comparison of oral and total communication modalities in the language training of young mentally handicapped children. *Education and Training of the Mentally Retarded, 18*, 103–110.

Zangari, C., Kangas, K. A., & Lloyd, L. I. (1988). Augmentative and alternative communication: A field in transition. *Augmentative and Alternative Communication, 4*, 60–64.

**Selected Materials/Resources**

Anthony, D. (1971). *Seeing Essential English.* Anaheim, CA: Educational Services Division, Anaheim Union School District.

Baker, C., & Cokely, D. (1991). *American Sign Language: A teacher's resource on grammar and culture.* Washington, DC: Clerc Books.

Bliss, C. (1975). *Semantography.* Sydney, Australia: Semantography.

Bolton, S., & Dashiell, S. (1989). *INCH: INteraction CHecklist for Augmentative Communication.* Wauconda, IL: Don Johnston Developmental Equipment.

Carlson, F. (1984). *Picsyms Categorical Dictionary.* Lawrence, KS: Baggeboda Press.

Carrier, J., & Peak, T. (1975). *Non-speech Language Initiation Program.* Lawrence, KS: H & H Enterprises.

Church, G., & Glennen, S. (Eds.). (1991). *The handbook of assistive technology.* San Diego, CA: Singular.

Clark, C., Davies, C., & Woodcock, R. (1974). *Standard rebus glossary.* Circle Pines, MN: American Guidance Service.

Cregan, A., & Lloyd, L. L. (1990). *Sigsymbols: American edition.* Wauconda, IL: Don Johnston Developmental Equipment.

Culp, D., & Carlisle, M. (1988). *Partners in augmentative communication.* Tucson, AZ: Communication Skill Builders.

Enders, A., & Hall, M. (Eds.). *Assistive technology sourcebook.* Washington, DC: RESNA Press.

Fant, L. J., Jr. (1972). *Ameslan: An introduction to American Sign Language.* Silver Spring, MD: National Association for the Deaf.

Humphries, T., & Padden, C. (1992). *Learning American Sign Language.* Englewood Cliffs, NJ: Prentice-Hall.

Johnson, J. (1986). *Self-talk: Communication boards for children and adults.* Tucson, AZ: Communication Skill Builders.

Johnson, R. (1981). *The Picture Communication Symbols.* Solana Beach, CA: Mayer-Johnson.

Johnson, R. (1985). *The Picture Communication Symbols—Book II.* Solana Beach, CA: Mayer-Johnson.

Lou, S., & Leff, R. (1990). *Talking Pictures.* Milwaukee, WI: Crestwood Company.

Maharaj, S. C. (1980). *Pictograph Ideogram communication.* Regina, Canada: George Reed Foundation for the Handicapped.

O'Rourke, T. (Ed.). (1978). *A basic course in manual communication.* Silver Spring, MD: National Association for the Deaf.

Prentke Romich Company. (1989). *How to obtain funding for augmentative communication devices.* Wooster, OH: Author.

Prentke Romich Company. (1990). *Intro Talker.* Wooster, OH: Author.

Prentke Romich Company. (1990). *Light Talker.* Wooster, OH: Author.

Prentke Romich Company. (1990). *Touch Talker.* Wooster, OH: Author.

Rakow, S.F.V., & Carpenter, C. B. (1993). *Signs of sharing: An elementary sign language and deaf awareness curriculum.* Springfield, IL: Charles C Thomas.

Shane, H. C. (1989). *Augmentative communication series.* San Antonio, TX: The Psychological Corporation.

Silverman, H., McNaughton, S., & Kates, B. (1979). *Handbook of Blissymbolics for instructors, users, parents, and administrators.* Toronto, Canada: Blissymbolics Communication Institute.

Stokoe, W. (Ed.). (1960). *Sign language structure: An outline of visual communication systems of the American deaf.* Buffalo, NY: University of Buffalo Press.

Vanderheiden, G., & Grilley, K. (1978). *Non-vocal communication techniques and aids for the severely physically handicapped.* Austin, TX: PRO-ED.

Woltosz, W., & Woltosz, G. (1989). *How to select a communication aid.* Lancaster, CA: Words+.

Wood, C., Storr, J., & Reich, P. A. (Eds.). (1992). Blissymbol reference guide. Toronto, Canada: Blissymbolics Communication International.

Woodcock, R., Clark, C., & Davies, C. (1979). *Peabody Rebus Reading Program.* Circle Pines, MN: American Guidance Service.

Words+. (1989). *Mores WSKE II.* Lancaster, CA: Words+.

# Oral Communication

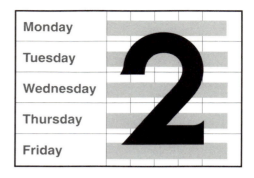

Meaningful communication, in both speech and writing, requires reasonably intact structural and neurological systems and the acquisition and internalization of culturally agreed-upon rules of production, order, and use, for both comprehending the communication of others and meaningfully producing spoken or written messages that are understood by others in the culture. One of the basic functions of language is its role in facilitating interpersonal communication and promoting effective and productive interpersonal relations. Since this curriculum is a life skills or functional curriculum, the interpersonal communication function assumes hegemony over other language functions.

The functional context and its role in language acquisition and use is the essence of this curricular area. This emphasis reflects the need and desire of developing people to understand their environment, to socialize with others, and to control the other people in their lives so that they may more effectively and efficiently meet their personal goals and objectives. Proceeding from this social interactionist perspective, the suggested instructional activities of this curriculum domain are designed for teachers, family members, and other trainers.

Because all languages rely on a set of rules that govern language understanding and language production, they are best understood and developed within a social context. A functional curriculum, by its very nature, emphasizes the interpersonal contexts in which people find themselves as they play out various social roles. Thus, language must be appropriate to the social situation. How language is used in different situations is called pragmatics (Bates, 1976). Pragmatics refers to the system of rules that governs the way language is used in diverse social contexts. The communicative intent of the speaker (or writer), therefore, plays a quintessential role in language facilitation and interpersonal communication. Pragmatics is concerned with the communicative components and strategies that assist an individual in achieving his or her needs, desires, and goals.

It must be remembered that in order to pragmatically use language, one must first acquire language. Initially, a child communicates with sounds or facial expressions or body movements and is able to take turns. As the child grows older, however, the sounds of the language, the words, and the structure are used to convey a more complicated message, suggest nuances, maintain a topic, and repair any misunderstandings. Functional communication depends on the acquisition of the basic language skills that provide the means through which an individual achieves his or her personal ends. Leonard and Fey (1991) suggest that a reciprocal relationship exists between grammar and pragmatics, where specific linguistic markers such as the auxiliary "do" may signal a contrast or a question and where the presentation of a question may require some type of modal auxiliary.

The cognitive and linguistic dimensions basic to interpersonal communication include comprehension of the linguistic, paralinguistic, and nonlinguistic elements of the communication act; perception of the underlying motives of others; estimation of the truthfulness and reliability of the participants in the communicative act; and internalization of the culturally determined rules for appropriate participation in communicative interactions.

The term *paralinguistic,* according to Owens (1992), refers to the vocal and nonvocal elements superimposed on the linguistic code that reinforce and clarify the speaker's message, while *nonlinguistic* refers to communicative devices such as gestures, posture, and facial expressions, which also play a significant role in communication (see Unit 1). Consequently, children and youth, whether they have disabilities or not, will be more successful communicators if, for example, they use language courtesies, greet others in appropriate ways, seek assistance only when needed and in an acceptable way, and are skilled in reinforcing others who can aid them in meeting their personal goals and objectives.

# LANGUAGE AS A RULE-GOVERNED BEHAVIOR

The three systems of rules that determine the form of a language are its phonology, morphology, and syntax (Bloom & Lahey, 1978). *Phonology* consists of the sound system and sound patterns employed in oral communication. Its rules specify what speech sounds (phonemes) can occur in a language and how these sounds can be combined to form words. Phonemes by themselves possess neither grammatical nor semantic meaning. They are the smallest units of speech (Gleason, 1961) that may be combined to form words that have semantic meaning and, in turn, that can be combined with other words to communicate an individual's intentions in rule-governed syntactic patterns.

Oral language proficiency depends on skilled auditory discrimination among and intelligible production of the phonemes in a language. A related skill is the ability to make phoneme-grapheme associations, which is essential to communicating in reading, writing, and arithmetic. (See Volume III, *Functional Academics* [Valletutti, Bender, & Sims-Tucker, in press].) Phonology also includes the study of the prosodic features of speech. These features include rate of delivery, vocal intonation patterns, and emphasis placed on specific syllables or words, as well as pauses and hesitations within communication units.

*Morphology* is the rule system that determines the meaning of words and their internal organization. Words consist of one or more units known as morphemes. A morpheme (not to be confused with a syllable) is the smallest grammatically meaningful language unit that cannot be divided into a smaller unit and still retain its meaning. Morphemes make it possible for speakers to modify word meanings and make semantic distinctions; they are sequenced into grammatical patterns. There are two kinds of morphemes: free and bound. Free morphemes form words that can stand alone and still possess meaning. Bound morphemes (grammatical morphemes) are attached or affixed to words to change their meaning (Gleason, 1961). The production of a morphological inflection is determined by its phonetic environment.

*Syntax* is the rule system that determines how morphemes are combined and sequenced to create meaningful phrases and sentences. Rules of syntax dictate the form or structure of a sentence. They govern word order, organization, and morphological relationships. Syntactic rules define which word combinations and word sequences are acceptable and which are not.

*Semantics* refers to a language's linguistic code, which communicates meaning to fellow speakers and writers of the language. The systematic study of semantics includes not only the study of symbols and their referents but also semantic-syntactic relationships. The linguistic code is culturally determined through the establishment of symbols that represent real objects, persons, events, and characteristics.

# PLAY ACTIVITIES AND LANGUAGE DEVELOPMENT

Play activities are said to be highly associated with language development (Bretherton, 1984; Fein, 1981; Hill & McCune-Nicolich, 1981; Kelly & Dale, 1989; Nicolich, 1977; Patterson & Westby, 1994; Westby, 1980, 1988, 1991). Object permanence is required before a child can acquire the name of an object, while means-end responses must be present before a child learns semantic relationships (e.g., an agent acting on an object, as in "Boy push") (Finch-Williams, 1984). Khan (1984), in his work with 24 children with profound retardation between the ages of 3 and 10 years, found that means-end achievement was important for learning individual words and two-word combinations.

Nicolich (1977) and Westby (1980) presented a detailed list of play accomplishments considered necessary for the development of language in a child. True communication is said to begin when a child begins to use toys appropriately, demonstrates tool use, and engages in autosymbolic activities. In the beginning, a child with a chronological age (CA) of 9–17 months, in his or her interaction with *objects,* finds an object under a scarf (Uzgiris & McVee Hunt, 1975), gives an object to another person, and then gives an object to another person to be acted upon (e.g., a jar of bubble solution is to be opened or a toy car is to be wound). The child (CA 17–22 months) continues by interacting with *toys* and demonstrating their appropriate use (e.g., the child throws a ball, bounces it, and catches it; builds with blocks; and pushes or drives a car). Play activities then evolve to the *pretend* or *autosymbolic* level, in which a child pretends actions involving himself or herself (e.g., the child pretends to be asleep or pretends to feed himself or herself (Nicolich, 1977; Westby, 1980).

Nicolich (1977) considers the *autosymbolic* level to be the second level of play development. The next level, level 3, is the *decentered* level, where the pretend behavior involves another person (Nicolich, 1977; Westby, 1980). The decentered level involves just *one scheme* (e.g., a child pretends to feed another person, brush a doll's hair, or wash a dish). Kelly and Dale (1989) found that all the single-word users in their study had only reached the one-scheme level of play development, in which the children were able to pretend to act on themselves or on another person. In their study with nondisabled children, Kelly and Dale (1989) found that only the children who were using words had reached the decentered level (level 3).

As a child proceeds in play development, he or she engages in *combinatorial symbolic games*. At this stage, a child is able to combine *two schemes*, such as pretending to drink from a bottle and then giving a doll a drink from the bottle (Nicolich, 1977), or to combine two toys in pretend play (Westby, 1980), such as pretending to open a milk container and then pouring the nonexistent contents in a cup.

By 24 months, children are able to pretend-play common everyday experiences, such as cooking, eating, setting the table, taking a bath, and going to work. Later, by 2½, their pretend play involves events that are less frequently experienced, such as going to the movies and going to the doctor's (Westby, 1980). These activities are called internally directed symbolic games by Nicolich (1977). By 3 to 3½ years, the pretend games become longer and events are related and sequenced: the child may start the game by pretending to mix the ingredients for a cake (near the flour canister), then putting the pretend batter into the oven, next removing the cake from the oven, and finally placing it on a plate that is then delivered to the kitchen table.

By 3½, the child may use dollhouses, garages, farms, and blocks for imaginative play and also may use one object to create or represent another. As an example, one child, Evan, picked up a napkin, stood its two sides on a table, and creased the peak, while declaring that he now had a tent in which he could sleep that night. Westby (1980) found that by 3½ to 4 years, children are learning to plan ahead and to work out problems they have not yet experienced (e.g., "If the car falls off the road, we will call a repair truck"). It is interesting to note that the modals "can," "will," and "might" are also emerging at this time as are the conjunctions "because" and "if."

## CURRICULAR EMPHASES

Goal I deals with developmental milestones that typically occur during the Preverbal Stage. Goal II considers the One-Word Stage, and Goal III addresses Stages I–V, reflecting the linguistic developmental model, based on the mean length of utterance, conceptualized and explicated by Brown (1973). Goals IV–XII deal exclusively with language use within the social context, which is the essence of a functional curriculum.

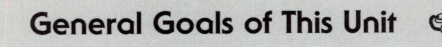

# General Goals of This Unit

I. The student will develop the basic visual, motor, auditory, vocal, play, and interactive skills that facilitate the development of oral language during the Preverbal Stage (0–12 months).

II. The student will progress through the One-Word Stage of oral language development (12–18 months).

III. The student will progress through Stages I–V of oral language development (18–48 months).

IV. The student will acquire the oral communication skills that will facilitate successful performance in various learning situations.

V. The student will acquire the oral communication skills that will facilitate successful performance in diverse interpersonal and social interactions.

VI. The student will acquire the oral communication skills that will facilitate successful performance in work situations.

VII. The student will acquire the oral communication skills that will facilitate successful performance in various leisure-time pursuits.

VIII. The student will acquire the oral communication skills that will facilitate successful performance as a member of a household.

IX. The student will acquire the oral communication skills that will facilitate successful performance as a friend and as a member of a family unit.

X. The student will acquire the oral communication skills that will facilitate successful performance as a member of a community.

XI. The student will acquire the oral communication skills that will facilitate successful performance as a consumer of goods and services and as a participant in various financial transactions.

XII. The student will acquire the oral communication skills that will facilitate successful interactions as a traveler within the community.

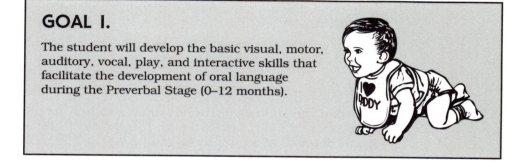

## GOAL I.

The student will develop the basic visual, motor, auditory, vocal, play, and interactive skills that facilitate the development of oral language during the Preverbal Stage (0–12 months).

Goal I deals exclusively with the Preverbal Stage of language development (0–12 months). The development of language during this period is an integration and synthesis of many basic prerequisite and interrelated skills. Among these skills are the following behaviors that may need to be addressed in an educational program designed to facilitate nonverbal and oral communication. (Approximate developmental ages are given in parentheses.)

1. The student moves in response to conversational speech (by 20 minutes of life) (Condon & Sanders, 1974).

2. The student imitates gross hand movements, opens his or her mouth, and protrudes the tongue (by first week) (Meltzoff & Moore, 1977).

3. The student looks at a caregiver's face (by 1 month) (Furuno, O'Reilly, Kosaka, Inatsuka, Allman, & Zeisloft, 1979).

4. The student imitates the gaze patterns of a caregiver who points to, shows, or moves an object (by 3 months) (Owens, 1992).

5. The student raises a hand to his or her mouth (by 4 months) (Furuno et al., 1979).

6. The student brings an object or toy to his or her mouth (by 5 months) (Furuno et al., 1979).

7. The student sits independently and is able to place both hands on a bottle (by 6 months).

8. The student begins to communicate through gesture (by 8 months).

9. The student looks, smiles, and hugs and is able to sequence a number of actions (by 8 months) (Sugarman, 1984).

10. The student holds his or her own bottle independently (by 9 months).

11. The student initiates an exchange of objects by showing, pointing to, and offering an object (by 10 months).

12. The student demonstrates object permanence (by 12 months).

13. The student begins to establish means-end behavior (by 12 months).

Stimulation of the student in specific areas will help to establish

1. visual contact for social integration;

2. hand movement for the development of gestural communication;

3. vocalization as the basis for verbalization;

4. intentionality so that sounds and gestures can be used to relay meaning; and

5. primitive verbalizations used to convey diverse intentions, whether to request an object, control a person's behavior, attract a person, or express feelings of pleasure or interest.

For Goals I, II, and III, the approximate chronological age when the skill is usually acquired is appended to each specific objective. This has been done to provide teachers, family members, and other caregivers with a developmental framework to help them in making decisions about instructional sequencing, whatever the chronological age of the individual whose oral communication skills are being stimulated and facilitated. Of course, when applying these objectives to various age groups, consideration must always be given to the age-appropriateness of both methods and materials.

Because of the elemental nature of the Preverbal Stage, suggested interventions are provided only for the infant and toddler level. These suggested interventions may be used at higher levels, when appropriate, if age-appropriate materials and activities are employed.

Finally, Teacher and Family Interventions are combined since they are basically the same, and, in fact, the teacher's role at this level, especially when working with the very young student, may simply be as a consultant who provides demonstrations and routines for the family member or members to implement.

## SPECIFIC OBJECTIVES

The student:

❏ A.  Coos and makes vowel-like sounds (by 2 months).

❏ B.  Engages in simple visual-motor rituals and routines such as playing "Peek-a-Boo" and "Pat-a-Cake" (by 4 months).

❑ C. Vocalizes in response to the vocalizations and verbalizations of caregivers (by 5 months) (Furuno et al., 1979).

❑ D. Babbles using reduplicated sounds such as "ba ba ba" (Rossetti, 1990). (Note: During the first year of life the following consonant sounds are typically produced: /m/, /p/, /b/, /n/, /t/, /d/, /k/, /g/, and /ng/ [by 6 months] [Lewis, 1951].)

❑ E. Pays attention to an object offered by a caregiver and when the caregiver verbally directs the child by saying, for example, "Look!" (by 6 months).

❑ F. Imitates pitch and intonation patterns (by 8 months) (Owens, 1992).

❑ G. Begins to aurally comprehend words frequently used by caregivers (by 9 months) (Reich, 1976; Anisfeld, 1984).

❑ H. Imitates adult vocalizations (by 9 months) (Rossetti, 1990).

❑ I. Imitates vocalizations and simultaneously uses gestures (by 9–10 months) (Bates, Benigni, Bretherton, Camioni, & Volterra, 1979).

❑ J. Requests an object by showing it to a caregiver (by 10 months) (Sugarman, 1984).

❑ K. Uses phonetically consistent forms (PCFs) that function as "words" for him or her (by 10 months) (Dore, Franklin, & Ramer, 1976; Reich, 1986).

❑ L. Uses sounds, intonations, and gestures to convey his or her intentions (by 10½ months) (Halliday, 1975).

❑ M. Gives an object to a caregiver either upon request or spontaneously (by 12 months) (Furuno et al., 1979).

❑ N. Produces a true word (by 12 months).

# SUGGESTED ACTIVITIES

## ☎ Specific Objective A

The student coos and makes vowel-like sounds (by 2 months).

## Teacher and Family Interventions

**Infant and Toddler Level.** If the student has begun to coo and make vowel-like sounds, play a vocalization game in which you imitate his or her vocalizations while "singing" a simple melody. Look directly into the eyes of the student, and smile as you enjoy cooing and vocalizing with him or her.

If the student has not yet begun to vocalize, engage him or her in a favorite activity such as cooing to a stuffed animal or doll. Draw the student's attention to your mouth movements, and place his or her hand on your vibrating throat. Show delight in any vocalization the student makes.

---

☎ ## Specific Objective B

The student engages in simple visual-motor rituals and routines such as playing "Peek-a-Boo" and "Pat-a-Cake" (by 4 months).

---

(See Sample Lesson Plan 1 at the end of Unit 2.)

A major emphasis of this specific objective as well as all the specific objectives, especially those for Goals I and II, is the establishment of intervention routines. Routines are important in the initial development of language because they are consistent; that is, they do not vary in the words used, in sentence structure, or in prosodic features such as intonation and stress. These routines always have the same initiation, development, and closure and are associated with specific events and behaviors. Routines may be done as a unit or may be broken into segments.

## Teacher and Family Interventions

**Infant and Toddler Level.** Play "Peek-a-Boo" and "Pat-a-Cake" with the student. Laugh and demonstrate your pleasure when playing "Pat-a-Cake," and demonstrate surprise and excitement when playing "Peek-a-Boo." Other chanting, singing, and movement activities that appeal to the student should also be engaged in on a regular basis.

---

☎ ## Specific Objective C

The student vocalizes in response to the vocalizations and verbalizations of caregivers (by 5 months).

---

## Teacher and Family Interventions

**Infant and Toddler Level.**   Hum, sing, chant, and talk to the student. Pause to give the student the opportunity to vocalize in turn. If the student vocalizes and thus joins in the vocalizing game, praise him or her and continue to enjoy the vocal play. If the student fails to imitate your vocalizations, play with one of his or her favorite toys.

During the play, vocalize as part of the play (e.g., make a tooting sound while playing with a train, a humming sound while playing with an airplane, and a "boom-boom" sound while playing with a toy drum). Sing while manipulating a doll, puppet, or stuffed animal that is "dancing" to the music. Basically, make vocalization part of the student's play activities.

 ### Specific Objective D

The student babbles using reduplicated sounds such as "ba ba ba." (Note: During the first year of life the following consonant sounds are typically produced: /m/, /p/, /b/, /n/, /t/, /d/, /k/, /g/, and /ng/ [by 6 months].)

(Note: The child will understand words more readily if they are part of his or her babbling repertoire [Stern, 1924].)

## Teacher and Family Interventions

**Infant and Toddler Level.**   Engage in play activities that lend themselves to vocal accompaniment. Vocalize duplicated sounds, especially those that are highly visible, such as "ma ma ma," "da da da," and "pa pa pa." Draw the student's attention to the repetitive movements of your lips and tongue. When making lip sounds (the bilabials /m/, /p/, and /b/ and the labio-dentals /f/ and /v/), you may want to move the student's lips in time with your vocalization of the duplicated sounds.

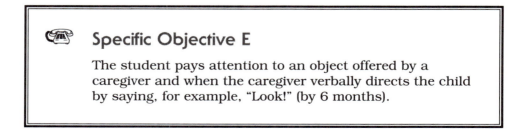 ### Specific Objective E

The student pays attention to an object offered by a caregiver and when the caregiver verbally directs the child by saying, for example, "Look!" (by 6 months).

## Teacher and Family Interventions

**Infant and Toddler Level.** Engage the student in a play activity, such as a mock tea party, that involves playing with several props. As you are having the tea party, say such things as "Look—I forgot to give you a napkin," "Look—we have some tasty sandwiches to have with our tea," or "Look—here is a wash basin to put our dirty dishes in." Reward the student for looking at the object offered and for then using it appropriately.

---

 **Specific Objective F**

The student imitates pitch and intonation patterns (by 8 months).

---

## Teacher and Family Interventions

**Infant and Toddler Level.** Sing some simple jingles and songs to the student and encourage him or her to join in. Listen to determine whether the student is using appropriate intonation patterns and pitches.

Play a game of "emotions" in which you express an emotion—for example, pleasure—vocally (without words) and then ask the student to show you with his or her voice that he or she is having a good time as well. Do the same for disappointment, sadness, and surprise.

If the student has some way of indicating "Yes" and "No," ask him or her a series of "Yes" or "No" questions, using a rising intonation pattern (e.g., "Do you have a nose?"). If the student fails to answer, demonstrate the statement vocal pattern (no rising intonation) by saying, "Yes, I see your nose. Here is your nose," while touching the student's nose. Follow up by asking the student, "Do you have a hand?" "Do you have a foot?"

---

**Specific Objective G**

The student begins to aurally comprehend words frequently used by caregivers (by 9 months).

## Teacher and Family Interventions

**Infant and Toddler Level.** Show the student a light switch, and direct his or her attention to an overhead light fixture or a nearby lamp. Turn the switch on and immediately say, "Light," as the bulb is illuminated. Turn the switch off and shrug your shoulders. Then, once more, turn the light on and say, "Light." Follow up by only turning the light on if the student looks up or toward the light after you have said, "Light."

---

☎  **Specific Objective H**

The student imitates adult vocalizations (by 9 months).

---

## Teacher and Family Interventions

**Infant and Toddler Level.**  Use a doll or hand puppet to say duplicated syllables such as "ma ma, ma ma, ma ___" or use a puppet or toy cow and say, "moo moo, moo moo, moo ___." Encourage the student to join you, by indicating with gestures that he or she should say the final sound.

You may follow up by singing, to the tune of "Mary Had a Little Lamb," something like the following: "Maa ma ma ma ma ma ___." The student then completes the line by singing, "Ma." Follow up by singing the actual words of the rhyme and encouraging the student to say the word that completes each of the ten lines of the refrain, for example, "Mary had a little ___," with the student saying, "Lamb."

---

☎  **Specific Objective I**

The student imitates vocalizations and simultaneously uses gestures (by 9–10 months).

---

## Teacher and Family Interventions

**Infant and Toddler Level.** Begin by demonstrating to the student commonly used vocalization-gesture combinations such as "Hi" and "Goodbye." Proceed to other gesture-vocalization combinations such as the "So big" gesture and throwing a kiss.

---

### ☎ Specific Objective J

The student requests an object by showing it to a caregiver (by 10 months).

---

## Teacher and Family Interventions

**Infant and Toddler Level.** Place two or three of the student's favorite toys out of his or her reach (e.g., a car, a ball, and a doll). Say, "Which one do you want? Do you want the car, the ball, or the baby?" Give the student the toy only after he or she has pointed to it. Accept eye movements and then move the student's hand to point and pick it up. Tell the student he or she may play with the toy for a while, and then repeat the game either with the same objects or with several new ones (e.g., a bell, a horse, and a truck).

Also, place several toys in front of the student, and tell the student that he or she must ask your permission to play with a toy by picking up the selection and showing it to you. Modify your response, sometimes giving permission ("Yes, you may throw the ball now") and sometimes denying it ("No, you may not bounce the ball. It is time for lunch. You can have the ball after lunch").

---

### ☎ Specific Objective K

The student uses phonetically consistent forms (PCFs) that function as "words" for him or her (by 10 months).

---

## Teacher and Family Interventions

**Infant and Toddler Level.** If the student begins to use a sound pattern to refer to an object or person in his or her environment, respond to that consistent sound pattern appropriately. For example, you might say to the student, "You said, 'Um-Um.' That means you would like a cookie. Yes, cookie, you want a cookie," or "You said 'Foo-foo.' Yes, give Fido a biscuit. Yes, he wants a biscuit," or "You said 'Nonnie' (since many children use this, it is acceptable as a true word). I guess you want to visit Grandma." (Note: You should teach the true word, but accept the student's PCF, if he or she has one.)

☎ Specific Objective L

The student uses sounds, intonations, and gestures to convey his or her intentions (by 10 1/2 months).

## Teacher and Family Interventions

**Infant and Toddler Level.**   If the student vocalizes with a rising inflection, look to see whether he or she is using gestures (such as pointing) and facial expressions, in order to determine his or her specific intent. (Note: The student may be using a rising intonation for varying intents, including asking a question, affirming a statement, or making a request.) If you believe that the intended question (as hypothesized from the sounds, intonation, gestures, and context) is, for example, "May I play with my teddy bear?" say to the student, "Yes, here is your teddy bear. Fine. Play with your teddy bear."

By interpreting the student's vocalizations, intonations, and gestures, you will establish the essence of communication; that is, you will be saying, "You want something to happen. You want me to do something. You must somehow let me know what it is, and I will try my best to understand what you want."

☎ Specific Objective M

The student gives an object to a caregiver either upon request or spontaneously (by 12 months).

## Teacher and Family Interventions

**Infant and Toddler Level.**   Place an object that you need or want to have somewhere near the student, and ask him or her to bring it to you (e.g., "I need a paper towel to clean my desk. Please bring me the *paper towels*," or "Please give me all the *cars* in the classroom so I can put them away where they belong"). Be sure to emphasize the key word so that the student is less likely to become confused by the other words in the request.

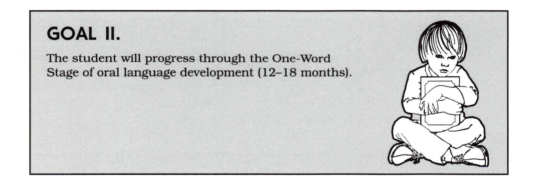

## Specific Objective N

The student produces a true word (by 12 months).

## Teacher and Family Interventions

**Infant and Toddler Level.** Identify the student's favorite toys, foods, and other objects. Frequently play with or use these objects. Be sure to say their names when using or playing with them. If the student says one of these words meaningfully and intelligibly, that is, so that it can be easily understood (articulatory accuracy is not necessary), respond by giving the student the item named and by demonstrating your delight in his or her first word.

### GOAL II.

The student will progress through the One-Word Stage of oral language development (12–18 months).

## SPECIFIC OBJECTIVES

The student:

- ❏ A. Comprehends approximately 50 words (by 13 months).
- ❏ B. Produces approximately 50 words formed with the sounds that he or she can produce, usually /m/, /p/, /b/, /n/, /t/, /d/, /w/, and /h/, later followed by /k/ and /g/ (by 18 months).

(Note: The International Phonetic Alphabet is not used in this curriculum in order to make understanding easier for those who are not conversant with it. The orthographic symbols found in most dictionaries are used instead.)

Because of the nature of the One-Word Stage, suggested interventions are provided only for the toddler level. These suggested interventions may be used at higher levels, when appropriate, if age-appropriate materials and activities are employed. Teacher and Family Interventions are combined, since they are basically the same, and, in fact, the teacher's role at this level may simply be as a consultant who provides demonstrations and routines for the family member or members to implement.

# SUGGESTED ACTIVITIES

---

☎ ## Specific Objective A

The student comprehends approximately 50 words (by 13 months).

---

A child's comprehension of a first word typically occurs approximately 3 months before production, while his or her comprehension of 50 words generally occurs 5 months before the production of 50 words (Benedict, 1979). A child's comprehension of a word is likely to differ from that of an adult. It may be more limited or more restricted.

## Teacher and Family Interventions

**Toddler Level.** Observe the student to determine the people and objects (inanimate and animate) in his or her environment in which he or she shows interest. Frequently refer to these items by name (in the case of a person, it may be a relationship term such as "Mommy" or a nickname such as "Ali") when you play with the student. In the case of toys, arrange for the student to use inanimate objects functionally, relate to animate objects such as plants and animals, consume items in the case of food and beverages, and interact with the people in his or her environment.

Appeal to as many senses as possible when stimulating comprehension, for example, e.g., when developing comprehension for the word "apple," experience its shape, color, touch, taste, and smell.

---

☎ ## Specific Objective B

The student produces approximately 50 words formed with the sounds that he or she can produce, usually /m/, /p/, /b/, /n/, /t/, /d/, /w/, and /h/, later followed by /k/ and /g/ (by 18 months).

---

| One-Word Intentions | Sample Child's Utterances |
|---|---|
| Terms for items that move | "Car." "Ball." |
| Terms for items that the child is able to handle | "Doll." "Cookie." |
| Terms for agents (people) who cause actions | "Daddy." "Mommy." |
| Requests for actions that change location | "Up." "Down." "Out." |
| Requests for actions that change an object | "One" (door). "Blow" (balloon). |
| Requests for actions that alter a person's attention | "See." "There." |
| Terms for the possessor of an object | "Pop-Pop." "Nana." |
| Social words | "Hi!" "Bye-Bye." |
| Terms that describe an object | "Big." "Dirty." |
| Specific nominals (i.e., someone's name) | "Bonnie." "Tami." "Ali." |

**FIGURE 2.1.** One-word intentions and sample child's utterances.

Whatever the variation in the sounds articulated, the words should be produced in a consistent pattern. It should also be noted that a one-word utterance may express a whole idea (a holophrase); for example, "Up!" may be used to express "Come over here and pick me up!" Furthermore, a child's one-word utterance may extend beyond an adult's understanding of a word (overextension) (Clark, 1973; Rescorla, 1980); that is, the child may say "car" for a car, motorcycle, bicycle, or even an airplane. A child's one-word utterance may also be more restrictive (underextension); in other words, the child may say "car" only for moving cars or toy cars or cars that are not moving (Bloom, 1970).

By 18 months a child, in his or her speech production, uses one-word intentions. See Figure 2.1.

## Teacher and Family Interventions

**Toddler Level.** Continue the activities in Specific Objective A. This time encourage the student to supply the word for the object or person in response to a request such as "Show me the ___!" or "Give me the ___!"

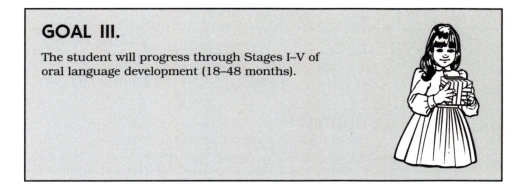

# GOAL III.

The student will progress through Stages I–V of oral language development (18–48 months).

Teacher and Family Interventions for each of the Stage I–V specific objectives are combined, since they are essentially the same. The teacher's role in the student's acquisition of these developmental sequences may primarily be as a consultant to parents and other family members who provides demonstrations and routines for these caregivers to implement in their daily interactions with the student.

# STAGE I

A morpheme is the smallest linguistic unit that has meaning. It may be one word (e.g., "girl," "house," or "doll") or even a multisyllabic word (e.g., "saddle," "cereal," or "apple"), or it may be part of a word that contains more than one morpheme (e.g., the "s" in the two-morpheme word "bikes," "un" in the two-morpheme word "unhappy," "est" in the two-morpheme word "biggest," or "er" and "s" in the three-morpheme word "teachers"). Children in Stage I use semantic rules with a number of morphemes in an utterance (MLU) of 1.75 with an upper limit of five morphemes. The approximate age is 18–27 months (Brown, 1973).

Students during this stage can make statements and comments, ask questions, and use negatives. Students in Stage I must be helped to pay attention to word order, that is, "Bobby hit" has a different meaning than "Hit Bobby" (Slobin, 1978). Children's two-word combinations have intentions, and these intentions must be identified and facilitated by teachers, other trainers, and family members.

The student during Stage I:

❏ A. Uses two-word combinations (the beginning of syntax) of his or her first words to communicate intentions (18–27 months).

❏ B. Uses two-word combinations to express a variety of ideas, states, and observations as well as his or her intentions (18–27 months) (Dore, 1975; Halliday, 1975).

❑ C. Comprehends "Yes" or "No" questions and *some* "Wh" questions (20 months) (Bellugi, 1965).

❑ D. Asks questions, progressing from the use of one or two words with a rising inflection to the use of a "Wh" interrogative pronoun (18–27 months) (Bellugi, 1965).

# SUGGESTED ACTIVITIES

Children in Stage I usually do not use prefixes or suffixes; that is, they do not inflect nouns to show possession or verbs to indicate past tense. Stage I interventions are suggested for only the toddler and preschool levels. These suggested interventions may be used at higher levels, when appropriate, if age-appropriate materials and activities are employed.

---

 ## Specific Objective A

The student uses two-word combinations (the beginning of syntax) of his or her first words to communicate intentions (18–27 months).

---

(See Sample Lesson Plan 2 at the end of Unit 2.)

Initially, the child may use just a few combinations of his or her first words to indicate his or her intentions. For example, the child may use one word as a pivot and add different words to the pivot word (Braine, 1963). For examples, see Figure 2.2.

## Teacher and Family Interventions

**Toddler Level.**   Play the "All Gone" game, in which you play with a toy and then remove it and say, "All gone." Do the same with food and beverages that have been consumed. Review each of the intentions in Figure 2.2 and demonstrate each one in reality contexts, such as rejection of an object. Do this by setting up situations in which the student offers you something (e.g., a cookie when you are on a diet), and you say, "No cookie. I don't want a cookie. Thank you."

**Preschool Level.**   At this level, continue the activities identified for the toddler level with the express purpose of increasing the number of intentions the student uses as well as his or her comprehension and expressive vocabulary.

| Child's Syntactic Utterances | Adult Interpretation | Intention | Pattern |
|---|---|---|---|
| "All broke." | All the toys are broken. | Change of state | "All" + verb |
| "All clean." | My hands are clean. | Change of state | "All" + adjective |
| "All gone." | Nothing is left. | Nonexistence | "All" + verb |
| "All go." | Let's all go. | Request for action | "All" + verb |
| "No bed." | I don't want to go to bed. | Rejection of place | "No" + noun |
| "No nap." | I don't want to take a nap. | Rejection of action | "No" + noun |
| "No down." | I want you to continue holding me. | Regulation of action—continuation | "No" + preposition |
| "No fix." | It's not fixed; it's still broken. | State of the object | "No" + verb |
| "No more." | Stop tickling me! | Regulation of action—termination | "No" + adverb |
| "More car." | Push the car (toy) again. | Regulation of adult behavior | "More" + noun |
| "More cookie." | I want another cookie. | Repeat object demand | "More" + noun |
| "More sing." | Let's sing the song again. | Repeat action demand | "More" + verb |
| "More Rosy." | Let's play "Ring-Around-a-Rosy." | Repeat action demand | "More" + noun |
| "More Daddy." | I want to go with Daddy. | Request for accompaniment | "More" + noun |

**FIGURE 2.2.**   Sample two-word child's utterances and their intentions.

| Grammatical Category | Semantic Relations | Child's Utterance |
|---|---|---|
| Noun + verb | Agent + action | "Daddy drive." (Father is driving.) |
| Verb + noun | Action + object | "Eat cookie." "Wash dog." |
| Noun + noun | Agent + object | "Mommy cake." (Mother baked or bought a cake.) |
| Noun + noun | Possessor + object | "Daddy coat." (This is Daddy's coat or Daddy has a coat.) |
| Noun + noun | Conjunction: "and" | "Hat coat." (I want my hat and coat.) |
| Adjective + noun | Attribute + object | "Big flower." "Red truck." |
| Adverb + noun | Recurrence | "More hug." (I want you to hug me again.) "More cat." (The cat is here again.) |
| Negative + noun | Nonexistence | "No dog." (The dog isn't here or The dog is gone.) |
| Negative + verb | Rejection | "No nap." (I don't want to take a nap.) |
| Negative + noun | Denial | "No toy." (That's not my toy.) |
| Pronoun + noun | Interrogative | "That ball?" (Asking for information, usually produced with a rising inflection.) |
| Verb + pronoun | Demand or request | "Want it." (Substitution of pronoun for noun.) |
| Verb + noun | Experiencer | "See dog." ( I see the dog.) |
| Pronoun + verb | Agent + action | "I push." (Look at me, I'm pushing the ___.) |

**FIGURE 2.3.**   Two-word utterances and sample statement. Based on Bellugi, 1965; Bloom, 1970; Fillmore, 1968; and Halliday, 1975.

---

## ☎  Specific Objective B

The student uses two-word combinations to express a variety of ideas, states, and observations as well as his or her intentions (18–27 months).

The student may use two words to make statements and express intentions. For examples, see Figure 2.3 on page 124.

## Teacher and Family Interventions

**Toddler Level.**   Review the intentions identified in Figure 2.3. Design learning experiences that involve the use of two-word utterances in their reality contexts (e.g., when the student is being driven to a recreational site, ask the parent to say, "Mommy drive. Mommy is driving the car").

**Preschool Level.**   At this level, continue the activities identified for the toddler level with the express purpose of increasing the number of statements the student makes to express ideas, states, and observations and his or her comprehension and expressive vocabulary.

---

### ☎ Specific Objective C

The student comprehends "Yes" or "No" questions and *some* "Wh" questions (20 months).

---

An expansion in the comprehension (and subsequent use) of interrogatives proceeds from the comprehension (and subsequent use) of one or two words with a rising intonation pattern to the comprehension (and use) of "Wh" interrogative pronouns, such as "what," "where," and "who" (see Figure 2.4).

| "Wh" Pronoun | Adult Intention | Adult Utterance |
|:---:|:---|:---|
| "Where" | Asking for location | "Where is your hat?" |
| "What" | Asking for information about an object | "What's in your hand?" |
| "What" | Asking for information about an action | "What are you doing?" |
| "Who" | Asking for information about a person | "Who is coming in?" |
| "Whose" | Asking about ownership | "Whose book is this?" |

**FIGURE 2.4.**   "Wh" interrogative pronouns: their intentions and sample utterances.

## Teacher and Family Interventions

**Toddler Level.** Ask the student the questions you need to ask as you interact with him or her on a daily basis (e.g., you or the parent asks "Yes" or "No" questions such as "Are you hungry?" and "Do you want to go out?").

**Preschool Level.** Begin to ask more questions that start with the "Wh" interrogatives "where," "what," "who," and "whose" (e.g., Parent: "Where are my car keys?" "What did you put in your mouth?" "Who loves you?" or "Whose dirty socks are these on the floor?" Teacher: "Where are the blocks?" "What is this toy called?" "Who is going on the field trip?" or "Whose lunch box is this?").

---

 ## Specific Objective D

The student asks questions, progressing from the use of one or two words with a rising inflection to the use of a "Wh" interrogative pronoun (18–27 months).

---

The child may use only a rising intonation pattern to ask a question before progressing to the use of "Wh" interrogative pronouns (see Figure 2.5). The child may then proceed to the use of a "Wh" interrogative pronoun to initiate a question (see Figure 2.6).

| Grammatical Category | Child's Utterance |
|---|---|
| Noun + noun | "Daddy cookie?" (Does Daddy want a cookie?) |
| Noun + verb | "Boy sleep?" (Is the boy sleeping?) |
| Verb + noun | "See car?" (Do you see the car?) |
| Negative + noun | "No wagon?" (What happened to my wagon?) |
| Pronoun + verb + noun | "I ride train?" (May I go for a ride on the train?) |

**FIGURE 2.5.** Sample child's utterances with rising inflection alone.

| Grammatical Category | Child's Utterance | Intention |
|---|---|---|
| "Who" + pronoun | "Who that?" (Who is that stranger?) | Asking for person |
| "What" + pronoun | "What that?" (What is that object's name?) | Asking for object's name |
| "What" + verb<br>"What" + noun + verb | "What doing?" (What are ___ doing?)<br>"What boy doing?" (What is that boy doing?) | Asking about an action |
| "Where" + noun + noun | "Where Mommy shoe?" (Where is Mommy's shoe?) | Asking for location |
| "Where" + noun phrase + verb | "Where my milk go?" (Where is my milk; is it all gone?) | Asking for location |
| "Where" + noun | "Where horse?" (Where did the horse go?) | Asking for location |
| "Where" + noun + verb | "Where horse go?" (Where did the horse go?) | Asking for location |

**FIGURE 2.6.**  Sample child's utterances using "Wh" interrogative pronouns. Based on Bellugi, 1965; Bloom, 1970; Brown, 1973; Dore, 1975; Fillmore, 1968; and Halliday, 1975.

## Teacher and Family Interventions

**Toddler Level.**  Role-play various situations in which the student must ask a question; for example, hide the student's lunch and tell him or her to ask you where it is.

**Preschool Level.**  Play a variation of a "Pantomime" game in which the student must ask you "What doing?" when he or she is unable to guess what you are acting out.

In summary, students in Stage I use linear semantic rules with an MLU of 1.75 and an upper limit of five morphemes. They can make statements and comments, ask questions, and use negatives. They can talk about agents, objects, experience, and nonexistence. They are able to reject, deny, regulate, greet, label, inform, and request actions and objects. Their word combinations have intentions and these intentions must be recognized and enhanced by teachers, family members, and other trainers. Children in Stage I must be helped to pay attention to the *order* of word presentation.

# STAGE II

Children in Stage II use semantic rules with an MLU of 2.25, with seven morphemes representing the upper range of speech production. The approximate age of Stage II is 21–34 months (Brown, 1973).

The student during Stage II:

- ❏ E. Comprehends prepositions that designate position in space or location of objects (21–34 months). (Note: Comprehension of "in" and "on" sometimes occurs as early as 18 months [Wilcox & Palermo, 1974].)

- ❏ F. Uses personal pronouns and the demonstrative pronoun "that" (21–28 months) (Morehead & Ingram, 1973; Waterman & Schatz, 1982).

- ❏ G. Comprehends and uses the present progressive tense of verbs (without the use of the auxiliary "to be") to indicate duration or a continuous happening (21–34 months).

- ❏ H. Comprehends and expresses plurality (28–34 months).

- ❏ I. Progresses in his or her use of the "Wh" interrogative pronouns and now may include the use of "why" when asking for a reason or explanation ("Why you laughing?"), while still omitting the auxiliary verbs "to be" and "to do" (21–34 months).

- ❏ J. Uses the negative auxiliary (preverb) forms "don't" and "can't" to express rejection ("I don't want it"), to give a command ("Don't leave me"), and to indicate inability ("I can't catch you") (21–34 months) (Klima & Bellugi, 1973, p. 342). (Note: At Stage II, the child is not able to add the auxiliary verb "to be" or "to do" [Norris, 1994].)

- ❏ K. Uses "no" and "not" to indicate rejection ("I no want medicine") and denial ("That no red, that blue") (21–24 months) (Bloom, 1970).

- ❏ L. Uses a combination of the negative and interrogative to ask why an action is not occurring ("Why not dog bark?") or why an action cannot occur ("Why not her dance?") (21–34 months).

- ❏ M. Uses catenatives, for example, "I wanna go," for the infinitive construction "I want to go" (24–34 months) (Miller, 1981).

- ❏ N. Uses the conjunction "and" to combine or serialize items (24–34 months).

# SUGGESTED ACTIVITIES

Because of the nature of Stage II, suggested interventions are provided only for the preschool and primary levels. These suggested interventions may be used at higher levels, when appropriate, if age-appropriate materials and activities are employed.

---

☎ ### Specific Objective E

The student comprehends prepositions that designate position in space or location of objects (21–34 months). (Note: Comprehension of "in" and "on" sometimes occurs as early as 18 months.)

---

(See Sample Lesson Plan 3 at the end of Unit 2.)

## Teacher and Family Interventions

**Preschool Level.**  Place an object of interest in front of the student. Say, "I am going to put the ___ on your desk so you can look at and examine it." (Put the object on the student's desk with a flourish.) After the student has played with or examined the object, say, "Now, put the ___ on my desk." Once the student comprehends "on," teach the preposition "in." Ask the student to help you store various objects (e.g., "Put the milk *in* the refrigerator," "Put your coat *in* the closet," or "Put the crayons *in* the box").

**Primary Level.**   At this level, add to the student's vocabulary other prepositions that indicate position or location. Play a variation of "Simon Says" and say, "Simon says stand *in back of* your partner" and "Simon says stand *next to* your partner." Continue by telling the student, "Put the bread *on* the shelf *next to* the eggs" and "Put the milk *on* the first shelf *in back of* the juice."

   (Note: Be sure that each item has an inherent front and back. For example, we agree which part of a person is his or her front or back, but we may not agree on what is the front of a round bottle. The front depends on where we are standing.)

| Type of Pronoun | Examples | Identifying Case |
|---|---|---|
| Subject pronoun | "I," "it," "you" | The child can indicate that he or she does the action or has the experience. |
| Object pronoun | "Me," "you," "it" | The child can indicate the object of an action or what has been experienced or what is desired. |
| Possessive pronoun | "My," "mine" | The child can indicate possession or ownership. |
| Demonstrative pronoun | "That" | The child can designate an item for someone to attend to. |

**FIGURE 2.7.** Pronouns acquired early and their cases. Based on *Language Development: An Introduction,* by R. E. Owens, Jr., 1992, New York: Merrill/Macmillan.

---

## ☎ Specific Objective F

The student uses personal pronouns and the demonstrative pronoun "that" (21–28 months). (See Figure 2.7.)

---

## Teacher and Family Interventions

**Preschool Level.** At this level concentrate on the use of the pronoun "I." Ask the student to do something and while doing it to tell you what he or she is doing (e.g., "I comb hair"). Then ask the student to do something and tell you afterward what he or she has done (e.g., "I jumped up and down").

Continue in the same manner with the subject pronouns "it" (perhaps to describe the action of a toy or other inanimate object) and "you" (to describe an action of yours or of another student). You may wish to introduce the object pronouns "me," "you," and "it."

At this level, the child may use the phrases shown in Figure 2.8.

**Primary Level.** At this level, introduce the possessive pronouns "my" and "mine" and the demonstrative pronoun "that." Put several objects that belong to you in front of you and several objects that belong to the student in front of him or her. Pick up each item and say, "My ___." Indicate to the student that you want him or her to do the same with his or her belongings.

| Combination of Categories | Semantic Relations |
|---|---|
| Possessive pronoun + noun | "My book." "My doll." "My cookie." |
| Subject pronoun + possessive pronoun | "It mine." |
| Noun + possessive pronoun | "Truck mine." |
| Verb + object pronoun | "Give me." "Kiss you." |
| Subject pronoun + verb | "You go." |
| Subject pronoun + possessive pronoun + adjective + noun | "It my big book." |
| Subject pronoun + verb + object pronoun + possessive pronoun + noun | "You give me my book." |
| Demonstrative pronoun | "That mine." |

**FIGURE 2.8.** Combining pronouns into grammatical categories to establish semantic relations.

Repeat this activity, but this time say, "This is mine." Ask the student to do the same. Repeat the activity once more; this time, however, place the belongings at a distance, point to each in turn, and say, "That ___ is mine" or "That is my ___."

---

### ☎ Specific Objective G

The student comprehends and uses the present progressive tense of verbs (without the use of the auxiliary "to be") to indicate duration or a continuous happening (21–34 months).

---

Note: For example, the student may say, "Evan eating" or "Ali laughing" (person + action) and "I dancing" (pronoun + action).

## Teacher and Family Interventions

**Preschool Level.** Engage in an action and as you are performing it, say, "I am ___ing." Then tell the student to perform the same action and say what he or she is doing. Next, engage in an action and ask the student to tell you what you are doing.

**Primary Level.**　Show the student videotaped sequences of classmates, siblings, and friends, and ask him or her to tell you what each person on the tape is doing.

---

### ☎ Specific Objective H

The student comprehends and expresses plurality (28–34 months).

---

The words "cars" and "card" both end with a consonant blend. "Cars," however, has two morphemes (the morpheme "s" signals the plural, or more than one car, while the word "card" has just one morpheme). The written grapheme "s," which indicates plurality, is pronounced in three different ways: /s/ as in "boats," /z/ as in "trees," and /iz/ as in "witches." By the end of Stage II, the student should be cognitively aware of the difference between one and more than one and be able to express this awareness.

The student should be able to point (respond receptively through gestures) to one apple and to two or more apples and then give you (respond expressively through gestures) one apple and two or more apples. In order to use the plural in a productive pattern, the student should be able to articulate the /z/ after a vowel (as in "toes") and after a final consonant to form a consonant cluster or blend (as in "beds"). He or she should be able to articulate the /s/ to form a consonant cluster in words ending in the voiceless stop-plosives /p/, /t/, and /k/ ("caps," "mats," and "books"). (See Figure 2.9.)

| /z/ | /s/ | /iz/ |
|---|---|---|
| eye, eyes | hat, hats | bush, bushes |
| boy, boys | cap, caps | match, matches |
| bow, bows | rack, racks | garage, garages |
| tie, ties | | cage, cages |
| bed, beds | | |
| cab, cabs | | |
| rag, rags | | |

**FIGURE 2.9.**　Phonemic patterns of nouns that form their plurality with the letter "s" or "es."

## Teacher and Family Interventions

**Preschool Level.**  At this level, begin with the commonly occurring nouns that are said in the plural form with the phoneme /s/ or /z/. Put several samples of an object in front of you (perhaps toy cars). Pick one up and say, "Car." Then pick up several and say, "Cars," while stressing the /z/ phoneme. Do the same with a word that ends with the /s/ phoneme, such as "cap," as you pick up one baseball cap and "caps," stressing the /s/ phoneme, as you pick up several.

**Primary Level.**  At this level, introduce some commonly occurring nouns that are said in the plural form with the phonemes /iz/. Repeat the activity of the toddler level with such items as boxes, dishes, and watches.

 **Specific Objective I**

The student progresses in his or her use of the "Wh" interrogative pronouns and now may include the use of "why" when asking for a reason or explanation ("Why you laughing?"), while still omitting the auxiliary verbs "to be" and "to do" (21–34 months).

During Stage II, the student continues to use "Wh" interrogative pronouns that were developing in Stage I. He or she may use the "Wh" interrogative pronouns to ask a location ("Where my blocks?"), to ask for a name ("What doll name?"), to ask for an action or an event ("What happen now?"), to ask for a person ("Who made that?"), and to ask for a reason ("Why Mommy crying?").

## Teacher and Family Interventions

**Preschool Level.**  Continue to facilitate the development of the "Wh" interrogative pronouns. Introduce the interrogative pronoun "why" in asking about obvious (observable) cause-and-effect relationships. For example, if a dish or glass falls and breaks, ask and then answer your own question: "Why did the dish break? Because it fell down and crashed on the hard floor." "Why did Johnny cry? Because he cut himself."

**Primary Level.**  At this level, you might begin to ask "why" questions when the cause-and-effect relationships are not as obvious (not observable), for example, "Why is Nikki smiling? Because it is her birthday," "Why is Carly yelling? She is angry because someone took her toy away from her."

---

 ## Specific Objective J

The student uses the negative auxiliary (preverb) forms "don't" and "can't" to express rejection ("I don't want it"), to give a command ("Don't leave me"), and to indicate inability ("I can't catch you") (21–34 months). (Note: At Stage II, the child is not able to add the auxiliary verb "to be" or "to do.")

---

## Teacher and Family Interventions

**Preschool Level.** Explain that there are times when somebody offers us something and we don't want it or asks us to do something that we don't want to do. Explain, also, that we must use a nice voice when we tell somebody that we don't want something or don't want to do something. Role-play situations in which the student refuses (rejects) an offer or suggestion ("I don't want the doll" or "I don't want to play").

**Primary Level.** At this level, role-play situations in which the student is being interfered with or bothered and asks the person to stop what he or she is doing ("Don't take my crayons!" "Don't make so much noise," or "Don't touch me there").

If you have an inability (or pretend to have one), stage a situation in which you need help that the student is able to provide. Explain a problem, such as cutting a straight line, and say, "I can't cut a straight line. Please help me." Follow up by selecting a skill with which the student is experiencing difficulty. Ask the student to seek help by asking you nicely for that help, for example, "I can't open the box of cereal. Please help me."

---

 ## Specific Objective K

The student uses "no" and "not" to indicate rejection ("I no want medicine") and denial ("That no red, that blue") (21–24 months).

---

## Teacher and Family Interventions

**Preschool Level.**   Place two items in front of you, one that is a favorite item and one that is a disliked item. Pick up the favorite item, and say, "I want this toy ___. Then gently push the disliked item away, and say, "I don't want this game." Identify a favorite and disliked item of the student's and offer him or her the disliked item. Persist in offering the item until the student indicates rejection by using "no" or "not."

**Primary Level.**   At this level, role-play "A Trip to the Circus," with a classmate of the student's playing the part of a clown. Tell the "clown" to do silly things such as saying, "Look at this picture of an elephant," while showing you a picture of a lion. Respond to these incorrect comments by saying, "That's not an elephant. It's a lion." After several such exchanges, ask the "clown" to play the silly game with the student.

---

### ☎  Specific Objective L

The student uses a combination of the negative and interrogative to ask why an action is not occurring ("Why not dog bark?") or why an action cannot occur ("Why not her dance?") (21–34 months).

---

## Teacher and Family Interventions

**Preschool Level.**   Bring a radio to class and fail to plug it in. Show it to the student, and put the power on. When it fails to play, ask the student, "Why doesn't the radio play?" Assist the student in responding and putting the plug in a nearby socket, if necessary. Then give the student a broken toy and ask him or her to ask you why it doesn't work.

**Primary Level.**   Role-play a situation in which you are unable to do something, for example, because a part of a game or toy is missing. Then ask, "Why can't I roll this car along the floor?" If necessary, provide the answer. Then give the student a flashlight whose batteries are dead. Encourage the student to ask why it doesn't work.

☎ **Specific Objective M**

The student uses catenatives, for example, "I wanna go" for the infinitive construction "I want to go" (24–34 months).

Examples of other catenatives are: "gonna," "gotta," and "hafta." These occur before true infinitives such as "have to go." See Specific Objective BB.

## Teacher and Family Interventions

**Preschool Level.** If there is an activity in the community that would be of interest to the student, tell him or her about it and express your interest, as well, by saying, "I want to go to the junior soccer league game." Then ask the student to tell you if he or she wants to go, too.

**Primary Level.** Introduce other catenatives, for example, by asking the student to tell you what he or she has to do before going to bed or where he or she is going to go for a vacation.

☎ **Specific Objective N**

The student uses the conjunction "and" to combine or serialize items (24–34 months).

The conjunction "and" may be used to combine or serialize items ("bread and butter," "cake and candy"). Previously, items may have been serialized without the use of a conjunction, as either compound direct objects ("Wear hat coat") or compound subjects ("Nikki Alex play").

## Teacher and Family Interventions

**Preschool Level.** Make a list of frequently used expressions that are joined together by the conjunction "and," such as "peanut butter and jelly," "salt and pepper," "ham and eggs," and "red, white, and blue." Play a game in which you say the first word plus "and" and pause for the student to finish the series.

**Primary Level.** Use the expressions collected for the preschool level. At this level, use these expressions in a quiz format, for example, say, "I want to make my food taste better. What can I ask you to pass to me?" "I am very hungry, and I want something special for breakfast with my eggs. What can you cook for me?" or "I saw the American flag. What colors did I see?"

# STAGE III

Children in Stage III use semantic rules with an MLU of 2.75, with nine morphemes representing the upper range of speech production. The approximate age of Stage III is 23–37 months (Brown, 1973).

The student during Stage III:

❏ O. Continues to develop subject pronouns to indicate gender, plurality, and possession (23–37 months) (Owens, 1992). (Note: "I" and "you" were established in earlier stages.)

❏ P. Uses the articles "a," "an," and "the" (23–37 months).

❏ Q. Uses the frequently heard past tense of commonly used irregular verbs, such as "ate," "went," and "ran" (23–37 months).

❏ R. Uses the conjunction "but" to indicate a difference or an exception (23–37 months).

## SUGGESTED ACTIVITIES

Stage III suggested interventions are provided only for the toddler, preschool, and primary levels. These suggested interventions may be used at higher levels, when appropriate, if age-appropriate materials and activities are employed.

---

☎ ## Specific Objective O

The student continues to develop subject pronouns to indicate gender, plurality, and possession (23–37 months) (Owens, 1992). (Note: "I" and "you" were established in earlier stages.)

---

(See Sample Lesson Plan 4 at the end of Unit 2.)

## Teacher and Family Interventions

**Toddler Level.** Since the student comprehends and uses the present progressive tense of verbs (without the use of the auxiliary verb "to be") to indicate duration or a continuous happening (see Specific Objective G) with nouns and the pronoun "I" + action, ask a male classmate and a female classmate to perform an action. Demonstrate the use of the gender-specific pronouns "he" and "she" in describing the action.

Follow up by asking the student to describe various actions as they are performed by boys, girls, men, and women. Use the auxiliary verb when asking or answering the question. Model the correct pattern.

**Preschool Level.** At this level introduce the pronoun "we" by performing the task with the student and asking him or her to perform it simultaneously with you; then describe the action, using the plural "we." Follow up by asking the student to join a member of his or her family or a classmate in performing various actions together.

**Primary Level.** At this level, continue the development of the possessive pronoun category by working on the student's recognition of ownership by someone else. Pick up an object owned by a classmate and say to the classmate, "Your doll." Ask the student to pick up an object belonging to a classmate and say, "Your ___."

Once the student begins to use the possessive pronoun "your" appropriately ("your" + noun), introduce the use of "yours," which shows possession without using a noun (e.g., "It yours" or "That yours").

---

### ☎ Specific Objective P

The student uses the articles "a," "an," and "the" (23–37 months).

---

The use of articles may not appear to be important but they serve a number of purposes:

1. They preserve the intonation pattern of the English language. Contrast the sentences, "The boy ate a cookie" and "Boy ate cookie." The former maintains the rising and falling intonation pattern of a declarative sentence, while the latter is said with a staccato, abrupt intonation pattern.

2. The articles "a" and "an" signal a general indefinite determination or new information and also assume a

numerical equivalent of "1" as opposed to additional quantities.

3. The article "the" signals a definite determination and provides special emphasis.

4. Articles signal nouns, thus helping a student to recognize where a plural marker might belong. They also set a structure for the appearances of adjectives, for example, "I saw a red ball" (any ball of that color) and "I saw the big tree in your garden" (the pride of your garden).

## Teacher and Family Interventions

**Toddler Level.** Introduce "the" to signal a specific person as you show the student a picture book or photographs. Say such things as "The boy is running." Continue by referring to animals that often appear in storybooks ("The wolf is mean") and then objects ("The basket is filled with food for Grandma").

**Preschool and Primary Levels.** Introduce "a" to signal a general determinant by discussing a category ("A letter carrier brings the mail to my house" or "A police officer helps protect us"). At these levels, provide experience in the contrasting use of these articles whenever the student uses one of them incorrectly.

---

### ☎ Specific Objective Q

The student uses the frequently heard past tense of commonly used irregular verbs, such as "ate," "went," and "ran" (23–37 months).

---

The use of commonly occurring irregular verbs in their past tense does not necessarily indicate an understanding of the concept of time in the past. It may be an indication of memorized speech patterns that were used in specific contexts. The specific verbs used by the student apparently are dependent on the experiences and the words used in his or her environment ("Daddy ate," "We went Grandma house," or "He ran home").

The order of acquisition may be as follows: the irregular verb form (e.g., "ate"), the regular form in Stage IV or Stage V (e.g., "jumped"), and the overgeneralization of the regular morpheme suffix "ed" to irregular verbs ("ated" or "eated"), followed by use of the correct form of many irregular verbs.

## Teacher and Family Interventions

**Toddler Level.** Listen to the student as he or she is speaking to identify which irregular verbs are used. If the student does not use the past tense of these verbs correctly, demonstrate the correct form in reality contexts, for example, "Martha (a classmate or sibling) ate all her vegetables. She can now have dessert."

**Preschool and Primary Levels.** Show the student pictures that show the passage of time, for example, a picture of a cat and a full bowl of milk and then a second picture with an empty bowl and a contented cat. Ask the student to tell you what happened ("The cat drank the milk"). As a further example, show a picture of a girl riding a bike and then a second picture showing the girl at a store with the bike chained to a fence outside the store ("The girl rode her bike to the store").

---

### ☎ Specific Objective R

The student uses the conjunction "but" to indicate a difference or an exception (23–37 months).

---

## Teacher and Family Interventions

**Toddler Level.** Ask the student to select something by contrast ("Take all the red cars, but not the green ones," "Give me all the big blocks, but leave the small ones there," or "Put the apples in the refrigerator, but put the cereal in the closet").

**Preschool and Primary Levels.** Ask the student to discuss something that is different from one's normal expectations, for example, "She usually smiles, but she is crying now" (she fell down) or "She is usually clean, but she spilled the applesauce on her dress at lunch."

# STAGE IV

Children in Stage IV use semantic rules with an MLU of 3.50, with 11 morphemes representing the upper range of speech production. The approximate age of Stage IV is 35–40 months (Brown, 1973).

The student during Stage IV:

☐ S.   Uses the past tense of regular verbs (35–40 months).

☐ T.   Uses the copula verb "to be" (35–40 months).

☐ U.   Uses the auxiliary verb "to be" (35–40 months).

☐ V.   Uses the auxiliary verb "to do" (35–40 months).

☐ W.   Expresses negation when using the copula verb "to be" and the auxiliary verbs "to be" and "to do" (35–40 months).

☐ X.   Expresses ability, possibility, and willingness and makes predictions by using the verbs "can" and "will" (35–40 months).

☐ Y.   Inverts auxiliary verbs to ask questions (35–40 months) (Bellugi, 1965).

☐ Z.   Asks questions using interrogative "Wh" pronouns and an auxiliary verb (35–40 months).

☐ AA.  Uses the pronouns "they," "her," "him," "his," "them," and "hers" in his or her connected speech (35–40 months).

☐ BB.  Uses simple infinitive clauses (35–40 months) (Miller, 1981).

☐ CC.  Begins to use complex sentences, including sentences with infinitives, extended "Wh" questions, and conjoined clauses (34–37 months).

☐ DD.  Uses cognitive transitive verbs such as "think," "guess," "wish," "wonder," "know," "mean," "remember," and "pretend" (by 40 months).

## SUGGESTED ACTIVITIES

Stage IV suggested interventions are provided only for the toddler/preschool and primary/intermediate levels. These suggested interventions may be used at the secondary level, when appropriate, if age-appropriate materials and activities are employed.

☏  ### Specific Objective S

The student uses the past tense of regular verbs (35–40 months).

| /t/ | /d/ | /id/ |
|---|---|---|
| /p/ as in "wrapped" | /b/ as in "rubbed" | |
| /k/ as in "picked" | /g/ as in "tagged" | /t/ as in "painted" |
| /s/ as in "passed" | /z/ as in "buzzed" | /d/ as in "raided" |
| /sh/ as in "pushed" | /zh/ as in "garaged" | |
| /ch/ as in "watched" | /j/ as in "aged" | |
| /f/ as in "sniffed" | /m/ as in "combed" | |
| | /n/ as in "rained" | |
| | /l/ as in "called" | |
| | /r/ as in "cared" | |
| | /o/ as in "owed" | |
| | /i/ as in "eyed" | |
| | /ow/ as in "bowed" | |

**FIGURE 2.10.**   Sounds that precede the bound morpheme "ed."

The bound past-tense morpheme for regular verbs is written as "ed" but is produced orally as /t/ as in "jumped," /d/ as in "hugged," and /id/ as in "hunted." See Figure 2.10 for examples of sounds that precede the bound morpheme "ed." The use of the past tense depends on cognitive awareness of the past tense and the linguistic ability to produce the bound past-tense morpheme.

## Teacher and Family Interventions

Repeat the suggested activities for Specific Objective Q. This time, however, assist the student in discriminating between the three sound patterns identified in Figure 2.10. Discover which regular verbs are used by the student in his or her everyday communication patterns. Make certain that the student says them, using the correct sound pattern. Provide assistance as needed.

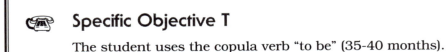

## Specific Objective T

The student uses the copula verb "to be" (35-40 months).

| Predicate Adjectives | Predicate Nouns |
|---|---|
| "I am cold." | "I am a boy." |
| "He is big." | "He is a man." |
| "She is small." | "She is a woman." |
| "It is heavy." | "It is a car." |
| "You are pretty." | "You are a teacher." |
| "They are happy." | "They are Girl Scouts." |
| "I was sick." | "I was the baby sitter." |
| "He was tall." | "He was a dancer." |
| "She was brave." | "She was the pitcher." |
| "It was soft." | "It was a birthday cake." |
| "You were slow." | "You were a Cub Scout." |
| "They were strong." | "They were players." |

**FIGURE 2.11.** The copula verb "to be" and its use in sentence patterns (pronoun + copula + predicate adjective or predicate noun).

(See Sample Lesson Plan 5 at the end of Unit 2.)

The copula verb "to be" is used with both predicate adjectives and predicate nouns. (See Figure 2.11.)

## Teacher and Family Interventions

**Toddler/Preschool Level.** Since the main verb "to be" is acquired first in situations where it cannot be contracted, at this level, begin by asking questions such as "Who is pretty?" "I am." "Who is the president?" "She is."

**Primary and Intermediate Levels.** Repeat the suggested activity for the toddler/ preschool level. At these levels, use the contracted form of the copula, for example, "It's heavy" (the package I am carrying), "He's tired" (a yawning classmate), "She's a Girl Scout," or "You're a nice teacher."

> ☎ **Specific Objective U**
>
> The student uses the auxiliary verb "to be" (35–40 months).

"I am hopping."    "I was sleeping."

"He is driving."    "He was drawing."

"She is drinking."    "She was singing."

"You are dancing."    "You were running."

"They are baking."    "They were jumping."

**FIGURE 2.12.**    Sample utterances with the auxiliary verb "to be" and the main verb plus "ing."

The use of the auxiliary "to be" signals the beginning of the development of the auxiliary systems. Other auxiliaries such as "to have" and "to do" and modal auxiliary verbs such as "can," "will," and "may" develop later. The auxiliaries and modals are needed for the production of negatives such as "He isn't painting" and "He can't write." They are also needed for the production of interrogatives such as "Is he jumping?" and "Will she fall?" (See Figure 2.12.)

## Teacher and Family Interventions

**Toddler/Preschool Level.**    Repeat the activities in Specific Objective O for the toddler and preschool levels. At this stage, require the student to use the auxiliary verb.

**Primary and Intermediate Levels.**    Show the student videotapes and photographs of people or animals performing different actions, and ask the student to tell you what he or she sees (e.g., "The boy is rubbing the magic lamp," "The lion is roaring," "The girl is playing baseball," or "The man is running"). Accept contractions, as in "He's riding a bike."

### ☎ Specific Objective V

The student uses the auxiliary verb "to do" (35–40 months).

## Teacher and Family Interventions

**Toddler/Preschool Level.**   Check first with the parents to determine whether the student performs certain household, grooming, and other tasks. Then ask the student questions that he or she should answer using the auxiliary verb "to do" in an affirmative response (e.g., "Do you brush your teeth when you get up in the morning" "Do you take out the garbage?" or "Do you help unpack the groceries?").

At the preschool level, provide the student with opportunities to use the pronouns "you," "we," and "they" with the auxiliary "do."

**Primary and Intermediate Levels.**   At these levels, again ask the student questions that he or she should answer with the auxiliary verb "to do," by using the third-person-singular "does" to refer to the action of another person (e.g., "Does your brother make his bed?" or "Does Mary swim well?"). (Note: If the student responds with a different syntactic pattern that is correct, praise him or her and ask if there is another way to answer.)

Do this until the student uses the correct form of the auxiliary "to do." For example, if the student responds, "Yes, Mary swims well," continue on with the activity until the student says, "Mary does swim well" or "She does swim well."

---

☎ ## Specific Objective W

The student expresses negation when using the copula verb "to be" and the auxiliary verbs "to be" and "to do" (35–40 months).

---

The negative forms "no" and "not" cannot directly follow the subject but rather must follow or be contracted with a form of the copula "to be" (e.g., "He is not angry," "It's not here," or "She isn't tired"), with an auxiliary verb "to be" or "to do" (e.g., "She is not yelling," "She isn't yelling," "I do not want it," "I don't want it"), *or* with an auxiliary verb (e.g., "She cannot climb," "She can't climb").

Negative morphemes signal different meanings. The modal auxiliary verbs "can't" and "won't" begin to appear as negative markers but do not fully develop until Stage V. See Specific Objective HH and Figure 2.13.

## Teacher and Family Interventions

**Toddler/Preschool Level.**   Review Figure 2.13 and provide the student with opportunities to express negatives to describe real occurrences. For example,

| Negative Categories | Child's Early Productions | Child's Later Productions |
|---|---|---|
| Nonexistence or disappearance | "No doll." | "The doll's not here." |
| Nonoccurrence | "No fix." | "The toy hasn't been fixed." |
| Cessation | "No round." | "It's not going around anymore." |
| Rejection | "No want." | "I don't want the carrots." |
| Prohibition | "No push." | "Don't push me." |
| Denial | "No cat." | "It's not a cat." |

**FIGURE 2.13.** Negative intentions and children's early and later productions. Based on *An Introduction to Children with Language Disorders,* by V. Reed, 1994, New York: Macmillan.

hide one of the student's favorite toys and expect him or her to use a complete sentence to indicate nonexistence or disappearance ("My truck is not here").

Work also on rejection, by asking the student if he or she would like something that he or she dislikes ("I don't want to go to Aunt Camilla's house"). Continue on with prohibition, by attempting to take a toy away from the student as he or she is playing with it ("Don't touch my Slinky").

**Primary and Intermediate Levels.**   At these levels, once again review Figure 2.13, and provide the student with opportunities to express negatives to describe real situations involving nonoccurrence ("Dinner isn't ready yet"), cessation ("The light doesn't go on anymore" [the bulb may need to be replaced]), and denial ("I didn't belch. Bobby did it").

---

### ☎  Specific Objective X

The student expresses ability, possibility, and willingness and makes predictions by using the verbs "can" and "will" (35–40 months). (See Figure 2.14.)

---

## Teacher and Family Interventions

**Toddler/Preschool Level.**   Review with the student the skills that he or she possesses. Play the "I Can" game in which you and the student take turns naming

| Modal | Intention | Examples of Usage |
|-------|-----------|-------------------|
| "Can" | Ability | "I *can* do it." (I'm able to!) |
| "Can" | Possibility | "You *can* do it." (It's possible if you try hard enough.) |
| "Will" | Volition or willingness | "I *will* do it." (I want to.) |
| "Will" | Prediction | "She *will* win the prize." |

**FIGURE 2.14.** The modals "can" and "will" and their intentions. Based on *A Comprehensive Grammar of the English Language*, by R. Quirk, S. Greenbaum, G. Leech, and J. Sartvik, 1989, White Plains, NY: Longman.

the things that each of you can do, using a sentence. Once the student has been successful in describing his or her abilities (this is a good self-esteem activity: "I'm OK!"), proceed to identify things both of you think a third party (a classmate or sibling, for example) can probably do (this is a good activity for improving the view of others: "They're OK, too!"), for example, "Lucy can climb to the top of the jungle gym" or "Mark can button his shirt without help."

**Primary and Intermediate Levels.** At these levels, work with the modal "will" to indicate willingness (e.g., "I will wash the dishes tonight") and to indicate a prediction (e.g., "I will be able to use a walker real soon").

---

### ☎ Specific Objective Y

The student inverts auxiliary verbs to ask questions (35–40 months).

---

Previous to Stage IV, children express questions by using a rising intonation. At this level, children begin to use more adult-like questions, by inverting the subject and the auxiliary verb. Also, at this point, use of the auxiliary verb "to do" and the modal auxiliary verb "can" begins in the declarative, negative, and inverted forms of questions. (See Figure 2.15.)

## Teacher and Family Interventions

**Toddler/Preschool Level.** At these levels, expect the student to use inverted auxiliaries to ask questions, using a form of the auxiliary "to be" in the

| Early Production (No Auxiliary) | Inclusion of Auxiliary | Later Production (Inversion) |
|---|---|---|
| "I going?" | "I am going?" | "Am I going?" |
| "He cleaning?" | "He is cleaning?" | "Is he cleaning?" |
| "She biting?" | "She is biting?" | "Is she biting?" |
| "It banging?" | "It is banging?" | "Is it banging?" |
| "You watching?" | "You are watching?" | "Are you watching?" |
| "We leaving?" | "We are leaving?" | "Are we leaving?" |
| "They fighting?" | "They are fighting?" | "Are they fighting?" |

**FIGURE 2.15.**    Early and later question production using pronouns or nouns and verb forms.

present progressive tense. See examples in Figure 2.15. At the preschool level, introduce the auxiliary "to be" in the past progressive tense (e.g., "Were they fighting?" or "Was she going to school when she fell?").

**Primary and Intermediate Levels.**    At these levels, expect the student to use inverted auxiliaries to ask questions, using a form of the auxiliary "to do" (e.g., "Do you wash your hands after going to the bathroom?" "Does he like to eat spinach?" or "Did she pass out the paper when she was supposed to?").

---

### ☎ Specific Objective Z

The student asks questions using interrogative "Wh" pronouns and an auxiliary verb (35–40 months).

---

In Stage II (see Specific Objective I), children formed interrogatives by using a "Wh" interrogative pronoun plus a main verb ("What happening?") or a noun phrase ("Where Mommy boots?"). No auxiliaries or copulas were used at this stage. As the student progresses, auxiliaries or copulas are included in early sentence production, with inversions occurring in later sentence production. See the examples in Figure 2.16.

| Early Sentence Production | Later Sentence Production |
|---|---|
| "Where Jerry working?" (no auxiliary "to be") | "Where is Jerry working?" |
| "Why Evan kicked the ball?" (no auxiliary "to do") | "Why did Evan kick the ball?" |
| "How Nikki carry her books?" (no modal auxiliary) | "How can Nikki carry her books?" |
| "What Joe is eating?" "Why Serge did break that?" (auxiliary present but no inversion) | "What is Joe eating?" "Why did Serge break that?" |
| "Why Alex can't fly?" "Where Carly will hide?" (modal auxiliary present but no inversion) | "Why can't Alex fly?" "Where will Carly hide?" |

**FIGURE 2.16.**  "Wh" interrogative pronouns in early and later sentence production.

## Teacher and Family Interventions

**Toddler/Preschool Level.**  At this level, concentrate on the production of questions using a form of the verb "to be." (See the examples in Figure 2.16.)

**Primary and Intermediate Levels.**  At these levels, concentrate on the production of questions using the modal "can" and a form of the verb "to do." (See the examples in Figure 2.16.)

---

### ☎ Specific Objective AA

The student uses the pronouns "they," "her," "him," "his," "them," and "hers" in his or her connected speech (35–40 months).

---

## Teacher and Family Interventions

**Toddler/Preschool Level.**  At this level concentrate on the use of the nominative plural pronoun "they." Ask two, then three or more, people (other than you and the student) to perform an action. Describe the action using the pronoun "they." Then ask these other people to perform other actions, and require the student to describe what he or she sees. Continue by describing a group of people using the pronoun "they" (e.g., "They are Boy Scouts" or "They [basketball players] are tall").

**Primary and Intermediate Levels.**    At these levels, concentrate on the objective pronouns in both their singular form ("him" and "her") and their plural form ("them"). Ask the student to play the part of a teacher in the "Playing School Game." Ask the student to give other students directions such as "Give the book to him!" and "Pass the crayons to her." At the intermediate level especially, work on the possessive pronouns "his," "her," and "hers." Have the student, acting as the teacher, ask questions such as "Is this his lunch box?" "Are these her books?" and "Are they hers?" while holding up some of the person's possessions.

 ## Specific Objective BB

The student uses simple infinitive clauses (35–40 months).

See Specific Objective M. A simple infinitive clause has two main verbs, and the subject of each verb is the same. For example, in the sentence "I want to eat," the subject of "to eat" is not included. The redundant subject is deleted before the infinitive. At this stage, children begin to use more complex sentences, including a gradual transition from the use of catenatives such as "gonna," "wanna," "hafta," and "gotta" into simple infinitive clauses. Thus, "I wanna play" now becomes "I want to play." "I hafta go" now becomes "I have to go." And "I'm gonna watch TV" now becomes "I'm going to watch TV."

## Teacher and Family Interventions

**Toddler/Preschool Level.**    Ask the student questions that are likely to stimulate the development of the infinitive, for example, "What do you want to do?" ("I want to play"), "What do you have to do?" ("I have to go to the bathroom"), and "What are you going to do?" ("I'm going to watch TV").

**Primary and Intermediate Levels.**    Ask the student to discuss household rules, regulations, and routines assigned to each member of his or her family, for example, "The young children go to bed every night by six," "I have to wash the dishes every other day," and "My brother has to take out the garbage."

☎   ## Specific Objective CC

The student begins to use complex sentences, including sentences with infinitives, extended "Wh" questions, and conjoined clauses (34–37 months).

## Teacher and Family Interventions

**Toddler/Preschool Level.**   At this level, begin by facilitating the use of the conjunction "and" to combine sentences. For example, the sentences "We went to the circus" and "We had ice cream" should be combined to form the sentence "We went to the circus, and we had ice cream."

**Primary and Intermediate Levels.**   At these levels, concentrate on the use of conjunctions such as "because" and "since." ("Because" indicates the reason and "since" indicates the passage of time.) Stimulate sentences such as "I didn't get any dessert because I didn't finish my vegetables" and "Since my father got a new job, I hardly ever get to see him."

☎   ## Specific Objective DD

The student uses cognitive transitive verbs such as "think," "guess," "wish," "wonder," "know," "mean," "remember," and "pretend" (by 40 months).

These cognitive transitive verbs are often used with embedded subordinate clauses. The embedded clause is usually the object clause that answers "what," for example, "I remember [what?] that he is going to visit," "I hope [what?] that he can play," and "I think [what?] that you are nice." In late Stage V, children may omit "that" and produce sentences such as "I wish you would stay." Subordinate clauses containing cognitive transitive verbs also may serve as indirect or embedded "Wh" questions, thus serving an object function (Lund & Duchan, 1993; Owens, 1992; Miller, 1981). For example:

| Statement | Embedded Clause | Information Requested |
|---|---|---|
| "I wonder | *what* she said." | Object |
| "I know | *where* it is." | Location |
| "I remember | *when* he did it." | Time |

## Teacher and Family Interventions

**Toddler/Preschool Level.**   Ask the student to share some of his or her memories with you in an effort to facilitate the development of embedded clauses, for example, "I remember that my grandfather used to give me nice presents." Also, ask the student to tell you what he or she knows, for example, "I know how to tie my shoes all by myself."

**Primary and Intermediate Levels.**   Ask the student to tell you some of the things he or she wishes or hopes for, for example, "I wish that I could sleep at Johnny's house" or "I hope that he will play ball with me." Also, ask the student about some of the things he or she wonders and thinks about, for example, "I wonder what Carly is going to do next?" or "I think that Alexis Rose is pretty."

# STAGE V

Children in Stage V use semantic rules with an MLU of 4.00, with 13 morphemes representing the upper range of speech production. The approximate age of Stage V is 41–46 months (Brown, 1973).

The student during Stage V:

- ❐ EE. Uses the pronouns "its," "our," "myself," "ours," "their," and "theirs" in his or her connected speech (41–46 months) (Owens, 1992).

- ❐ FF. Uses the modal auxiliary verbs "could," "would," "may," "might," "should," and "must" (41–46 months).

- ❐ GG. Uses the conjunctions "because" and "if" to form complex sentences (by 46 months).

- ❐ HH. Uses relative pronouns to introduce relative clauses to form complex sentences (by 46 months).

# SUGGESTED ACTIVITIES

Stage V suggested interventions are provided only for the preschool, primary, and intermediate levels. These suggested interventions may be used at the secondary level, when appropriate, if age-appropriate materials and activities are employed.

---

🕿 **Specific Objective EE**

The student uses the pronouns "*its*," "*our*," "*myself*," "*ours*," "*their*," and "*theirs*" in his or her connected speech (41–46 months). (See Figure 2.17.)

---

## Teacher and Family Interventions

**Preschool Level.** At this level, concentrate on the use of "its," which is a nonperson possessive pronoun (e.g., "Its [the car's] fender is dented") and the gender-neutralized plurals "our" and "their" (e.g., "Our garden [the family's] is beautiful" and "Their [another class's] room is very attractive").

**Primary Level.** At this level, concentrate on the use of "ours" and "theirs." "Ours" and "theirs" are independent possessives that indicate more than one owner of the object possessed (e.g., "That car is ours" and "Those [band] uniforms are theirs").

**Intermediate Level.** At this level, concentrate on the use of the reflexives "myself" and "yourself" (e.g., "I hurt myself" and "Can you do that by yourself?").

| Pronouns | Intentions | Examples of Utterances |
|---|---|---|
| "Its" | Possessive | "*Its* (the car's) fender is dented." |
| "Our" | Possessive | "*Our* house is white." |
| "Their" | Possessive | "*Their* garden is pretty." |
| "Him" | Objective | "I like *him*." |
| "Ours" | Possessive | "These toys are *ours*." |
| "Theirs" | Possessive | "Those supplies are *theirs*." |
| "Myself" | Reflexive direct object | "I hurt *myself*." |
| "Yourself" | Reflexive indirect object | "You first told *yourself* to stop and think." |

**FIGURE 2.17.** Commonly used Stage V pronouns and their intentions.

---

📞   ## Specific Objective FF

The student uses the modal auxiliary verbs "could," "would," "may," "might," "should," and "must" (41–46 months).

---

(See Sample Lesson Plan 6 at the end of Unit 2.)

In Stage IV, most children have developed the modal auxiliary verbs "can" and "will." (See Specific Objective X.) These other modals also start to emerge in Stage IV but occur with greater frequency in Stage V. Each of the modals carries its own meaning, but not all of the subtleties of meaning are used by the children. (See Figures 2.18–2.21.)

## Teacher and Family Interventions

**Preschool Level.**   At this level, concentrate on the modals "can," "could," "can't," and "couldn't." See Figure 2.18.

| Modal | Intention | Examples of Utterances |
|---|---|---|
| "Can" | Ability | Q: "Is he able to do it?" <br> A: "Yes, he *can* jump." |
| "Could" | Ability | Q: "Do you think she is able to run from here to there?" <br> A: "She *could* run a mile." |
| "Can" | Possibility | Q: "Where will she have lunch?" <br> A: "She *can* eat with us." |
| "Could" | Possibility | Q: "Will he be there?" <br> A: "He *could* be late." |
| "Can't" | Inability or lack of permission | "I *can't* play." |
| "Couldn't" | Inability | "I *couldn't* even if I tried." |
| "Can't" | Inability | "*Can't* you tie a knot?" |
| "Can't" | Request for information | "Why *can't* you go?" |

**FIGURE 2.18.**   The modals "can," "can't" "could," and "couldn't": Intentions and sample utterances. Based on *A Comprehensive Grammar of the English Language*, by R. Quirk, S. Greenbaum, G. Leech, and J. Sartvik, 1989, White Plains, NY: Longman.

| Modal | Intention | Examples of Utterances |
|-------|-----------|------------------------|
| "Will" | Prediction | "You *will* find the key." |
| "Would" | Prediction | "I *would* go if I had the money." |
| "Won't" | Refusal | "I *won't* do it." (present) |
| "Wouldn't" | Refusal | "He *wouldn't* help me." (past) |
| "Will" | Volition—intention | "*Will* you send it?" |
| "Would" | Volition—willingness | "*Would* you do that?" |

**FIGURE 2.19.** The modals "will," "would," "won't," and "wouldn't": Intentions and sample utterances. Note: "Would" is not a frequently used modal. Based on *A Comprehensive Grammar of the English Language,* by R. Quirk, S. Greenbaum, G. Leech, and J. Sartvik, 1989, White Plains, NY: Longman.

**Primary Level.** At this level, concentrate on the modals "will," "would," "won't," and "wouldn't." See Figure 2.19.

**Intermediate Level.** At this level, concentrate on the modals "may," "might," "should," and "must." See Figures 2.20 and 2.21.

 ## Specific Objective GG

The student uses the conjunctions "because" and "if" to form complex sentences (by 46 months).

| Modal | Intention | Examples of Utterances |
|-------|-----------|------------------------|
| "May" | Permission | "*May* I have this?" |
| "May" | Possibility | "It *may* happen." |
| "Might" | Possibility | "It *might* happen." (more tentative than *may*) |

**FIGURE 2.20.** The modals "may" and "might": Intentions and sample utterances. Based on *A Comprehensive Grammar of the English Language,* by R. Quirk, S. Greenbaum, G. Leech, and J. Sartvik, 1989, White Plains, NY: Longman.

| Modal | Intention | Examples of Utterances |
|-------|-----------|------------------------|
| "Should" | Obligation | "You *should* do the dishes." |
| "Should" | Seeking advice or guidance | "*Should* I write to her?" |
| "Must" | Obligation | "You *must* be on time to work." |
| "Must" | Necessity | "You *must* water that plant" (or it will die). |

**FIGURE 2.21.** The modals "should" and "must": Intentions and sample utterances. Note: "Shall" is not a modal that is used by many people in the United States. Based on *A Comprehensive Grammar of the English Language*, by R. Quirk, S. Greenbaum, G. Leech, and J. Sartvik, 1989, White Plains, NY: Longman.

In earlier stages, children developed compound sentences, that is, two equally joined sentences using the conjunctions "and" (for addition, as in "I bought peanut butter and I bought jelly") and "but" (for contrary statements, as in "I can go but I don't wanna"). With the advent of the use of "because" and "if" as conjunctions, the child is using *subordinators* and is continuing the development of complex sentences. (See Figure 2.22.)

## Teacher and Family Interventions

**Primary Level.**   At this level, review with the student events whose cause is fairly obvious, such as "The light went off because we pushed the switch," "The glass broke because I dropped it," and "I cut my finger because the scissors are sharp."

**Intermediate Level.**   At this level, ask the student to give the reason why less obvious or more subtle things occur, such as "My mother is angry because I didn't listen" and "Because I didn't share my toys, I can't have a cookie."

| Conjunction | Intention | Sentence |
|-------------|-----------|----------|
| "Because" | Causality—statement of a reason | "It broke *because* I dropped it." |
| "If" | Statement of a condition | "I swim *if* the sun is out." |

**FIGURE 2.22.** The conjunctions "because" and "if." Based on *A Comprehensive Grammar of the English Language*, by R. Quirk, S. Greenbaum, G. Leech, and J. Sartvik, 1989, White Plains, NY: Longman.

**Secondary Level.**  Play a pretend game in which the student is asked to imagine a situation and to state what he or she would do under specified conditions, for example, "If you were watching a movie and someone was talking loudly, what would you do?" and "If you were cooking and your clothes caught fire, what would you do?" Make certain that the student uses a complex sentence in his or her response.

---

### ☎ Specific Objective HH

The student uses relative pronouns to introduce relative clauses to form complex sentences (by 46 months).

---

Relative clauses are introduced by relative pronouns and refer to or modify the noun that immediately precedes them. Relative pronouns that modify the object are learned first, for example, "I saw the *girl* who lives down the street."

At a later time, relative clauses that modify the subject begin to appear, for example, "The *boy*, who is running, is my brother" (Kamhi & Nelson, 1988; Scott, 1988). Owens (1992) noted that a child uses the first relative pronouns with a nonspecific noun such as "one" or "kind," so that a sentence such as "I want *one* that I can eat" may appear. Relative pronouns that introduce relative clauses include "who," "whom," "whose," "which," and "that." A zero marker may also be employed (Quirk, Greenbaum, Leech, & Sartvik, 1989). (See Figure 2.23.) A zero marker is an optional construction, for example, "Nikki and Alex played the game (that) I gave them." The sentence may be spoken or written with or without the relative pronoun.

## Teacher and Family Interventions

**Primary Level.**  Concentrate on the personal relative pronoun "who." Begin with the sentence structure in which the relative pronoun "who" is used to refer to the object of a sentence. Show the student photographs of different people, and ask him or her to indicate a preference, for example, "I like the boy who is wearing a red shirt" when shown two photographs, one of a boy wearing a red shirt and the other of a boy wearing a yellow shirt, or "I like the girl who has long hair" when shown two photographs, one of a girl with long hair and one of a girl with short hair.

Continue, using the same or similar photographs, with the sentence structure in which a relative pronoun is used to refer to the subject of the sentence, for example, "The boy who is wearing the red shirt is sitting" and "The girl who has long hair is eating."

| Relative Pronoun | Intention | Sentence |
|---|---|---|
| "Who" | Personal: refers to the object or subject of the sentence | "I like the teacher *who* is smiling." "The girl *who* is happy is having a party." |
| "Whose" | Possessive | "The barn *whose* roof leaked is fixed." |
| "Which" | Nonperson reference | "The spider, *which* I found, is black." |
| "Whom" | Personal: refers to the object | "This is a person *whom* I really like." |
| "That" | Nonperson reference | "The dog *that* I like is small." |
| Zero | Marking is not stated but is understood | "The dog I own is small." |

**FIGURE 2.23.** Relative pronouns and sample complex sentences.

**Intermediate Level.** Introduce the possessive relative pronoun "whose," beginning with a person reference, for example, "The boy whose book I tore is angry." Engage several of the student's classmates in a number of role plays in which one of the participant's belongings plays a key role, for example, "The girl whose dress was dirty asked her friend to help her clean it," "The man whose wallet was stolen called the police," and "The woman whose hat fell off thanked the boy who caught it." Continue by working with "whose" when there is a nonperson reference.

Show the student before-and-after pictures of objects. Ask him or her to comment on the second picture. For example, show the "before" picture of an intact barn and then the "after" picture of the same barn with a missing roof, and ask the student to tell you *what happened and what needs to be done* ("The barn, whose roof was blown off, needs to be repaired"). Before-and-after pictures of various objects should be used, leading to such sentences as "The house, whose window was broken, needs a new window" and "The store, whose chimney fell down from the tornado, must be fixed."

(Note: At this level, you may also decide to work on the personal relative pronoun "whom.")

**Secondary Level.** Work on the nonperson-referenced relative pronouns "that" and "which." It is especially important to begin work on the use of the zero marker. Repeat the activities identified at the primary level. This time encourage the use of the personal relative pronoun marker "who," followed by its omission in an alternative sentence structure, for example,

"The boy who is wearing a red shirt is the one I like," followed by "The boy wearing a red shirt is sitting."

Continue with the nonperson relative pronoun marker "that," followed by its omission in an alternative sentence structure, for example, "The watch that I am wearing is new," followed by "The watch I'm wearing is new."

## GOAL IV.

The student will acquire the oral communication skills that will facilitate successful performance in various learning situations.

# SPECIFIC OBJECTIVES

The student:

☐ A. Continues a behavior when praised, encouraged, and otherwise orally reinforced.

☐ B. Stops an undesirable or inappropriate behavior when asked or warned to do so.

☐ C. Responds appropriately to oral commands.

☐ D. Responds correctly to oral instructions.

☐ E. Obeys the commands and instructions of others in emergency situations.

☐ F. Asks for clarification and further explanation when needed.

☐ G. Provides assistance to others who request it and asks for assistance when needed.

☐ H. Asks for a desired object, toy, or game and needed instructional materials and equipment.

☐ I. Reinforces peers and others who are performing or behaving in an appropriate or successful manner.

☐ J. Informs others when he or she is ill, not feeling well, or in pain.

❐ K. Indicates desires relevant to free play and other activities, snack preferences, and food served at school breakfasts and lunches.

❐ L. Delivers oral messages to others.

❐ M. Identifies desired objects from the school library and from a school or training-site store or commissary.

❐ N. Shares his or her thoughts and feelings with others in simple conversational exchanges.

❐ O. Internalizes and follows activity schedules and obeys rules and regulations that have been discussed and described orally and behaves accordingly.

---

 ## Specific Objective A

The student continues a behavior when praised, encouraged, and otherwise orally reinforced.

---

(Note: Orally reinforce students for attempts as well as successes, even when more tangible reinforcers are being used as part of a behavioral management program. Reinforcers and reinforcement schedules should be addressed from a programming perspective, that is, the eventual goal is to minimize tangibles as reinforcers and to emphasize praise as a reinforcer. Teachers and other trainers should be generous with their praise and develop a wide range of verbal reinforcers. "Okay" is a feeble reinforcement and an overused "Good" easily loses its magic!)

## Teacher Interventions

**Infant and Toddler/Preschool and Primary Levels.**  At these levels, be sure to praise the student for attempts as well as successes and concentrate on the basic activities of daily living such as toileting, dressing and undressing, eating and drinking, grooming, and safety and health.

**Intermediate and Secondary Levels.**  At these levels, concentrate on using a variety of words of praise, emphasize the successful meeting of performance challenges, stress the use of praise given intermittently, and be especially aware of behaviors that represent successful adaptations to appropriate performance in the community as a worker, as a participant in leisure-time pursuits, and as a member of a family and other personal communities.

## Family Interventions

**Infant and Toddler/Preschool and Primary Levels.**   At these levels, encourage the parents to praise their child for both attempts and successes as they concentrate on the activities of daily living (toileting, dressing and undressing, eating and drinking, personal hygiene and grooming, household management and maintenance, and safety and health).

**Intermediate and Secondary Levels.**   At these levels, encourage the parents to use a variety of words of praise, to emphasize successes, and to be especially aware of behaviors that represent independence and that promise a successful transition to adult life.

---

☎  **Specific Objective B**

The student stops an undesirable or inappropriate behavior when asked or warned to do so.

---

## Teacher Interventions

**Infant and Toddler/Preschool and Primary Levels.**   As early as possible, physically stop a student whenever he or she engages in an undesirable or inappropriate behavior. As an essential part of this action, couple it with a word or words of reprimand or warning. Be sure to also explain the reason why the behavior is undesirable or inappropriate, even if the student does not comprehend the oral message. It is hoped that the student will "read" the nonverbal clues such as vocal intonation, facial expression, and other body language.

At the primary level, follow up explanations that are understood with role plays that demonstrate and reinforce appropriate behaviors, such as covering one's mouth when coughing, going to the bathroom to pass wind, and treating school property with care.

**Intermediate and Secondary Levels.**   At these levels, concentrate on eliminating behaviors that are likely to interfere with the student's successful transition to adult life and with his or her need to establish and maintain successful interpersonal relations, acquire and maintain employment, have enriching and fulfilling leisure-time activities, and live as independently and productively as possible.

## Family Interventions

**Infant and Toddler/Preschool and Primary Levels.** Impress upon the parents that they should physically stop their child whenever he or she engages in an undesirable or inappropriate behavior. Remind them to couple the physical act with a reprimand or warning and to explain the reason why the demonstrated behavior is undesirable or inappropriate, even if they believe that the child does not comprehend their words.

**Intermediate and Secondary Levels.** At these levels, ask the parents to concentrate on eliminating behaviors that will hinder their youngster's transition to adult life. Remind them not to embarrass their youngster when he or she engages in inappropriate or undesirable behavior in the presence of others. Tell them that instead, they should explain as soon as possible, when they are alone with the child, why the behavior was inappropriate and to suggest an appropriate behavior that might have been substituted.

---

☎ **Specific Objective C**

The student responds appropriately to oral commands.

---

## Teacher Interventions

**Infant and Toddler/Preschool Level.** Take an inventory of the student's fine and gross motor skills. Once you have determined what skills he or she possesses, incorporate them into one-part commands, for example, "Clap your hands!" "Close the door!" "Pick up the crayon!" and "Stand up!" Follow up by singing action songs such as "If You're Happy and You Know It" and acting out finger plays such as "I Have a Little Turtle." Also, at this level, include the situation-bound definite adverbs "here" and "there."

**Primary Level.** At this level (see Figure 2.24), include in your commands (a) adjectives that denote differences in visual, auditory, gustatory, proprioceptive, olfactory, and tactile qualities; (b) prepositions that denote specific locations such as "on," "in," "over," "under," "next to," "in front of," and "behind"; (c) personal pronouns; and (d) the demonstrative pronouns "this," "that," "these," and "those."

**Intermediate Level.** At this level, include in your commands adjectives that denote color, shape, space, time, distance, and seriation (see Figure 2.25.)

| Sensory Modality | Polar Adjectives |
|---|---|
| Visual | Big, small; tall, short |
| Auditory | Loud, soft |
| Gustatory | Sweet, sour |
| Proprioceptive | Heavy, light |
| Tactile | Wet, dry; warm, cool; hot, cold |
| Olfactory | Nice, bad |

**FIGURE 2.24.**   Representative polar adjectives.

**Secondary Level.**   At this level, include in your commands (a) both comparative and superlative adjectives; (b) adverbs that end in "ly"; (c) the indefinite and instrumental prepositions "near," "by," and "at"; and (d) the situation-bound indefinite adverbs "anyplace" and "somewhere."

## Family Interventions

**Infant and Toddler/Preschool Level.**   Tell the parents to ask their child to perform, during play activities, such actions as "Drive the car!" "Rock the baby!" "Clap your hands!" and "Bounce the ball!" Also, remind the parents to ask the child to put things or do something in a definite place in the home.

**Primary Level.**   Encourage the parents to refer to family members and objects found in the home by using personal pronouns. Review with the parents the

| Quality | Nonpolar Adjectives |
|---|---|
| Color | Primary—red, yellow, and blue<br>Secondary—green, violet, and orange |
| Shape | Round, square |
| Space | Top, middle, bottom, deep, shallow |
| Numerals | One, two, three |
| Seriation | First, second, third, . . . last |

**FIGURE 2.25.**   Representative nonpolar adjectives.

use of the various forms of the seven personal pronouns, "I," "you," "he," "she," "we," "they," and "it." Urge them to describe typical happenings, for example, "I feel sleepy," "You must put away your toys!" "It (the soup) is too hot to eat!" "He (Daddy or a brother) is mowing the lawn," "She (Mommy or a sister) is walking the dog," "We are going shopping after lunch," and "They (the neighbors) are taking a walk."

Encourage them, also, to work with prepositions that denote specific locations when giving directions relevant to household chores, with polar adjectives, and with demonstrative pronouns. (See Figure 2.24.)

**Intermediate Level.** Ask the parents to identify the nonpolar qualities of objects in the home and the community. Tell them to give their youngster commands relevant to these qualities, for example, "Water the plant that has yellow flowers!" "Please bring me the square placemats!" and "Put the book on the bottom shelf!"

**Secondary Level.** At this level, ask the parents to give their youngster commands such as "Walk slowly!" "Put your crayons away quickly!" "Please give me the largest bag of pretzels!" "Put the plant near the table!" and "Just put your toys somewhere out of the way!"

---

☎ ## Specific Objective D

The student responds correctly to oral instructions.

---

## Teacher Interventions

**Primary Level.** Play a modified version of "Simon Says" using two-part commands. At this level, begin to give the student classroom responsibilities that require him or her to follow specific directions, for example, "Erase the chalkboard and then wash it with the sponge" and "Clear your desk and then pass out the containers of milk."

**Intermediate Level.** Give the student two or more commands involving classroom chores and activities. After the student performs a task, thank him or her for being a good worker. Requests might include, for example, "Please collect the books and put them on the top shelf of the bookcase."

**Secondary Level.** At this level, give the student directions for carrying out various functional tasks such as taking care of the classroom plants, making a birdhouse as a gift, and assembling a piece of furniture or an appliance that has been purchased for classroom use.

## Family Interventions

**Primary Level.**   Ask the parents to give their child directions for simple household tasks, for example, "You open the box of cough drops by finding the cellophane tab and pulling it around the top."

**Intermediate and Secondary Levels.**   At these levels, encourage the parents to give their youngster directions for various household chores, for example, following a recipe from oral directions, assembling an item such as a bookcase, doing simple household repairs, and doing a multistep chore such as sorting clothes, washing and drying them, ironing some of the items, and putting them away in the proper storage area.

---

☎   ## Specific Objective E

The student obeys the commands and instructions of others in emergency situations.

---

## Teacher Interventions

**Infant and Toddler/Preschool and Primary Levels.**   Explain to the student what a fire drill is. Be sure not to overemphasize the danger and to make the student unnecessarily apprehensive. Get permission to conduct a fire drill separately from the rest of the school. (The rest of the school might be told that it is a special fire drill to give some of the younger students additional practice.)

Also, take the student on trips in the community to locate "Exit" signs, fire exits, emergency notices in buildings, and other examples of community provisions for emergency situations, such as fire alarm boxes, emergency telephones, fire extinguishers, fire hydrants, and emergency shelters.

**Intermediate and Secondary Levels.**   Discuss with the student other emergency situations that might arise, especially those related to special geographic areas, like hurricanes, tornadoes, forest fires, mudslides, floods, and earthquakes. Be sure to describe and practice evacuation procedures. As part of your instruction, show the student photographs, videotapes of news broadcasts, and movies that depict these natural disasters and people's responses to them.

## Family Interventions

**Infant and Toddler/Preschool and Primary Levels.** Ask the parents to establish a fire escape plan for the family home. Ask them to explain the plan to their child and to conduct periodic drills.

**Intermediate and Secondary Levels.** Remind the parents to continue to practice home fire drills at these levels. Ask them also to establish plans for handling emergencies, especially those that are relevant to their geographic area, both in the home setting and when moving about or traveling in the community.

---

 ## Specific Objective F

The student asks for clarification and further explanation when needed.

---

## Teacher Interventions

**Primary and Intermediate Levels.** Once the student has developed sufficient proficiency to understand simple commands, directions, and instructions, give him or her directions that he or she might not understand because of the length of the language unit or because of new vocabulary.

When the student becomes confused, encourage him or her to ask for clarification or further explanation. Explain that everyone may become confused at times when given directions and that, when this occurs, it is *always* appropriate to ask for the directions to be explained again until they are understood.

**Secondary Level.** At this level, give the student more complex tasks to complete, especially those that are related to possible work situations, leisure pursuits, and home management and maintenance. Encourage the student to ask for clarification whenever he or she does not understand the directions.

## Family Interventions

**Primary and Intermediate Levels.** Ask the parents to give one another or another family member directions that are not easily understood. Remind them to have arranged for the person who is "confused" to model asking for clarification and to explain that people often need to ask for further explanations. Encourage the parents to give the child directions that he or she will not easily comprehend. Tell them to make certain that this activity does not frustrate the child.

**Secondary Level.** At this level, tell the parents to give their youngster more difficult tasks to carry out, especially those that are related to possible job opportunities, leisure pursuits, and home management and maintenance. Encourage them to remind the youngster periodically that it is *always* appropriate to ask for further explanations since that might prevent accidents, damage to materials and equipment, and mistakes that could result in problems in the home, in the community, and on the job.

 ## Specific Objective G

The student provides assistance to others who request it and asks for assistance when needed.

## Teacher Interventions

**Infant and Toddler/Preschool and Primary Levels.** Set up classroom situations in which you need help, for example, "Please put your finger on the knot so I can finish wrapping this package for the 'Toys for Tots' campaign," "Please refill the watering can while I wipe up the water that I spilled," and "Please close the door behind you when we leave for lunch." Reward the student for being a good helper who provided you with assistance when you requested it. Follow up by assigning the student a task that he or she cannot possibly complete without help.

**Intermediate and Secondary Levels.** Show the student excerpts from television shows or teacher-made movies that depict people engaged in work situations who request help from others, for example, "I need help in carrying this heavy box," "Hold the ladder while I clean out the gutter," and "Show me once again how to operate this machine safely." Then engage the student in cooperative activities with his or her classmates. Monitor the activities to make certain that the student responds by assisting others in his or her group who request help.

Follow up by involving the student in several role plays in which the student plays different workers who ask for help, for example, a flight attendant ("I need some more ice to serve the cold drinks"), a cook ("Somebody help me clean up the soup I spilled"), and a nurse's aide to a patient ("Roll on your side so I can slip the clean sheet under you").

## Family Interventions

**Infant and Toddler/Preschool and Primary Levels.**   Ask the parents to arrange activities in which they need help, for example, "Please help me clear the dirty dishes," "Please hold the freezer door open so I won't spill the water in the ice cube tray onto the floor," and "Please help me set up the folding chairs for the 'Candy Land' game"). Remind them to praise their child for being a good family member. Ask them to follow up by giving the child household tasks for which he or she must request help.

**Intermediate and Secondary Levels.**   Ask the parents to share work and other experiences with their youngster that demonstrate how other people have responded to their requests for help. For example, the parent who is a teacher might say, "I asked Ms. ___, the other fifth-grade teacher, to help me put up a new bulletin board, and she was a great help," or the parent who is a sanitation worker might say, "I had to pick up a real heavy load so I asked my partner for help, and he helped prevent me from injuring myself."

Ask the parents to follow up by giving the youngster tasks that he or she will only be able to complete by asking other family members for help.

---

☎   ## Specific Objective H

The student asks for a desired object, toy, or game and needed instructional materials and equipment.

---

## Teacher Interventions

**Infant and Toddler/Preschool and Primary Levels.**   Identify objects, toys, games, materials, and equipment that the student enjoys playing and working with or will need to complete assigned tasks. Give the student permission to play or work with these items, and fail to supply one or more of the needed items. Do not supply the desired article unless the student asks for it in an intelligible manner; however, if this will lead to undue frustration, supply it when the student attempts to say the name of the item. Accept the initial sound or first syllable if the student is unable to say the entire word intelligibly, especially at the infant and toddler/preschool level.

**Intermediate and Secondary Levels.**   Give the student a variety of tasks to complete without supplying any of the needed materials or equipment. Make certain that a number of the items are not available in the classroom or are in a locked closet. Do not supply the needed or desired articles unless the student asks for them with intelligible speech, using whatever grammatical and syntactic patterns he or she is capable of producing.

## Family Interventions

**Infant and Toddler/Preschool and Primary Levels.**  Ask the parents not to automatically provide their child with desired food, beverages, toys, games, and other items unless he or she succeeds in asking for them in an intelligible way or attempts to ask for them, even if the child approximates just the first sound or syllable.

**Intermediate and Secondary Levels.**  Encourage the parents to assign their youngster tasks that he or she cannot complete without equipment or materials that are not available in the home or that have been placed in a storage area unknown to the child. Remind them to reward the youngster for attempts as well as successes in communicating his or her material and equipment needs.

---

☎  ## Specific Objective I

The student reinforces peers and others who are performing or behaving in an appropriate or successful manner.

---

## Teacher Interventions

**Infant and Toddler/Preschool Level.**  Model reinforcing the student and his or her classmates for behaving in appropriate and successful ways. Comment on your behavior by making a statement and then asking a follow-up rhetorical question, "I like to praise people who work hard and do well. Don't you?"

**Primary Level.**  At this level, point out the appropriate behavior of classmates and ask the student to join you in praising those classmates. Reinforce the student for praising others of his or her own accord.

**Intermediate and Secondary Levels.**  At these levels, assign the student the job of "teaching assistant," who is responsible for monitoring a classmate's work in an area in which the student shows a greater degree of skill. Instruct the student in how to use praise as a way of motivating the

performance of his or her peer. Follow up with discussions on how reinforcing others will contribute to success in interpersonal relations in a
variety of settings, including the work context. Share situations in your
own life when praising others proved to be valuable in meeting your own
needs.

## Family Interventions

**Infant and Toddler/Preschool and Primary Levels.**   Encourage the parents to be generous with their praise for their child and for other family members. Urge
them to remind the child to praise his or her family members when they
behave in appropriate and successful ways. Remind them that, if the
child praises a family member without prompting, they should reinforce
the behavior by saying, for example, "You are a good person who has
kind words for someone else."

**Intermediate and Secondary Levels.**   Ask the parents to share experiences with their
youngster that illustrate how praising someone else (such as a work
supervisor or a relative) helped them on the job or in improving relations
with friends, neighbors, and relatives. Encourage them to reinforce the
youngster whenever he or she praises others for working hard or for successes, including younger family members who have corrected inappropriate behavior.

---

☎  ## Specific Objective J

The student informs others when he or she is ill, not
feeling well, or in pain.

---

## Teacher Interventions

**Primary Level.**   Role-play "The Doctor's Office" or "The Hospital Clinic." Tell the student that he or she is sick, not feeling well, or in pain and that he or she
must tell this to the receptionist and doctor. Give the student various situations, for example, "You hurt your knee when you fell," "Your eye hurts
and you think the wind blew some dirt in it," or "You ate something that
may have been spoiled and your stomach hurts." (Note: This activity also
provides an excellent review of body parts in a truly functional way!)

**Intermediate and Secondary Levels.**   Discuss the prevention of accidents and dis-
eases. Include in your discussion the identification of symptoms that

point to physical problems, including pain and discomfort. Be sure to clarify when aches are normal, for example, following exercise, and when severe or prolonged pain or discomfort, such as chest and neck pains, should impel the student to tell appropriate others about it.

## Family Interventions

**Infant and Toddler/Preschool Level.**   Remind the parents to establish some communication strategy for the child, to indicate when he or she is feeling ill or is in pain, even if it is only nonverbal. (See Unit 1, "Nonverbal Communication," Goal II, Specific Objective K.)

**Primary Level.**   At this level, encourage the parents to demonstrate how they inform each other when they are ill or in pain and to share with the child when they make doctor's appointments in response to pain and discomfort that may point to a physical problem that needs professional attention. Encourage them to assist the student in communicating pain and illness through intelligible speech production.

**Intermediate and Secondary Levels.**   Tell the parents to assist their youngster in differentiating between aches and other physical symptoms that are benign (aching feet after wearing new shoes), those that require some attention but can be treated in the home (a cold with no fever that requires bed rest, fluids, and, perhaps, nonprescription medications), and those that require medical intervention (loss of consciousness after a bad fall or bleeding that cannot be stopped). Remind them to make certain that the youngster communicates pain and illness in a way that is appropriate.

---

☎  ## Specific Objective K

The student indicates desires relevant to free play and other activities, snack preferences, and food served at school breakfasts and lunches.

---

## Teacher Interventions

**Infant and Toddler/Preschool Level.**   As early as possible, ask the student to make choices between two different free play activities, for example, "Do you want to play with the car or the blocks?" Reward the student by giving him or her the selected item, even if he or she did not orally state the preference. When you judge that the student is able to say what he or she wants, however, require him or her to do so.

**Primary Level.**  At this level, give the student more than two choices of activities and snack or other food items. Expect an oral response (even if it is an approximation of the sounds) with or without an accompanying gesture. Do not accept a gesture if the student is able to use speech to indicate his or her preferences.

**Intermediate Level.**  Review the school lunch menu with the student on a daily basis. If choices are available, encourage the student to make his or her own selections.

**Secondary Level.**  Obtain menus from restaurants in the community. (For the student with limited functional reading skills, make up menus with pictures of food items. See Figure 2.26.) Use these menus for role plays, and follow up with visits to several restaurants for breakfasts, lunches, and din-

**Figure 2.26.**  Picture menu: main courses (entrées).

ners. As a variation, obtain a meal order form from a local hospital, and role-play being hospitalized and having to order one's meals.

## Family Interventions

**Infant and Toddler/Preschool Level.** Tell the parents to give their child choices between two different toys or activities, for example, "Do you want your stacking toy or drum?" or "Do you want to go to the playground or to the zoo?" Remind them to encourage verbalization.

**Primary Level.** At this level, encourage the parents to give their child more than two choices of activities and snack or other food items. Urge the parents to include the child in decisions about what might be served for daily meals, while keeping in mind nutritional and dietary factors and any food allergies.

**Intermediate and Secondary Levels.** Ask the parents to take their youngster to cafeterias, fast-food restaurants, buffets, and more formal restaurants that are located in the community. Tell them to read the menus to the youngster if he or she is unable to do so and to ask the youngster what he or she would like to order.

---

☎ ## Specific Objective L

The student delivers oral messages to others.

---

## Teacher Interventions

**Primary Level.** Give the student a simple message to tell to a classmate (who is out of the room when the student returns to the classroom) or to a nearby teacher, for example, "Please tell Mary Lou that we will be going to lunch early today" or "Please tell Mrs. Clark that her class is invited to have a morning snack with us."

**Intermediate and Secondary Levels.** At these levels, increase the complexity of the messages that the student will be expected to deliver to others, for example, "Please tell the nurse that Tommy is absent today and that I would appreciate it if she would call his home to find out what is wrong" or "Please go to the principal's office and invite her to see our play on Friday. Also, give her the invitation you made especially for her."

## Family Interventions

**Primary Level.** Ask the parents to give their child oral messages to deliver to a family member who is somewhere else in the home, for example, "Please tell Aunt Lucy that dinner will be ready in 10 minutes" or "Please tell Aimee to turn off or lower the volume on her radio. Baby Nicholas is sleeping."

**Intermediate and Secondary Levels.** At these levels, encourage the parents to give their youngster oral messages to give to neighbors, teachers, and others with whom he or she comes into contact, for example, "Go next door to the Garlitz's and ask if we can borrow their lawnmower" or "Tell your teacher, Mr. Kearney, that you will be absent on Friday because we will be attending Grandpa's funeral. Also, give Mr. Kearney this note."

---

☎ ## Specific Objective M

The student identifies desired objects from the school library and from a school or training-site store or commissary.

---

## Teacher Interventions

**Infant and Toddler/Preschool Level.** Take the student to the school library to pick out a magazine or picture book to take back to class. Give the student a choice of two or three magazines and ask him or her to identify the one he or she would like from the picture on the cover.

**Primary Level.** Take the student to the school or training-site store or commissary to determine what is available for purchase. Follow up by planning a meal or party, making up a short shopping list, and asking the student to ask the storekeeper for the items on the list.

**Intermediate and Secondary Levels.** Take the student for trips into the community in which he or she will need to ask salespeople for specific items, for example, "I looked on the counter and didn't find any size-16-collar, size-32-sleeve white shirts. Do you have any in stock?" or "I am looking for a lighter-weight jacket and can't find one. Can you please show me where I might find lightweight jackets?"

## Family Interventions

**Infant and Toddler/Preschool and Primary Levels.**  Ask the parents to take their child to a supermarket in the community. Ask them to search in vain for a desired item and then give the child the task of asking a store employee, for example, "Where can I find the jams and jellies?"

**Intermediate and Secondary Levels.**  Encourage the parents to give their youngster the task of locating specific items in stores that are unusual or that have special conditions, for example, "Do you have bitters in stock?" "My father wears big sizes. Do you have any short-sleeved sport shirts in size 3X?" or "My mother is looking for a wallet with a zippered change purse. Do you have one like that in genuine leather?"

---

☎  ## Specific Objective N

The student shares his or her thoughts and feelings with others in simple conversational exchanges.

---

## Teacher Interventions

**Infant and Toddler/Preschool Level.**  Give the student one of his or her favorite toys. Hold a simple conversation about that toy, for example, "This is a funny little dog. Do you like it? See how I make it move. Would you like to see me make it dance? What else would you like me to make it do?" (Note: Even if the student responds minimally, you are still setting the pattern for a conversational interchange.) (See Figure 2.43 in Goal VIII, Specific Objective L, for additional ideas.)

**Primary Level.**  Ask the student to bring in photographs of family members, the house, pets, toys, and other items that are found in the student's home environment for his or her own personal photograph album. Use these photographs and the album to hold simple conversations. (See Figure 2.43 in Goal VIII, Specific Objective L, for additional ideas.)

**Intermediate and Secondary Levels.**  Record and then play for the student pertinent news broadcasts and programs with a news format (e.g., "60 Minutes"), and read the student newspaper and magazine articles and editorials about current events and issues, especially those that may affect the student and his or her family or that are of interest to the student. Engage in follow-up conversations in which the student is encouraged to express his or her thoughts and feelings.

## Family Interventions

**Infant and Toddler/Preschool and Primary Levels.** Encourage the parents to hold family conversations about matters that directly affect the family and to include their child in these conversations (preferably on a daily basis at a set time). Ask them to include terms like "feelings" and "thoughts" in their conversations, for example, "I didn't know you *feel* that way, Michelle!" "I *think* that we should exercise more than we are doing now!" or "So, David, you are *thinking* that you should eat less fat in your diet."

Remind the parents that, at these levels, they are modeling conversational patterns and that they should not necessarily expect their child to actively participate and to express his or her feelings and thoughts.

**Intermediate and Secondary Levels.** Encourage the parents, at these levels, to expect their youngster to play a more participatory role in family conversations and discussions. Remind them to honor the feelings and thoughts expressed by the youngster, since ignoring them typically will result in diminished participation. Ask them to use materials and information from the media as sources of conversational topics, especially those that affect the youngster and the family.

---

 ## Specific Objective O

The student internalizes and follows activity schedules and obeys rules and regulations that have been discussed and described orally and behaves accordingly.

---

## Teacher Interventions

**Infant and Toddler/Preschool and Primary Levels.** As early as possible, establish routines, rules, and regulations for classroom and school behavior. Identify the consequences of appropriate and inappropriate behavior and apply them consistently. (See Figures 2.27 and 2.28.)

**Intermediate and Secondary Levels.** Set up daily and weekly schedules, using wall and personal calendars. Ask the student to tell you his or her schedule of activities at the beginning of each school week and each day, and to review the experiences at the end of the school week. Also, ask the student to indicate scheduled activities that occur after school hours and on nonschool days.

| Rules for Appropriate Behavior | Possible Positive Consequences |
|---|---|
| Students must raise their hand whenever they wish to gain the teacher's attention or when they wish to answer a teacher's question. | The teacher will respond and will give them their fair share of opportunities to respond. The teacher will praise them for obeying. |
| Students must stay in their seat when doing quiet activities and obtain the teacher's permission to leave their seat or leave the room. | The teacher will give them opportunities to play with games and toys of their choice or to read a book or magazine that interests them. |
| Students must respect the property of the school, the teachers, and their fellow students. | The teacher will give them token reinforcements that they can later exchange for a tangible item of their choice. |
| Students must treat their classmates and the teachers and staff with respect. | The teacher will schedule special treats such as showing them a video of a favorite or interesting movie. |
| Students must complete all assigned tasks within the established timelines, whenever possible. | The teacher will give them occasional healthy treats when they complete their assignments. |
| Students must sit in their seat in a proper manner. | The teacher will give them extra play periods so that they can have opportunities to use all their muscles in fun activities. |
| Students are responsible for keeping the area around their desk neat and clean and must return all materials to their proper storage areas. | The teacher will keep the classroom as attractive and uncluttered as possible and will post the names and photographs of students who keep their desk clean on the class bulletin board. |

**FIGURE 2.27.** Classroom rules and possible positive consequences.

## Family Interventions

**Infant and Toddler/Preschool and Primary Levels.** Ask the parents to establish routines, rules, and regulations for behavior in the home and the community. Tell them to identify consequences for both appropriate and inappropriate behavior and to be sure to apply them consistently.

Encourage the parents to involve their child in setting the routines and rules and to require the child to repeat them and to say them from memory, whenever possible, until they are internalized and observed.

| Rules for Appropriate Behavior | Possible Negative Consequences |
|---|---|
| Students must raise their hand whenever they wish to gain the teacher's attention or when they wish to answer a teacher's question. | The teacher will either ignore them when they fail to follow the rule or will reprimand them and only call on them when they observe the rule. |
| Students must stay in their seat when doing quiet activities and obtain the teacher's permission to leave their seat or leave the room. | The teacher will take away their privilege of playing with games or toys of their choice. |
| Students must respect the property of the school, the teachers, and their fellow students. | The teacher will take away points or tokens earned. |
| Students must treat their classmates and the teachers and staff with respect. | The teacher will deny them the opportunity to join their classmates on field trips. |
| Students must complete all assigned tasks within the established timelines, whenever possible. | The teacher will not give them a special privilege (like erasing the board) until they complete their assignments. |
| Students must sit in their seat in a proper manner. | The teacher will take away scheduled play periods. |

**FIGURE 2.28.** Classroom rules and possible consequences for inappropriate behavior.

**Intermediate and Secondary Levels.** At these levels, remind the parents to establish daily and weekly schedules. Ask them to review these schedules with the youngster until he or she can say them correctly. Encourage them to monitor the youngster to make sure that he or she is observing the established schedule without reminders.

Ask the parents to expect the youngster to establish personal schedules (with minimum assistance) as an aid to helping with the transition to adult life, for example, working out a morning schedule in order to get to work on time.

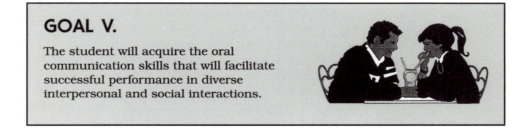

## GOAL V.

The student will acquire the oral communication skills that will facilitate successful performance in diverse interpersonal and social interactions.

# SPECIFIC OBJECTIVES

The student:

❏ A. Uses language courtesies.

❏ B. Apologizes for accidental mishaps and inappropriate behavior.

❏ C. Joins others in singing activities at parties and social events and during religious services, when appropriate.

❏ D. Requests and follows directions and instructions and provides directions and instructions to others upon request.

❏ E. Seeks and provides comfort, advice, guidance, and counsel.

❏ F. Expresses needs, feelings, and thoughts and responds appropriately to the expression of wants, feelings, and thoughts of others.

❏ G. Expresses himself or herself with intelligible speech and in the language patterns expected of adults who are successfully functioning in the community.

# SUGGESTED ACTIVITIES

---

☎ ## Specific Objective A

The student uses language courtesies.

---

(See Figure 2.29, Specific Objective B, and Sample Lesson Plan 7 at the end of Unit 2.)

## Teacher Interventions

**Infant and Toddler/Preschool Level.** Set up situations in which the student requests a favored object or food or beverage item. Even if the student uses a gesture (pointing) to indicate the desired item, expect him or her to say or approximate the word "Please." In the beginning, you may wish to refer to "Please" as the "magic word." Complete the sequence by asking the

"Please!"                    "Pardon me!"

"Thank you!"                 "I beg your pardon!"

"You're welcome!"            "I'm sorry!"

"Bless you!"                 "Forgive me!"

"Excuse me!"                 "No, thank you!"

**FIGURE 2.29.**   Common language courtesies.

student to say "Thank you" when receiving the item and then saying, "You're welcome" in turn.

The emphasis at this level is on the use of the language courtesies "Please" and "Thank you." Also, introduce saying, "Bless you" when someone sneezes.

**Primary Level.** At this level, sometimes reverse the pattern, with the student responding to your request for a desired item, supplying the item, and then saying, "You're welcome." For example, you may ask the student, "Please give me your log book so I can see if your parents responded to the note I sent home."

Vary this activity by asking the student to complete a task such as hanging his or her coat in the closet and by saying, "Thank you" when the task has been done. At this level, also introduce the use of the words "Excuse me" or "Pardon me" when interrupting someone who is speaking or busy.

**Intermediate Level.** At this level, in realistic role plays, involve the student in saying, "Thank you!" in situations other than in response to obtaining a desired object, for example, in response to a compliment or to a person providing assistance.

Also introduce the language courtesies involving the use of the words "Excuse me," "Pardon me," and "I beg your pardon." Begin by introducing these expressions for wishing to pass someone who is blocking the way or for passing in front of a person or between people when no other passage is possible.

Set up two tables with clothing items or appliances as mock display counters. Make a narrow aisle between them, and engage the student in a role play in which he or she must pass a shopper (a classmate) who is standing in the aisle while examining an article on display. Repeat by arranging the tables with a wider aisle in which two shoppers (classmates) are standing talking, and the student must pass between them.

**Secondary Level.** If not covered at earlier levels, discuss the need to say "Excuse me" or "Pardon me" when belching, burping, hiccuping, or passing wind. Explain why it is courteous to excuse oneself and rude to fail to do so. Discuss the possible negative consequences that might result whenever people at home, at school, in the community, and in the workplace are disturbed by these behaviors and/or the student's failure to excuse himself or herself.

Also, introduce saying, "No, thank you!" in response to questions that ask whether one would wish to do something, for example, "Would you like to go swimming?" when the person asked does *not* wish to. Practice this concept by asking the student a series of "Would you" questions.

## Family Interventions

**Infant and Toddler/Preschool Level.** Ask the parents to take their child to a bank that gives lollipops to young children and to tell the child to say "Please" to request a lollipop and "Thank you!" when the teller gives the child the lollipop.

**Primary, Intermediate, and Secondary Levels.** Review the Teacher Activities for these levels. Encourage the parents to (a) model these language courtesies, (b) expect their youngster to demonstrate them whenever the appropriate situations arise naturally in the home and the community, (c) praise the youngster for being "a courteous person," and (d) reprimand the youngster when he or she fails to use the courtesies.

---

☎ ## Specific Objective B

The student apologizes for accidental mishaps and inappropriate behavior.

---

## Teacher Interventions

**Infant and Toddler/Preschool Level.** Model having accidental mishaps such as spilling fruit juice and saying, "I'm sorry! It was an accident. Please help me clean it up!" Whenever the student has a similar mishap, be sure not to overreact and make certain that he or she does not overreact either. If necessary, calm the student down and say, "I know you didn't mean to; it was just a simple accident. Just say, 'I'm sorry' and let's get it cleaned up!"

**Primary, Intermediate, and Secondary Levels.** At each of these levels, wait for inappropriate behaviors to occur. When they occur, stop the student from continuing the behavior, reprimand the student, engage the student in a discussion or explanation of why the behavior is inappropriate, and expect the student to apologize by saying either "I'm sorry for (the inappropriate behavior described)" or "Please forgive me for (the inappropriate behavior described)!"

Remember to be consistent in stopping inappropriate behavior and in expecting an apology.

## Family Interventions

**Infant and Toddler/Preschool Level.** Ask the parents to respond to any mishaps they might have, such as dropping and breaking glassware, plates, or dishes, by saying such things as "Oops, I'm sorry! I hope I didn't frighten you. It was an accident. I'll clean up the mess and be really careful not to cut myself or to leave any of the pieces on the floor!" Urge the parents to remind their child, whenever he or she has a similar mishap, to say, "It was an accident. I'm sorry!"

**Primary, Intermediate, and Secondary Levels.** At each of these levels, encourage the parents to respond to their youngster's inappropriate behavior by stopping the behavior, reprimanding the child, engaging him or her in a discussion of why the behavior is inappropriate, and requiring an apology such as "I'm sorry for (the inappropriate behavior described)" or "Please forgive me for (the inappropriate behavior described)!"

---

☎ **Specific Objective C**

The student joins others in singing activities at parties and social events and during religious services, when appropriate.

---

## Teacher Interventions

**Infant and Toddler/Preschool Level.** Schedule musical activities at different times during the day. Join the student in singing nursery rhymes that have been set to music, such as "Mary Had a Little Lamb" and "Jack and Jill." Also sing simple commercial jingles that appeal to the student.

**Primary Level.**   Join the student in singing action songs in which he or she acts out a song while singing it, for example, "Monkey See, Monkey Do," which involves engaging in an action that a monkey sees and imitates. "If You're Happy and You Know It" is also an action song that young students enjoy singing and acting out.

**Intermediate and Secondary Levels.**   Determine recent and current songs that are enjoyed and sung by students at these levels. Learn these songs, and ask the student to sing them along with you and with several of his or her classmates.

   If the school has a choir, encourage the student to audition and join the choir. If there is no choir, help to organize one.

## Family Interventions

**Infant and Toddler/Preschool Level.**   Encourage the parents to sing to their child at bedtime. If necessary, teach them some simple nursery rhymes that have been set to music as well as familiar lullabies. Remind them to ask the child to join in singing these songs at different times of the day. During family birthday celebrations, encourage the parents to sing "Happy Birthday to You" along with their child.

**Primary Level.**   If the parents participate in religious observances, ask them to encourage their child to join in the singing of favorite hymns and to teach the child songs that are sung at holiday times and in different seasons, such as "In the Good Old Summertime," "April Showers," "Frosty the Snowman," "Jingle Bells" (Christmas or winter), "Here Comes Peter Cottontail" (Easter), and "Dreidel, Dreidel, Dreidel" (Hanukkah).

**Intermediate and Secondary Levels.**   If the family incorporates singing during parties and celebrations, remind the parents to encourage their youngster to join in singing, for example, Christmas songs and carols and even to go Christmas caroling.

---

 ## Specific Objective D

The student requests and follows directions and instructions and provides directions and instructions to others upon request.

---

(See Goal IV, Specific Objectives C, D, and E, for additional suggested activities.)

## Teacher Interventions

**Infant and Toddler/Preschool and Primary Levels.**  Give the student a task that he or she cannot easily perform unless some oral directions are provided. Ask the student if help is needed. If he or she asks for help, only provide the directions needed to complete the task.

Begin with simple directions (e.g., directions for opening a box of cereal) and proceed to more complex ones (e.g., directions for wrapping pennies, nickels, dimes, and quarters in coin wrappers to take to a bank) as the student makes progress in understanding directions and in working out the required motor and cognitive plan.

**Intermediate and Secondary Levels.**  At these levels, identify tasks that the student can do with facility, and then role-play these tasks with you asking for help. If necessary, assist the student in stating the directions in an organized, sequential, and understandable way. Be sure to give the student an opportunity to practice the skill of giving oral directions without guidance from you or others.

## Family Interventions

**Infant and Toddler/Preschool and Primary Levels.**  Encourage the parents to give their child household chores that he or she cannot easily perform unless some oral directions are provided. Tell them to ask the child if he or she needs help and to provide directions only if asked.

Urge the parents to begin with simple directions (e.g., directions for putting knives, spoons, and forks in the appropriate compartments in a silverware storage tray) and to proceed to more complex ones (e.g., replacing a burned-out light bulb with the appropriate bulb) as the child improves in his or her understanding of directions.

**Intermediate and Secondary Levels.**  At these levels, ask the parents to pretend that they cannot do a household task that their youngster is able to do, such as correctly planting seeds for a vegetable garden. Remind them to ask the youngster for help and to reward him or her for giving clear and correct directions and for being patient.

| ☎ | Specific Objective E |
|---|---|
| | The student seeks and provides comfort, advice, guidance, and counsel. |

## Teacher Interventions

**Infant and Toddler/Preschool Level.**   Role-play using a doll or stuffed animal that is "sad" or in "discomfort" and needs to be comforted. Demonstrate holding and comforting the doll or stuffed animal and then ask the student to also provide a comforting hug.

Next, tell the student that there may be times when he or she is upset and will want to be comforted. Demonstrate body language clues that indicate the need to be comforted and say typical accompanying words such as "I don't feel well and I can sure use a hug."

(Note: Be sure to make clear to whom the student should go for comfort and the difference between a comforting hug and one that is not appropriate!)

**Primary and Intermediate Levels.**   At these levels, role-play situations in which you must make a decision and are unable to do so without some advice. For example, at the primary level, you might say, "My nephew is visiting me and I want to take him somewhere for some fun. Do you think I should take him to see the baseball game or go bowling instead? What do you think?" At the intermediate level, you might say, "It looks as though it may rain soon and the weather report says we should expect rain today. Do you think we should go for a walk in the nearby state park or should we postpone it for another day? Tell me what you think we should do."

Also, role-play situations in which the student is experiencing difficulty in making a decision and seeks the guidance of others.

**Secondary Level.**   At this level, role-play situations (with you acting as the student's same-age peer) that are serious or potentially dangerous and for which you are seeking the student's counsel. For example, you might say, "A friend of mine wanted me to lie to my parents and say I am going to sleep at her house when we are really going to go to a boy's house to be with him and one of the other members of his basketball team. What do you think I should do?"

Follow up by giving the student a situation for which he or she seeks your counsel in a role play, for example, "My friend wants me to go to the shopping mall and shoplift some records. What do you think I should do?"

## Family Interventions

**Infant and Toddler/Preschool Level.** Ask the parents to demonstrate how to comfort a family member who is upset or sad and to describe what they are doing. Remind them to show the appropriate way of comforting others with suitable words as well as by physically holding or hugging the person. Encourage them to indicate to their child that there may be times when he or she is upset and will want to be comforted.

(Note: Be sure to emphasize that the parents should make clear to whom the child should go for comfort and the difference between a comforting hug and one that is not appropriate!)

**Primary and Intermediate Levels.** At these levels, ask the parents to seek the advice of their child in helping them to make a decision, for example, at the primary level, they might say, "I'm not sure which blouse goes better with this skirt. Which one do you prefer?" At the intermediate level, they might say, "We've been invited to Grandma Laurie's house for Thanksgiving dinner at the same time as Grandma Michelle's dinner. What do you think we can do not to upset either one?"

Also, ask the parents to be especially cognizant of when the youngster is experiencing difficulty in making a decision and to remind the child that it is usually helpful to seek the advice of others.

**Secondary Level.** Encourage the parents not to avoid dealing with actual problems that are serious or potentially dangerous for which they are seeking the youngster's counsel, for example, "Our neighbor's dog has bitten several of the neighborhood children and the neighbors have ignored our complaints and the complaints of others. What do you think we should do now?"

Tell them to follow up by giving the youngster situations for which he or she seeks their counsel in a role play, for example, "My friend wants me to go 'all the way.' What do you think I should do?"

---

### ☎ Specific Objective F

The student expresses needs, feelings, and thoughts and responds appropriately to the expression of wants, feelings, and thoughts of others.

---

## Teacher Interventions

**Infant and Toddler/Preschool Level.** At this level, concentrate on the expression of needs. Begin by asking the student to get you something you need, for example, "Please get me the stapler from my desk. I need it to put this beautiful picture of spring on the bulletin board.

Follow up by giving the student a task to complete with a missing item that he or she must ask for; for example, say, "We can't play this game because we don't have all the checkers!"

**Primary Level.**  At this level, concentrate on the expression of feelings. Discuss situations that have occurred in your life that have engendered feelings of happiness and sadness, for example, "I was so happy when my daughter had a healthy baby boy!" or "It made me very sad when my friend was badly injured in the collision." Follow up by asking the student to tell you about something that has made him or her happy or sad.

**Intermediate and Secondary Levels.**  At these levels, concentrate on the expression of thoughts. Express an opinion about a current issue facing the school or the local community, and then ask the student to express his or her opinion on the same issue, for example, "The county council is debating whether to have a leash law for cats. I don't agree. Cats are different from dogs. What are your thoughts on this matter?"

## Family Interventions

**Infant and Toddler/Preschool Level.**  At this level, ask the parents to concentrate on the expression of needs. Tell them to begin by asking their child to get them something they need, for example, "Please get me the hammer. I need to fix this piece of wood that has separated from its base." Remind them to also give the child a chore to do with a missing item that he or she must ask for, for example, "I've made the bed, but I need to know where the clean pillowcases are."

**Primary Level.**  At this level, ask the parents to concentrate on the expression of feelings. Tell them to share life experiences with their child, especially those that have been shared or observed by the child, for example, "Remember how happy we were at Aunt Susie and Uncle Buster's anniversary party!" or "Remember how terrible we felt when our neighbor's barn burned down!" Remind them to follow up by asking the child to tell them about things that have made them happy or sad as well as those that have frightened them or made them angry.

**Intermediate and Secondary Levels.**  At these levels, ask the parents to concentrate on the expression of thoughts. Encourage them to express an opinion about an issue facing the family or local community and then ask the youngster to express his or her opinion on the same issue, for example, "Daddy wants to either go swimming today or go to see the soccer game. I think we should go swimming. What do you think we should do?"

---

☎ **Specific Objective G**

The student expresses himself or herself with intelligible speech and in the language patterns expected of adults who are successfully functioning in the community.

---

## Teacher Interventions

**Infant and Toddler/Preschool Level.** At this level, concentrate on language stimulation activities such as singing, talking, and reading to the student. Do not correct any misarticulations but rather reward successful sound production, for example, "I like the way you put your lips together and made a good /b/ when you asked me to roll the ball to you."

**Primary, Intermediate, and Secondary Levels.** At these levels, reward the student for improving the intelligibility and syntactic patterns of his or her speech. Be sure to always be a good speech and language model. As the student progresses, be sure to expand your own vocabulary usage as well as the length and structural sophistication of your language units.

Remember that precise articulation is not the goal but rather intelligibility of speech. Say such things as "I like the way you said that. I had no difficulty understanding what you were saying. You said that so clearly that I didn't have to ask you to repeat what you said!" and "You said what you wanted so clearly that I didn't have to ask you to explain what you meant!"

## Family Interventions

**Infant and Toddler/Preschool Level.** At this level, show the parents how to conduct interesting language-stimulation activities. Be sure to emphasize that they should not compare their child's performance to that of other children and should simply encourage the child to verbalize in play situations and other functional interactions (e.g., during mealtimes). Remind them that they should speak naturally and not modify their speech or language even if the child does not understand everything that is being said.

**Primary, Intermediate, and Secondary Levels.** At these levels, tell the parents to reinforce their youngster for improving the intelligibility and syntactic patterns of his or her speech. Remind them to provide a good speech and language model and that accurate articulation and perfect syntax are not the objectives, but rather intelligibility of speech and clarity and effectiveness of communication.

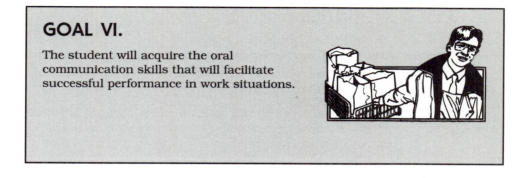

## GOAL VI.

The student will acquire the oral communication skills that will facilitate successful performance in work situations.

# SPECIFIC OBJECTIVES

The student:

❑ A. Responds appropriately to oral directions and instructions given by work supervisors and asks for clarification and further explanation when needed.

❑ B. Continues a behavior when praised, encouraged, or otherwise orally reinforced and stops an undesirable or inappropriate behavior when asked or warned to do so.

❑ C. Provides assistance to supervisors and co-workers when appropriate and seeks the assistance of co-workers and supervisors when needed.

❑ D. Internalizes and follows work schedules and obeys work rules and regulations.

❑ E. Asks for needed work materials and equipment when they are not readily available.

❑ F. Informs the appropriate individual when he or she will be late or will be absent from work.

❑ G. Transmits messages to co-workers and supervisors when asked to do so.

❑ H. Shares his or her thoughts and feelings with co-workers in simple conversational exchanges and expresses to co-workers and supervisors any concerns or grievances about work conditions, including safety and health factors.

❑ I. Discusses salary, fringe benefits, promotion, and other work-related matters with supervisors.

❑ J. Provides appropriate information, including work history and qualifications, to a prospective employer in a job interview.

# SUGGESTED ACTIVITIES

> ☎ ## Specific Objective A
>
> The student responds appropriately to oral directions and instructions given by work supervisors and asks for clarification and further explanation when needed.

## Teacher Interventions

**Primary Level.** Assign the student work-related tasks to do in the classroom. Be simple, direct, and explicit in your directions. Model the kind of directions a work supervisor might give a worker, for example, "After I erase each of the chalkboards, you wash them with this sponge" or "After I place the invitations to our art show in an envelope, you seal it and then give it to (a classmate's name) to paste a stamp on."

**Intermediate and Secondary Levels.** Continue assigning work-related classroom tasks. At these levels, make the directions increasingly complex so that the student is likely to need further exploration or clarification. For example, in an assembly task (e.g., building storage cabinets or bookshelves for the classroom), ask the student to hand you a piece of wood shelving or a screw without indicating the size of the item.

If the student asks for clarification, praise him or her for doing so. If the student does not ask, remind him or her to ask for clarification whenever directions are not clear rather than make a mistake. Remind the student that he or she may have a job in the future where there may be a need to assemble a piece of equipment or machinery.

## Family Interventions

**Primary Level.** Ask the parents to give their child household chores. Remind them to be simple, direct, and explicit. Encourage them to use their own job-related experiences in setting up these tasks and in giving directions to the child.

For example, tell the parents to set up an assembly line operation in which various members of the household have different assignments as, for instance, in the four separate tasks that follow a meal: clearing the dinner dishes, washing them, drying them, and returning the dishes, eating utensils, and cooking utensils to their storage areas.

**Intermediate and Secondary Levels.** At these levels, ask the parents to make the directions increasingly complex so that their youngster is likely to need further exploration or clarification. Tell them to draw parallels, whenever possible, between the jobs one does at home and those that might be done in a work situation (e.g., a person prepares and serves meals in the home and might prepare and serve meals when working at a restaurant).

For example, ask the parents to assign household management and maintenance tasks to the youngster (see Volume I, *Self-Care, Motor Skills, Household Management, and Living Skills* [Bender, Valletutti, & Baglin, in press]) and to talk about how experience in household management and maintenance may be similar to the maintenance requirements of work sites.

---

 ## Specific Objective B

The student continues a behavior when praised, encouraged, or otherwise orally reinforced and stops an undesirable or inappropriate behavior when asked or warned to do so.

---

## Teacher Interventions

**Infant and Toddler/Preschool and Primary Levels.** As part of your behavior management program, be sure to praise the student for appropriate behavior. Even if you are using tangible reinforcers, couple these reinforcers with praise. Stop a student who engages in inappropriate behavior from continuing the behavior and warn him or her to stop.

**Intermediate Level.** Plan a trip in the community. Prior to taking the trip, identify the rules of behavior for the trip and the positive and negative consequences that will follow. (See Figure 2.30.) Then take the student on the trip and apply the established consequences.

**Secondary Level.** Discuss the importance of following rules and regulations when on a job. (See Figure 2.31.) Role-play situations in which the student plays the role of someone who loses his or her job because of inappropriate behavior and failure to stop the behavior following a warning from a supervisor. For example, the student engages in horseplay near dangerous machinery, is warned to stop, fails to do so, and is fired. Follow up by reading and discussing newspaper accounts of people who failed to behave appropriately while at work.

Do not wander away from the class or leave the group to go with anyone else. Keep your teacher, an adult volunteer, or a parent who is also on the trip in view at all times.

Obey the rules and regulations of the place being visited, for example, "Do not take food or beverages into this store" or "Please be quiet. People are reading."

Obey the rules of the transportation vehicle being used, for example, "Do not talk to the bus driver while the bus is in motion" or "No eating or carrying food or beverages in the subway."

Do not run, laugh loudly, act in a rowdy manner, or behave in a way that causes people to pay undue attention to you or the group when in a public place.

Respect the people you meet and the property of others while on the trip.

Behave safely at all times, especially when crossing streets, using public and private transportation, and using escalators and elevators.

**FIGURE 2.30.**   Rules for taking a trip in the community.

## Family Interventions

**Infant and Toddler/Preschool and Primary Levels.**   Encourage the parents to establish household rules and regulations (see Figure 2.32) and their positive and negative consequences. Urge them to be consistent and fair in their application of consequences.

Behave safely at all times, especially when working around electrical and heavy equipment. Be sure to use any required safety equipment.

Be punctual at all times and notify a supervisor or his or her representative when you are going to be unavoidably late.

Go to work on workdays unless there is a legitimate reason for being absent.

Work cooperatively with fellow workers. Follow the directions and instructions of work supervisors and respond favorably to constructive criticism.

Complete all assigned tasks in the allotted time and meet the standards required of the job.

Take rest periods and use the bathroom facilities at appropriate times.

Return all materials and equipment to their proper storage areas.

Keep your work area clean and neat.

Dress appropriately for the job.

**FIGURE 2.31.**   Sample work rules and regulations.

Hang up your clean clothing in your closet.

Put all clothing that needs to be cleaned in the laundry basket.

Make your bed as soon as possible after getting up in the morning.

Put away all grooming items after their use and clean the bathroom counter after you finish grooming yourself.

Close the bathroom door for privacy when you are using the commode for voiding or evacuation.

Throw all garbage that cannot be recycled in the trash can and all items that can be recycled in the recycling container.

Complete all assigned household chores in a timely fashion.

Return cleaning supplies and equipment to safe storage areas.

Provide requested assistance to other members of the household.

**FIGURE 2.32.** Sample household rules and regulations.

**Intermediate Level.** Ask the parents to establish rules and consequences for behavior outside of the home, whether it is in a public place in the community or a private home. (See Figure 2.33.) Urge them to be diligent in applying the identified consequences.

**Secondary Level.** Ask the parents to share with their youngster specific rules and regulations as they apply to their current and previous employment. Remind them to share these anecdotes and to be sure to point out the

Respect the home of the person being visited; that is, use the furniture as it is meant to be used and do not touch the knickknacks.

Do not enter rooms in the home whose doors are closed or go to another area of the house without permission.

Be sure to flush the toilet and clean bathroom areas after using the toilet.

Do not run or engage in rowdy or outdoor behaviors while in a person's home.

Do not open closet doors or look in the refrigerator.

Ask permission to look at magazines, books, and photographs or to use entertainment materials (toys or games) or equipment (television, radio, or stereo sets).

Offer to help clean up, if you have been served refreshments.

**FIGURE 2.33.** Some rules and regulations for visiting the homes of others.

consequences that might have occurred when rules of behavior were observed and when they were not.

---

☎  ## Specific Objective C

The student provides assistance to supervisors and co-workers when appropriate and seeks the assistance of co-workers and supervisors when needed.

---

## Teacher Interventions

**Infant and Toddler/Preschool and Primary Levels.**   Engage in a classroom task and ask the student to assist you in completing the task, for example, "Please get a new pen from my desk drawer. This one has run out of ink, and I want to finish writing this note telling your parents how well you did today" or "Please put your finger here on the cord so I can tie the knot on this package of clothing we are donating to the homeless."

**Intermediate Level.**   Share with the student situations that you have had as a teacher and that required you to ask the help of a fellow teacher, for example, "My computer screen says, 'Please Wait,' and I have been waiting for a long time and nothing happens. Please show me what to do so I can resume my typing." Then share experiences that involved you asking a supervisor for help, for example, "When a student of mine began to have seizures in the classroom, I called Ms. (principal's name) for help, since the school nurse was not in."

**Secondary Level.**   At this level, review with the student the appropriate way to ask for help. Role-play various situations in which the student: (a) provides assistance to a co-worker or supervisor when asked (e.g., "Please get me some sandpaper so I can smooth out the rough spots on this piece of wood" or "Please call the maintenance department for me while I try to figure out what to do") and (b) seeks the assistance of a co-worker or supervisor when the student needs help (e.g., "I know you have done this particular job before. What advice do you have?" or "I don't remember what I had to do next. Please help me").

## Family Interventions

**Infant and Toddler/Preschool and Primary Levels.**   Ask the parents to arrange situations in which they call on various members of the household to provide

| Occupation | Request for Assistance |
|---|---|
| Nurse's aide | "Please help me move the patient from her bed to the wheelchair." |
| Mechanic's helper | "Please check to see what made the tire flat." |
| Waiter's assistant | "Please clear the dishes on table 4." |
| Supermarket clerk | "Please mop up the spill in aisle 2." |
| Maintenance worker | "Please change the fluorescent lights in Mr. Han's office." |
| Horticultural worker | "Please weed the front lawn." |

**FIGURE 2.34.**   Sample occupations and sample requests for assistance.

them with needed assistance. For example, at the infant and toddler/ preschool level, they might say, "I spilled some dirt from the flowerpot. Please get me the dustpan." At the primary level, they might say, "I am very busy, and these letters must be mailed today before the last mail pickup. Please, (household member's name), take these letters and mail them at the corner mailbox" or "I cut my finger. Please, get me the Band-Aids from the medicine cabinet."

**Intermediate and Secondary Levels.**   Ask the parents to share work situations that they have had in which they were asked for assistance as well as those for which they sought needed help. Encourage them to follow up by engaging their youngster in role plays in which he or she plays the part of a particular worker who seeks or provides typically requested help. (See Figure 2.34.)

---

☎   **Specific Objective D**

The student internalizes and follows work schedules and obeys work rules and regulations.

---

## Teacher Interventions

**Primary Level.**   Establish a daily schedule of school activities. Use the expression "What are we going to *work* on today," rather than "What are we going to *learn* today," when talking about learning activities. After the student has

| Occupation | Sample Work Rules |
|---|---|
| Veterinarian's aide | Exercise the dogs (number of times a day). |
| Stock clerk | Record the number of items by their stock numbers after each new delivery and after each order is filled. |
| Supermarket bagger | Remember to ask the customer whether he or she wants paper or plastic bags. |
| Fast-food restaurant worker | Remember to put napkins in all take-out orders, but no more than two napkins per serving. |
| Factory worker | Remember to separate all defective parts and to return equipment to the proper storage areas. |

**FIGURE 2.35.**   Representative occupations and sample work rules.

followed the schedule over a period of time and the schedule has been sufficiently reviewed, ask the student to state what his or her daily schedule of activities is. Reward the student for following the schedule without being reminded. Periodically ask the question, "What do we do next?"

**Intermediate Level.**   Give the student a work task that involves several sequential steps that must be completed over a period of time, for example, cutting wood to specifications, sanding it, painting it, applying a second coat, and then using it to create a finished product such as a birdhouse as a Father's Day gift for his or her grandfather.

**Secondary Level.**   Role-play different occupations and typical work rules and regulations, especially as they apply to task completion. (See Figure 2.35.) Give the student a hypothetical occupation and a rule or rules, and ask him or her to demonstrate one or more rules in several role plays.

## Family Interventions

**Primary Level.**   Encourage the parents to set up a daily schedule of group household activities (e.g., meals, discussions, and leisure-time activities) and individual household activities (e.g., cleaning and food preparation). Tell them that after their child has followed the schedule over a period of time and the schedule has been sufficiently reviewed, they should ask the child to relate his or her daily schedule of individual and collective activities.

Urge the parents to reward the child for following the schedule without being reminded and to periodically ask the question, "What's on our schedule now?"

**Intermediate Level.**  Remind the parents to assign their youngster household tasks that involve several sequential steps that must be completed over a period of time, for example, cleaning the attic or garage or doing an inventory of household items currently available in the home (e.g., food, first-aid materials and medicines, linens, tools, cleaning materials and supplies, and emergency equipment such as flashlights, candles, batteries, fuses, and replacement bulbs).

**Secondary Level.**  Encourage the parents to talk to their youngster about the specific rules and regulations of their current and former employment and the ways they make certain that they follow these rules, for example, "I am expected to clean up and to return all my tools to their proper place. I remember to do so by saying to myself each day before I wash my face and hands, 'Not only are my hands soiled by the work done today, but my work area is also soiled. I must clean my work area before I wash my hands.'"

Suggest that the parents follow up by engaging their youngster in role plays that depict different occupations and typical work rules and regulations. (See the Teacher Interventions.)

---

### ☎ Specific Objective E

The student asks for needed work materials and equipment when they are not readily available.

---

## Teacher Interventions

**Infant and Toddler/Preschool and Primary Levels.**  Give the student a task to do without supplying all the needed materials. For example, at the infant and toddler/preschool level, you might ask the student to help you wrap some gifts for a holiday grab bag and fail to give him or her the Scotch tape dispenser. At the primary level, you might ask the student to print the first letter of his or her first name and fail to give him or her a pen or pencil.

**Intermediate and Secondary Levels.**   Discuss different occupations and the tools and equipment associated with them. Then engage in role plays in which the student is asked to carry out a task and is not given the needed equipment. For example, ask the student to be a waiter or waitress without a tray to carry the food, a carpenter without a hammer, or a plumber without a plunger.

Play a matching game in which you name an occupation and the student gives you a "tool of the trade"; then play its counterpart, in which you name the tool and the student names its associated occupation. (See Figure 2.36.)

## Family Interventions

**Infant and Toddler/Preschool and Primary Levels.**   Encourage the parents to give their child household tasks with which he or she is familiar without supplying all the needed materials. For example, at the infant and toddler/preschool level, they might ask the child to wipe the table and fail to give him or her a sponge or dish cloth. At the primary level, they might ask the child to help clean the windows and fail to give him or her the window-washing fluid.

**Intermediate and Secondary Levels.**   Ask the parents to discuss the tools and equipment of their own current and former occupations. Encourage them to engage their youngster in role plays in which he or she is assigned an occupation and is expected to carry out a task, but is not given the needed equipment; for example, the student is a hairdresser without a pair of scissors or a comb, a short-order cook without a spatula, or a nurse's aide without a thermometer.

---

☎   ## Specific Objective F

The student informs the appropriate individual when he or she will be late or will be absent from work.

---

## Teacher Interventions

**Primary Level.**   Whenever the student is on time to school, say, "This is the start of our day, and you have arrived to class *on time*. It is a good thing to be *on time*." Continue by saying, "Because you are *on time*, you can participate in the first activity of the day."

After the student begins to understand the concept of being on time, wait for an occasion when he or she is not on time. At these moments

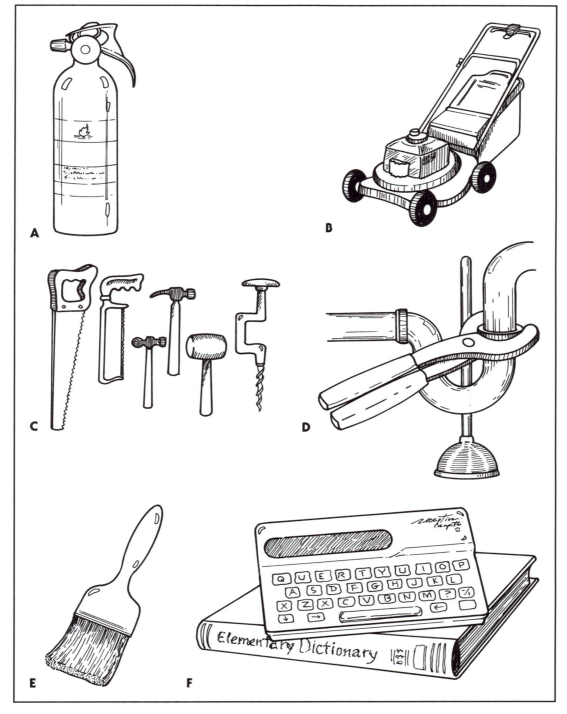

**FIGURE 2.36.** Tools of the trade: (a) fire fighter, (b) gardener, (c) carpenter, (d) plumber, (e) painter, and (f) teacher.

say, "You are *not on time*, so we started our first activity without you. You made us wait because you were *not on time*, so now you must wait until we finish. It is really *not* a good thing to be late."

Once the student understands the concept of not being on time, say, "Another way of saying *not on time* is to say *late*. When people are *not on time*, they are *late*." Reprimand the student when he or she is late, and begin developing the idea that there are times when people cannot avoid being late and that when these situations arise, it is important to let the people who are expecting you know that you are going to be late.

**Intermediate Level.**   Engage in several role plays in which you play the part of a person who expects to be late and telephones to inform someone else of his or her expected lateness. For example, say, "I'm sorry, but I will arrive at the restaurant around 10 minutes late. Please wait for me. I'll get there as soon as I can!" Then role-play different social and leisure-time activities in which the student cannot avoid being late and must use the telephone to report on the expected lateness and indicate the likely time of his or her arrival.

At this level, also introduce the idea that there may be times when one cannot arrive at all to a destination and will be *absent*. Role-play scenes in which you telephone someone (the student or a classmate) to indicate that you will be absent. Follow up by engaging the student in playing the part of the person who is going to be absent, while you play the part of the person who is expecting him or her.

**Secondary Level.**   At this level, role-play different situations involving reporting to a work site where one is going to be late or absent. (See Figure 2.37.) Make certain to indicate that when someone is hired for a job, he or she must find out, as early as possible, to whom the telephone call should be made whenever he or she expects to be late or absent. Also, review which reasons are acceptable and which are not appropriate, as suggested in Figure 2.38.

## Family Interventions

**Primary Level.**   Ask the parents to explain those circumstances when they could not avoid being late. Remind them that when they are late in the company of their child, they should first tell the child that they must make a telephone call to explain that they are going to be late and then make the telephone call in the child's presence. Encourage them, when they are unexpectedly delayed en route to an appointment, to make sure their child is present and then to say, for example, "We're sorry we're late, but there was an accident on Route 60 and the traffic was backed up for miles."

| Acceptable Reasons | Unacceptable Reasons |
|---|---|
| Poor traveling conditions: "The buses are running late because of the icy roads." | "I was out late, and I was so tired that I slept a little longer." |
| Personal situation: "I will be late because I cut my finger and waited until the bleeding stopped!" | "I left my watch home on my bureau, and I didn't know what time it was." |
| Family situation: "My mother is sick, and I had to make breakfast for the rest of the family." | "I was playing a game with my friend and was having a good time. When I checked the clock, I realized I was going to be late." |
| Equipment problems: "The electricity went out during the night in my community, and my electric alarm clock didn't go off on time." | "I am at the record store. I was coming to meet you, but since it was on my way, I stopped to pick up a record I've been wanting to buy." |

**FIGURE 2.37.**  Acceptable and unacceptable reasons for being late.

**Intermediate Level.**  Encourage the parents to explain to their youngster reasons why they have been absent for work in the past and might be absent for work or have to cancel an appointment in the future. (See Figure 2.38.)

**Secondary Level.**  Ask the parents to engage their youngster in role plays involving real-life situations that are pertinent to the youngster and to the family as a whole. For example, they might say, "You need to call Dr. Salpino to cancel your counseling session since you have to be at Aunt Lisa's wedding at that time."

---

☎ Specific Objective G

The student transmits messages to co-workers and supervisors when asked to do so.

---

## Teacher Interventions

**Primary Level.**  Orally give the student messages that he or she must transmit either orally or by hand to a classmate, a fellow teacher, a school admin-

| Acceptable Reasons | Unacceptable Reasons |
|---|---|
| Personal illness: "I twisted my ankle yesterday. I am in terrible pain and can hardly walk. So I won't be in today." | "I don't feel very well today. I guess I stayed out too late last night. |
| Family illness: "My father is being operated on Friday, and I am taking him to the hospital. I'll have to be out on Friday." | "My friends are going to the beach today, and I thought I would like to go, too." |
| Death: "My Aunt Susie's funeral service is Wednesday morning. I won't be in school on Wednesday." | "Tomorrow is the first day of the baseball season and I'd like to be there for the opening game, so I won't come to school tomorrow." |
| Civic duty: "I have been called for jury duty so I will be absent tomorrow." | "The tickets for the rock concert will go on sale tomorrow and I'm going to stand on line to get tickets, so I probably won't come to work tomorrow." |
| Personal situation: "I am a witness in a trial so I will be absent for work tomorrow." | "I have an ugly pimple on my chin, so I guess I'll stay out a couple of days." |

**FIGURE 2.38.**  Acceptable and unacceptable reasons for being absent.

istrator, or a member of the school staff. Reward the student for being a "good messenger."

**Intermediate Level.**  Play the game of "Gossip," in which you whisper a message in the ear of the student and he or she must pass it on to another person who passes it on in turn. Comment on how the message is distorted when that occurs and point out the need to make sure that you deliver the message exactly as given.

**Secondary Level.**  Role-play situations in which you give the student an important message to pass on to someone else, for example, "You are a railroad worker and have been told to warn the engineer of the approaching train that there is a disabled car on the railroad tracks" or "Your sister has fallen downstairs and wants you to call 911 to get help, since she can't get to the telephone."

## Family Interventions

**Primary Level.** Ask the parents to give the child messages to deliver to another family member who is in a different location in the home, for example, "Please go upstairs and tell Johnny that dinner is ready and to wash his hands and face and come right down."

**Intermediate and Secondary Levels.** Ask the parents to give their youngster messages to transmit over the telephone to a relative or close friend during actual situations, for example, "My hands are messy from mixing the ground meat for tonight's meat loaf, and I forgot to call Uncle Tony and Aunt Lil to remind them to pick up Grandma Rose for dinner tonight. Please, Theresa, call Uncle Tony and Aunt Lil and give them the message."

---

 ## Specific Objective H

The student shares his or her thoughts and feelings with co-workers in simple conversational exchanges and expresses to co-workers and supervisors any concerns or grievances about work conditions, including safety and health factors.

---

## Teacher Interventions

**Primary Level.** Give the student a variety of cooperative tasks in which decisions have to be made by the team members, for example, "You are to create the bulletin board that honors Black History Month. You talk it out and decide on what the bulletin board should look like and what materials you will need" or "You have been asked to plan and prepare a luncheon for Grandparents' Day. Discuss the menu and make the plans to make this celebration a success."

**Intermediate and Secondary Levels.** Role-play situations in which the student pretends that he or she must join co-workers (fellow students) in making decisions about working conditions or grievances (e.g., "What should we do about the company's idea to increase our contribution to the health plan?") and work-related activities (e.g., "Our company is planning a company picnic. What do you think of this idea? Who do you think should be invited other than the workers? Should family members be invited? What activities do you think should take place at the picnic, and what food and beverages do you think should be served?").

# Family Interventions

**Primary Level.**   Encourage the parents to involve their child in family discussions concerning family chores and other cooperative group activities, for example, "We need to plan how to celebrate Lisa's graduation. Let's talk about the various ways we can celebrate and then make plans for the actual celebration" or "We need to set up a schedule to visit Aunt Helen while she is recuperating from her recent accident. What do you think we should do?" Also, ask the parents to hold conversations that deal with any disputes, disagreements, or grievances that are causing family problems.

**Intermediate and Secondary Levels.**   Encourage the parents to share with their youngster experiences they have had with co-workers in which they have had to share their thoughts and feelings, for example, "I had to discuss what I thought were safety hazards with some of my co-workers because I wanted to hear what they thought and to find out whether we should take the problem to a supervisor" or "I was upset when the mother of one of our co-workers died and no one did anything. I asked some of my co-workers to meet me to discuss whether we needed to establish a policy on expressing our sorrow to co-workers on sad occasions such as the death of a close family member and expressing our congratulations to co-workers on happy occasions such as the birth of a baby." Suggest that the parents follow up these examples with complementary role plays.

---

☎ ## Specific Objective I

The student discusses salary, fringe benefits, promotion, and other work-related matters with supervisors.

---

# Teacher Interventions

**Secondary Level.**   Share with the student any incidents that you have heard about workers discussing salary, fringe benefits, and other work-related matters with supervisors. Ask the student and his or her classmates to share any similar incidents with you. Discuss the appropriate ways of handling such situations.

Show the student videotaped segments of mishandled labor disputes and teacher-made video vignettes of the proper way to deal with work-related issues. Follow up by engaging the student in similar role plays. Tape these role plays for the student to review and critique later.

## Family Interventions

**Secondary Level.**   Encourage the parents to discuss with their youngster how they handled work-related matters with their supervisors. Lend them tapes of their youngster's successful role plays (see Teacher Interventions) to review in the home and to share with other family members.

---

☎  ## Specific Objective J

The student provides appropriate information, including work history and qualifications, to a prospective employer in a job interview.

---

## Teacher Interventions

**Primary and Intermediate Levels.**   Discuss and model how to participate in a job interview. Show the student videotapes of former students with disabilities who have participated successfully in a role-played job interview. After this, require the student and his or her classmates to apply and interview for class jobs rather than simply giving them out, for example, "We need a classroom maintenance supervisor to make sure that our student custodians and maintenance workers have done their jobs satisfactorily. Who has some relevant experience and the qualifications for this job and would like to apply?" When the student applies for a job, hold an interview in which he or she must delineate his or her qualifications for the job in the ways shown in your demonstration and the videotapes.

**Secondary Level.**   Invite business people and human resource professionals to the classroom. Ask them to explain, as part of a role play, that they are interviewing for job openings that are of interest to the student and his or her classmates. Ask them to then engage the student in a role play in which the student interviews for the position they describe.

## Family Interventions

**Secondary Level.**   Encourage the parents to assist their youngster in locating potential jobs of interest to the youngster and for which he or she is qualified. Ask them to engage the child in practice interview sessions and, when feasible, to follow up successful interview sessions by arranging for actual interviews.

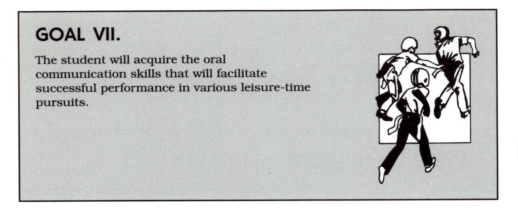

**GOAL VII.**

The student will acquire the oral communication skills that will facilitate successful performance in various leisure-time pursuits.

# SPECIFIC OBJECTIVES

The student:

    ❏ A. Follows instructions for playing with toys and indoor games.

    ❏ B. Follows instructions for engaging in outdoor games, sports, and physical fitness activities.

    ❏ C. Accepts oral invitations from others to participate in various leisure-time activities.

    ❏ D. Makes plans, in concert with others, for various recreational activities.

    ❏ E. Invites family members, friends, and neighbors to join him or her in various leisure-time activities, including games and sports, entertainment and sports events, shopping, and social events.

    ❏ F. Explains the rules and processes involved in a specific leisure-time pursuit to others who do not know the activity and with whom he or she wishes to participate.

    ❏ G. Engages in the communication involved in participating in various leisure-time events, for example, responding to and giving football play information, answering questions in a table game, or discussing items seen on a nature hike or walk.

    ❏ H. Purchases needed materials and equipment, including arts-and-crafts, hobby, and sports equipment, clothing, and materials.

    ❏ I. Makes the arrangements for specific recreational activities, including purchasing tickets to and making inquiries about and reservations for sports and diverse entertainment events.

# SUGGESTED ACTIVITIES

---

☎ ## Specific Objective A

The student follows instructions for playing with toys and indoor games.

---

## Teacher Interventions

**Infant and Toddler/Preschool Level.**   Identify toys the student has demonstrated an interest in. Use these toys to create several different organized activities. For example, when playing with toy cars, say to the student, "Make the car go!" "Make the car stop!" and "Put the car in the garage!" (with a suitable garage prop). When playing with a doll or puppet, say, "Make the doll dance!" "Put the doll in the crib!" and "The doll is hungry. Give it some milk!" (with a suitable doll-sized bottle as a prop). Praise the student for responding appropriately to the directions.

**Primary Level.**   Determine the toys and table games that the student enjoys playing. Be sure to include oral directions or questions as an integral part of activities with these toys and games. For example, while playing a game such as "Candy Land" or "Chutes and Ladders," tell the student, "Move three spaces!" A further example is the card game "Go Fish," in which the student must respond to the question, "Do you have any (face value of a desired card)?"

**Intermediate and Secondary Levels.**   Introduce the student to as many indoor or table games as possible. Be certain to include games with which he or she is not familiar. Provide instructions for the games, and reward the student for following these instructions and playing the games correctly. Introduce a variety of card games, such as "Rummy," "Hearts," and "Fan Tan," and classic board games, "Bingo," "Monopoly," and "Yahtzee," as well as newly popular ones.

## Family Interventions

**Infant and Toddler/Preschool Level.**   Demonstrate how to use typical childhood toys as a means of building oral language comprehension. Encourage the parents to make some of their child's interactions with favored toys into a verbal interchange. For example, when playing with a ball, tell them to say such things as "Roll the ball to me!" "Throw the ball to Daddy!" "Bounce the ball!" and "Catch the ball!"

**Primary Level.** At this level, ask the parents to make their directions more advanced than those at the infant and toddler/preschool level. For example, tell the parents that when they are playing with a stacking toy that involves putting rings of different sizes and different colors in a progressively smaller pattern, they should say such things as "Find the one that goes on next. It is the (name of color) one." Tell the parent, at this level, to involve the family in different card and table games as part of the family's leisure-time activities conducted in the home.

Encourage the parents to purchase or borrow books from a public library that describe how to play a variety of card and other table games. Tell them to teach their child and the other family members how to play these games.

**Intermediate and Secondary Levels.** Ask the parents to introduce new card and table games to their youngster, making certain that they select games that are appropriate to the youngster's age and interests and that require increasing skill in following directions as the youngster progresses in his or her ability to comprehend instructions.

---

☎ ## Specific Objective B

The student follows instructions for engaging in outdoor games, sports, and physical fitness activities.

---

(Note: In all games, sports, and other physical activities requiring strength, endurance, and agility, attention should be paid to any physical limitations of the individual student. The emphasis throughout must be on enjoyment and fitness rather than on winning and competing.)

## Teacher Interventions

**Infant and Toddler/Preschool Level.** Play *low-activity* games such as croquet and miniature golf, *balance* games such as "Twister" and "Blockhead," and *target* games such as "Ring Toss" and "Jarts" with the student. Reward the student for following directions correctly.

**Primary Level.** Engage the student in physical fitness activities, such as calisthenics, in which he or she must follow the directions for both the type of activity and the number of repetitions. Teach the student how to play "Simon Says" and similar games in which he or she must respond to your words or to words from an audiocassette or record player. Also, play games on the school playground such as "Shuffleboard" and "Hopscotch."

**Intermediate and Secondary Levels.** Introduce the student to various sports that require the comprehension of rules for playing them and for recording results. Start with games such as bowling, duckpins, Ping-Pong, and "Air Hockey" that involve limited and fairly simple rules. At the secondary level, introduce sports that are physically more demanding and have more complex rules, such as softball, baseball, soccer, and basketball.

## Family Interventions

**Infant and Toddler/Preschool Level.** Encourage the parents to engage family members in active games, sports, and other physical fitness activities. Ask them to select activities that take into consideration any physical limitations of their child as well as his or her level of oral language comprehension. At this level, children's toy sets such as plastic bowling pins and "Ring Toss" are appropriate because of the simplicity of their rules and the minimum physical requirements. Encourage the parents to take their child to a local playground so that the child can experience the play equipment and follow safety and other directions in using this equipment.

**Primary Level.** Ask the parents to accompany their child to view a variety of sports events in the community and to explain the rules of the game as the game progresses. Encourage them to be sure, if feasible, to attend Little League games and special events such as the Special Olympics. Ask them to begin to instruct their child in simple games such as Ping-Pong, bowling, and miniature golf.

**Intermediate and Secondary Levels.** At these levels, encourage the parents to put their youngster on a physical fitness regimen that involves proper nutrition, exercise, and rest. Tell them to concentrate on oral language comprehension activities as, for example, in learning how to do a stroke in swimming, following the coach's directions in a game of softball, carrying out a calisthenic routine, and following pathways on a hike or nature walk.

---

### ☎ Specific Objective C

The student accepts oral invitations from others to participate in various leisure-time activities.

---

## Teacher Interventions

**Infant and Toddler/Preschool Level.**   Schedule play activities at various times of the school day. Introduce these activities in different ways, for example, "Would you like to play (name of the game)?" "It's playtime. Today, we are going to learn how to play (name of the game)," or "Who would like to play (name of the game)?"

**Primary Level.**   Schedule free play times, and encourage the student to invite classmates to join in a game. Reward students who invited others to play with them in an appropriate way and students who accepted invitations and participated successfully in the activity.

**Intermediate and Secondary Levels.**   Arrange for various trips in the community in which the student participates in activities as a member of a pair (seats for the event are in pairs only) or as a member of a small group (students must participate in the activity as part of a designated group, e.g., group A will visit the museum shop while group B goes to the museum cafeteria). Assign a classmate the task of inviting the student to participate in the activity.

## Family Interventions

**Infant and Toddler/Preschool Level.**   Ask the parents to schedule various leisure-time activities and to extend an invitation to their child as an important first step in the activity. For example, ask them to say such things as "We are going to the movies to see ___. Would you like to go with us?" Tell them to ask this question when engaging in an activity that the child likes.

**Primary Level.**   Encourage the parents to give their child a choice of suitable leisure activities, for example, "Today is a nice day. We can go swimming at the pool in the State Park, or we can go for a ride and have a picnic by the lake. Which one would you like to do?"

**Intermediate and Secondary Levels.**   Encourage the parents to assist their youngster in establishing and maintaining friendships. Ask them to arrange for a friend (perhaps in cooperation with the friend's parents) to invite the youngster to various recreational activities. At the secondary level, if the youngster has an interest in dating and opportunities to do so, encourage the parents to engage in role plays in which the youngster is asked to go out on a date.

> ☎ Specific Objective D
>
> The student makes plans, in concert with others, for various recreational activities.

## Teacher Interventions

**Infant and Toddler/Preschool Level.**  Tell the student that he or she will be joining you in a fun activity. Give the student a choice of several activities and ask him or her to select one. Demonstrate how to plan for the selected activity by deciding together on needed materials and equipment, the amount of time needed and available, the location at which the activity will occur, the rules, and the responsibilities, including cleaning up and returning materials and equipment to their storage areas. See Figure 2.39.

**Primary Level.**  After you demonstrate how to plan an activity with the student several times, encourage the student to select a classmate with whom he or she would like to share a toy or play a game. In the beginning, provide some supervision and then require the student to join one or more classmates in planning activities for open periods during the school day.

**Intermediate Level.**  Discuss with the student and his or her classmates possible trips into the community for recreational activities. Demonstrate how to

---

Time factors—both needed and available

Safety and health factors

Money needed

Location where activity is to take place

Needed materials and equipment

Rules and responsibilities

Clean-up considerations

Storage of materials and equipment

Transportation needs

---

**FIGURE 2.39.**  Elements involved in planning recreational activities.

plan these activities by determining time constraints and requirements, costs involved, transportation needs, a schedule of activities, and any special clothing or materials needed. After several demonstrations, schedule a trip in the community and ask the student to join his or her classmates in planning for these trips.

**Secondary Level.** Engage the student in a role play in which the student and several classmates are expected to plan leisure-time activities that involve a great deal of planning, for example, a field trip to a nearby amusement park or sports event, a class party or school dance, or a luncheon for parents and grandparents. Whenever feasible, actually engage in these activities.

## Family Interventions

**Infant and Toddler/Preschool Level.** Encourage the parents to involve their child in planning family recreational activities. Tell them that even if the child does not actively participate in these sessions, he or she should be present and participate on some level, if possible, even if it is only to nod approval or smile in delight.

**Primary Level.** Tell the parents to involve the child in making decisions about leisure-time pursuits when there are several available choices. Encourage them to assign one of the planning elements to the child at his or her level, for example, deciding what food should be taken on a picnic or for what section of the sports stadium they should purchase tickets.

**Intermediate Level.** At this level, parents should give the youngster increased responsibility for planning leisure-time activities with other family members. Encourage the parents to utilize, as much as possible, a variety of activities. Remind them that they may need to supervise planning sessions in the beginning while gradually reducing their guidance until they merely review and evaluate the plans prior to their actual implementation.

**Secondary Level.** Ask the parents to share with their youngster the plans they make with friends, relatives, neighbors, and co-workers for their own leisure time as well as the way they arrived at these plans. At this level, tell the parents to encourage their youngster to make leisure-time plans with friends and classmates. Remind them to emphasize that joining friends, classmates, and co-workers in recreational activities is a good way of establishing and maintaining friendships and friendly relations. (See Goal IX, Specific Objective A, and Figures 2.44 and 2.45.)

> ☎  ## Specific Objective E
>
> The student invites family members, friends, and neighbors to join him or her in various leisure-time activities, including games and sports, entertainment and sports events, shopping, and social events.

## Teacher Interventions

**Infant and Toddler/Preschool Level.**   Plan a classroom activity to which another class will be invited (e.g., for a demonstration of the students' artwork or for a snack). Give the student a written invitation to take to the teacher of the class that is invited. Accompany the student, and tell him or her to deliver the invitation and, if possible, to simultaneously announce the invitation to the teacher and the students.

**Primary Level.**   Ask the student to tell you the names of friends and family members whom he or she has joined in leisure-time activities. Discuss some of the student's favorite activities and role-play these activities, requiring the student to use an unconnected telephone to invite friends and family members to join him or her in the activities. Suggest other possible activities for subsequent role plays.

**Intermediate and Secondary Levels.**   Plan activities that are open to family members and friends, for example, inviting parents to accompany the class on a field trip or inviting friends to join the class at a neighborhood playing field. Expect the student to invite these individuals as a home assignment and to inform the class of their acceptance or nonacceptance as part of the ongoing planning process.

Be sure to explore the various possible leisure-time pursuits available in the community and in nearby jurisdictions.

## Family Interventions

**Infant and Toddler/Preschool and Primary Levels.**   Ask the parents to plan a birthday party or other special-occasion celebration to which their child can invite friends and relatives. Encourage the parents to arrange for the child to do the actual invitation, in person or over the telephone.

**Intermediate and Secondary Levels.**   Encourage the parents to involve their youngster in family planning sessions relevant to leisure-time pursuits. Tell them to include a variety of activities appropriate to their budget and interests and the availability of the activities in the community.

Suggest activities such as games and sports, entertainment and sports events, shopping, and social events. At the secondary level, urge the parents to encourage the youngster to plan leisure-time activities for the purpose of inviting his or her own friends to join in recreational activities without the parents' participation.

---

### ☎ Specific Objective F

The student explains the rules and processes involved in a specific leisure-time pursuit to others who do not know the activity and with whom he or she wishes to participate.

---

## Teacher Interventions

**Primary Level.**   Teach the student a simple card or table game with which he or she is not familiar. Once the student is able to play the game, ask him or her to teach it to a classmate who is not familiar with the game. Provide assistance as needed.

**Intermediate Level.**   Teach the student a number of games such as bowling and miniature golf. After the student has mastered a game, ask him or her to teach a classmate who is not familiar with the game. Once you have determined that the classmate has understood the rules and processes, make arrangements for the child and the classmate to participate in the activity.

Do this with a variety of games and sports, including games to be played in the classroom as well as those to be played in the community.

**Secondary Level.**   Take the student for a trip in the community to purchase tickets to a sports event. Discuss and demonstrate the various steps involved, including the use of public transportation, the determination of available seats (including their location and costs), and the decision about which ones to purchase.

On the return to the class, ask the student to share the experience with one or more classmates. Follow up by asking the student to teach a classmate how to purchase tickets to a variety of paid recreational activities in role plays and, whenever feasible, in actual trips to these community sites.

## Family Interventions

**Primary Level.** Encourage the parents to teach their child the rules and processes of a simple game and then to require the child to teach them the game as part of a role play in which they pretend not to know how to play the game. Tell them that if the child is successful, they should follow up by asking the child to teach the game to someone else, preferably a friend with whom he or she can play the game during leisure time.

**Intermediate and Secondary Levels.** Encourage the parents to identify recreational activities that their youngster can engage in independently. Ask them to identify family members, friends, and neighbors who are unfamiliar with the activity (or willing to pretend ignorance), to whom the youngster can explain the rules and steps. Remind the parents to follow up by arranging for the youngster to join his or her "student" in the specified activity.

---

☎ ## Specific Objective G

The student engages in the communication involved in participating in various leisure-time events, for example, responding to and giving football play information, answering questions in a table game, or discussing items seen on a nature hike or walk.

---

## Teacher Interventions

**Infant and Toddler/Preschool Level.** Play a variety of games in which verbal exchanges are an integral part of the game. At this level, a game of "Picture Lotto" is appropriate, in which you show the student a picture of an object and say, for example, "Do you have a picture of an (animal name)?" and the student is expected to say, "Yes, I have a picture of that (animal name). Give me the card, please." The card game "Go Fish" is also an excellent choice for this activity.

**Primary Level.** Take the student for trips in the community. Comment on the sights, sounds, and smells, for example, "I like the new window display at (department store's name)," "Aren't the spring flowers beautiful?" "I liked the music that was being played when we passed the record store, didn't you?" or "Didn't it smell nice when we passed by the bakery?" Encourage the student to comment on things he or she experiences on the trip.

**Intermediate and Secondary Levels.** At these levels, engage the student in games and other recreational activities that stimulate conversation, for example, discussing strategies and plays in a football game, talking about choices of places to go for lunch, speaking about preferences in music and musical performers, or commenting on the latest fashions displayed in clothing stores and in clothing departments of department stores.

Later in the school day or on subsequent days, engage the student in a conversation that reminisces about the trip.

## Family Interventions

**Infant and Toddler/Preschool Level.** Ask the parents to involve their child in playing games that include some verbal exchanges, for example, puppet play, in which the child plays the part of one of the characters, and playing "House," in which the child assumes various roles, including the part of a parent or sibling.

**Primary Level.** Encourage the parents to take the child for trips in the community. Remind them to use these trips as occasions to model and stimulate language development. If needed and feasible, ask the parents to join you and the child on a trip in the community to observe how you make the trip a language experience, both during the trip and in talking about it at a later time.

**Intermediate and Secondary Levels.** Tell the parents to engage their youngster in recreational activities that are enhanced through verbal exchanges and conversations, for example, conversations at a family gathering, discussions while attending sporting events, and talks about movies, exhibits, and other shared experiences in follow-up conversations at home.

---

☎  ## Specific Objective H

The student purchases needed materials and equipment, including arts-and-crafts, hobby, and sports equipment, clothing, and materials.

---

## Teacher Interventions

**Infant and Toddler/Preschool Level.** Plan an arts-and-crafts project that requires you to order materials from the school secretary or art teacher. Take the student with you when you request these needed supplies. Follow up by purchasing supplies from petty cash funds when the supplies are not available in the school.

**Primary Level.**  If you have a hobby, show the student samples of this hobby (e.g., collections), and discuss the hobby with the student. Include in your discussion information on the supplies and materials needed and the pertinent costs. Engage the student in a role play in which he or she plays a person who is purchasing supplies for a hobby and you play the part of the salesperson.

**Intermediate and Secondary Levels.**  Show the student photographs of individuals (preferably his or her age peers) who are playing various sports. Comment on the uniforms or special clothing and equipment. Visit a local sporting goods store. On your return to school, set up a simulated sporting goods store and role-play purchasing sports equipment, materials, and clothing for several different sports, especially those that interest the student.

If the student already has a hobby, discuss this hobby with the student, making sure to review how and where he or she makes purchases needed to engage in that hobby.

## Family Interventions

**Infant and Toddler/Preschool and Primary Levels.**  Encourage the parents to arrange for their child to accompany them as they make purchases of special clothing, materials, and equipment for various leisure-time activities. Remind them to comment on the purchases after they have been completed, for example, "I am happy that the yarn I have been looking for to knit you a sweater was on sale" or "I finally was able to buy the fishing pole I needed. I saved money for several months to buy it."

**Intermediate and Secondary Levels.**  Encourage the parents to motivate their youngster to develop an interest in a hobby or in becoming a participant in sports and other physical activities (e.g., by joining a gym). Remind them to discuss the requirements and financial aspects of these activities.

Tell the parents, when appropriate and feasible (given financial and other constraints), to expect the youngster to budget for, save for, and make needed purchases.

---

☎ ## Specific Objective I

The student makes the arrangements for specific recreational activities, including purchasing tickets to and making inquiries about and reservations for sports and diverse entertainment events.

---

## Teacher Interventions

**Intermediate and Secondary Levels.** After you have demonstrated making arrangements for various leisure-time activities (including purchasing tickets to and making inquiries about and reservations for sports and diverse entertainment events), involve the student in making plans for these events. After the plans have been finalized, require the student to make any needed inquiries and reservations and to handle the necessary financial transactions.

## Family Interventions

**Intermediate and Secondary Levels.** Ask the parents to include their youngster in planning sessions concerning family leisure-time pursuits. Remind them to demonstrate making inquiries and reservations over the telephone and engaging in necessary financial transactions. Encourage them to give the youngster increasing responsibility for making arrangements as he or she demonstrates skills in arranging leisure-time activities.

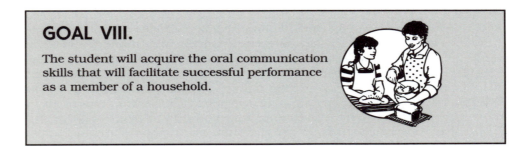

## GOAL VIII.

The student will acquire the oral communication skills that will facilitate successful performance as a member of a household.

# SPECIFIC OBJECTIVES

The student:

☐ A. Responds, with appropriate action, to requests for desired objects.

☐ B. Follows instructions for carrying out various household chores.

☐ C. Responds appropriately to questions asked by a household member who is seeking specific information about *where* an object is, *when* a household activity is to take place, *how to* cook a particular meal or *how much* soap powder should be placed in the washing machine, *how many* eggs are needed for the noodle pudding, *what* the oven should be set at, *who* is responsible for a particular chore, *to whom* something belongs, *whose* object something is, and *which* object or activity is being discussed or desired.

☐ D. Responds to requests for assistance, when appropriate, and seeks help, when needed.

☐ E. Gives messages to household members.

☐ F. Plans, with household members, various household maintenance and cleaning chores, including care of utensils, clothing, linens, furniture, and appliances.

☐ G. Plans snacks, meals, and parts of meals with household members and participates in making up shopping lists.

☐ H. Plans, with household members, various social and leisure-time activities that take place in the home and community.

☐ I. Communicates needs, thoughts, and feelings to pertinent members of the household.

☐ J. Shares information of importance obtained from the media and other sources with other members of the household.

☐ K. Makes telephone calls requested by household members or that deal with factors and issues pertinent to the household.

☐ L. Participates in simple conversations (small talk).

☐ M. Participates in important or serious discussions relative to the household, for example, making short- and long-range plans, budgeting, purchasing needed furniture and appliances, identifying home safety and security measures, and handling emergencies.

# SUGGESTED ACTIVITIES

---

☎ ## Specific Objective A

The student responds, with appropriate action, to requests for desired objects.

---

## Teacher Interventions

**Infant and Toddler/Preschool and Primary Levels.** Show the student the various objects that are located in the classroom. When showing each of the objects, name it, explain its purpose, and demonstrate its use, for example, "Pencil. This is a pencil. We write with a pencil. See how it makes marks on the paper." After several repetitions, say to the student, "Please give me the pencil."

**Intermediate and Secondary Levels.** At these levels, introduce items that are not as commonly found in the typical classroom environment; for example, in learning experiences involving household management, ask the student to give you the nutcracker, the potato peeler, and other kitchen gadgets used in baking and cooking.

## Family Interventions

**Infant and Toddler/Preschool and Primary Levels.** Ask the parents to show their child various objects found in their home. Tell them to show the child each of the objects, name it, explain its purpose, and demonstrate its use, for example, "Toothpaste. This is toothpaste. We use toothpaste to brush our teeth. Watch as I use the toothpaste to brush my teeth." Tell the parents to then say to the child, "Please bring me the toothpaste," when they wish to brush their teeth.

**Intermediate and Secondary Levels.** At these levels, tell the parents to introduce items that are less frequently used on a daily basis in the home, for example, a fuse to replace one that is burned out, a magnifying glass to view a road map, or candles to put on the table during a special meal. Remind them to review and emphasize safety factors.

---

☎ ## Specific Objective B

The student follows instructions for carrying out various household chores.

---

## Teacher Interventions

**Infant and Toddler/Preschool and Primary Levels.** As early as possible, assign classroom chores to the student, especially those that he or she can accomplish with a minimum of guidance and supervision. If possible, assign the student chores that are similar to household tasks, such as emptying the wastebasket and returning materials and supplies to their storage area.

Comment on the fact that the student can do the same thing at home. At these levels, provide the student with simple one-step instructions. (See Figure 2.40.)

| School Chore | Related Household Chore |
|---|---|
| Washing the chalkboard | Washing windows and mirrors |
| Storing school supplies | Storing food packages |
| Decorating the bulletin board | Hanging pictures |
| Watering plants | Gardening and caring for indoor plants |
| Giving out supplies | Dispensing medications, setting the table, and providing play and leisure-time materials and equipment |

**FIGURE 2.40.**   School chores and related household chores.

**Intermediate and Secondary Levels.**   At these levels, assign the student classroom tasks that involve multistep instructions and require greater skill, for example, tending to classroom plants, stacking the bookshelves, conducting an inventory of supplies, returning books to the library, or delivering invitations to a class play to the principal and teachers.

## Family Interventions

**Infant and Toddler/Preschool and Primary Levels.**   Encourage the parents to assign their child, as early as possible, at least one household task that he or she is capable of performing with minimal guidance and supervision. In the beginning, ask the parents to carry out a cooperative chore such as making the bed together, separating dirty laundry into piles, or unpacking groceries.

Remind the parents to use the same directions each time the task is performed, for example, "Help me make your bed. You put the pillow at the headboard," "Put all the white clothes in this pile," or "Unpack the grocery bag and put the cans on this counter." At the primary level, increase both the number of tasks to be done as a cooperative endeavor and the number of tasks that are to be done alone.

**Intermediate and Secondary Levels.**   Encourage the parents to gradually increase the complexity of the instructions along with the areas of responsibility, for example, dusting the furniture, drying and putting away the breakfast dishes, filling the ice cube trays, or preparing simple snacks and parts of meals.

☏ **Specific Objective C**

The student responds appropriately to questions asked by a household member who is seeking specific information about *where* an object is, *when* a household activity is to take place, *how to* cook a particular meal or *how much* soap powder should be placed in the washing machine, *how many* eggs are needed for the noodle pudding, *what* the oven should be set at, *who* is responsible for a particular chore, *to whom* something belongs, *whose* object something is, and *which* object or activity is being discussed or desired.

## Teacher Interventions

**Infant and Toddler/Preschool Level.** At this level, concentrate on the "what" and "where" questions by asking the student to tell you the name of an object, for example, "What is this?" (while pointing to or picking up an object) and also where something is in the classroom, for example, "Where is your lunch box?" or "Where is the fish food?"

**Primary Level.** At this level, concentrate on the "who," "whose," and "which" questions, for example, "Who needs to go to the bathroom?" "Whose lunch box is this?" or "Which one is your coat?"

**Intermediate Level.** At this level, concentrate on the "when," "how much," and "how many" questions, for example, "When do we go to music class?" "How much more time do you need to finish your work?" or "How many sandwiches do we need to make for our morning snack?"

**Secondary Level.** At this level, concentrate on the "how" and "to whom" questions, for example, "How do you set the table?" or "To whom does this umbrella belong?"

## Family Interventions

**Infant and Toddler/Preschool Level.** At this level, ask the parents to concentrate on the "what" and "where" questions by asking their child to tell them the name of a household object, for example, "What is this?" (while pointing to or picking up an object) and also where something is, for example, "Where is your shirt?" or "Where did you put your shoes?"

**Primary Level.**   At this level, ask the parents to concentrate on the "who," "whose," and "which" questions, for example, "Who broke the cup?" "Whose toothbrush is this?" or "Which one of you left the front door open?"

**Intermediate Level.**   At this level, ask the parents to concentrate on the "when," "how much," and "how many" questions, for example, "When is your favorite television program on?" "How much money do you need for the field trip?" or "How many games are you planning to play at the picnic?"

**Secondary Level.**   At this level, ask the parents to concentrate on the "how" and "to whom" questions, for example, "How do you set your alarm clock?" or "To whom does this key chain belong?"

---

☎   ## Specific Objective D

The student responds to requests for assistance, when appropriate, and seeks help, when needed.

---

## Teacher Interventions

**Infant and Toddler/Preschool Level.**   Identify one of the student's favorite toys or picture books. Begin to play with the toy and ask for the student's assistance in manipulating or playing with it. For example, while playing with a puppet, ask the student to assist you in picking something up with the puppet's hands, and when looking at a book, ask the student to help you turn the page.

**Primary Level.**   At this level, introduce the concept that the student might need help from others. Model asking for help in an appropriate manner and only when needed. Then identify a situation in which the student needs assistance, for example, in opening the thermos in his or her lunch box. Do not provide assistance until the student requests it.

**Intermediate and Secondary Levels.**   At these levels, concentrate on assisting the student in distinguishing between situations where the student is able to function independently and those where he or she requires help. If the student requests assistance when none is needed, be sure to indicate that he or she does not need help, and provide no assistance.

## Family Interventions

**Infant and Toddler/Preschool Level.** Tell the parents to ask their child for assistance during play and other household activities; for example, ask them to say such things as "Please hold the refrigerator door open so I don't spill the water from the ice cube tray while I put it in the freezer" and "Please wipe the spilled milk while I finish setting the table."

**Primary Level.** At this level, encourage the parents to assign their child household tasks that require him or her to seek and ask for help, for example, "Dad, please tell me where the plastic wrap is. I need to cover the leftovers before I put them in the refrigerator" or "Mom, I put my jacket on by myself, but I need your help in putting the zipper in its track so that I can zip it up."

**Intermediate and Secondary Levels.** At these levels, ask the parents to refuse to assist their youngster when assistance is not needed and to respond with help when he or she asks for help in an appropriate manner.

---

☏ ## Specific Objective E

The student gives messages to household members.

---

## Teacher Interventions

**Infant and Toddler/Preschool and Primary Levels.** Role-play a game of "House" with the student in which he or she must give a message to a parent, for example, while playing with a doll whose eyes close and that wets and cries, the student says, "The baby is wet," "The baby is sleepy," or "The baby is crying."

**Intermediate and Secondary Levels.** At these levels, role-play taking telephone messages to be given later to a parent or other family member when that individual returns home. As the student progresses, increase the length, complexity, and seriousness of the message, proceeding from personal messages to business ones. Include appointment and appointment cancellation messages, messages from an employer, and messages pertinent to leisure-time activities (e.g., airline reservations). (See Figure 2.41.)

> The appointment has been rescheduled (or cancelled).
>
> The goods will be delivered on Tuesday between 1:00 and 3:00 P.M.
>
> The ordered goods have arrived at the store.
>
> The work site is closed (or opening late) because of an ice storm.
>
> The supervisor seeks a return call.
>
> The softball tournament has been cancelled due to rain.
>
> The travel agent has made the requested airline reservations.
>
> The bank called—your new checks have arrived.

**FIGURE 2.41.** Sample business messages.

## Family Interventions

**Infant and Toddler/Preschool and Primary Levels.** Encourage the parents to arrange for their child to give messages to other family members at appropriate times, such as "Call your sister—dinner is ready," "Tell your brother to put out the trash can," "Remind Daddy to walk Rover," and "Ask Mommy where she put the newspaper."

**Intermediate and Secondary Levels.** Remind the parents to demonstrate giving other family members messages taken via the telephone. Ask the parents to follow up these demonstrations by deliberately calling home when their youngster is alone and asking him or her to deliver a message to a family member upon that person's return home. Encourage them to increase the length, complexity, and importance of the messages as the youngster makes progress in this skill.

☎ ## Specific Objective F

The student plans, with household members, various household maintenance and cleaning chores, including care of utensils, clothing, linens, furniture, and appliances.

## Teacher Interventions

**Infant and Toddler/Preschool and Primary Levels.** Discuss needed classroom maintenance and cleaning chores with the student. Include in your discussion the chores to be done, evaluation criteria, when the task is to be done, what materials and equipment are needed, and who is responsible for each task. Require the student to do at least one chore, and expect him or her also to participate in the planning.

As the student progresses, expect greater participation in the planning and decision-making process as well as in the assumption of tasks to be done independently.

**Intermediate and Secondary Levels.** At these levels, discuss with the student the need for him or her to participate in planning and implementing plans for keeping his or her home well maintained and clean. Especially at the secondary level, discuss alternative living arrangements such as living in a group residence or as a single person in an apartment or a home setting.

In your discussions and follow-up role playing, be sure to emphasize the differences between living in an apartment and living in a house. Then ask the student, along with one or more of his or her peers (with minimal assistance from you), to identify needed classroom and school maintenance and cleaning tasks and to carry out these tasks in a well-designed and well-orchestrated plan.

## Family Interventions

**Infant and Toddler/Preschool and Primary Levels.** Encourage the parents to discuss needed household maintenance and cleaning chores with their child. Remind them to include the chores to be done, levels of acceptable performance, when the task is to be done, what materials and equipment are needed, and who is responsible for each task.

Tell the parents that, as the child makes progress, they should expect increased participation in the planning and the assumption of tasks to be done independently.

**Intermediate and Secondary Levels.** At these levels, ask the parents to require the youngster to take a more prominent and active role in the planning of household maintenance and cleaning tasks. Encourage them to give the youngster, as appropriate, as much of a leadership or decision-making role as possible, especially when the plans involve his or her own room or preparation for events that are of special relevance and interest to the youngster, for example, a party for his or her friends or same-age relatives.

---

☎    # Specific Objective G

The student plans snacks, meals, and parts of meals with household members and participates in making up shopping lists.

---

## Teacher Interventions

**Infant and Toddler/Preschool and Primary Levels.**  Plan class snacks, luncheons, parties, and other celebrations that involve food preparation. Include the student in planning for the selection of the menu, the drawing up of the shopping list, the shopping trip, and the food preparation. As the student makes progress, gradually increase his or her role in both the planning process and its execution.

Encourage as much meaningful oral communication as possible. When making up the shopping list, ask the student to dictate the items to you as you write them down on the shopping list.

**Intermediate and Secondary Levels.**  At these levels, discuss with the student the need for him or her to participate in planning and implementing plans for household snacks, meals, and celebrations, including parties. Especially at the secondary level, discuss alternative living arrangements such as living in a group residence or as a single person in an apartment or in a home setting.

In your discussions and follow-up role plays, be sure to emphasize the need for effective communication when the student is making plans that involve one or more other residents whose opinions must be taken into consideration and who will share in carrying out the plans. Then ask the student, along with one or more of his or her peers, to plan a class meal without your input to which family members or other classes are invited.

## Family Interventions

**Infant and Toddler/Preschool and Primary Levels.**  Ask the parents to involve their child in planning family snacks, luncheons, parties, and other celebrations that involve food preparation. Remind them to encourage the child to (a) make suggestions for the food and beverages to be served, (b) review the food supplies on hand and recommend items to be placed on a shopping list, (c) accompany them on the shopping trip, and (d) assist in the food preparation. Tell them that as the child makes progress, they should gradually increase his or her role in both the planning process and its execution and encourage as much meaningful oral communication as possible.

**Intermediate and Secondary Levels.**   At these levels, encourage the parents to give their youngster increasing responsibility for planning and implementing plans for household snacks, meals, and celebrations, including parties. Especially at the secondary level, urge the parents to emphasize effective communication as the youngster assumes a dominant or leadership role in the planning while they act as interested and cooperative followers.

---

   ## Specific Objective H

The student plans, with household members, various social and leisure-time activities that take place in the home and community.

---

## Teacher Interventions

**Infant and Toddler/Preschool and Primary Levels.**   Involve the student in planning functional academic activities and other functional activities that are based on leisure activities that can be pursued in the home and in the classroom, for example, planning a "Card Party" as part of a functional academic game in which the participants practice reading numerals, colors, and symbols (suit designations) and making decisions based on the information decoded. (Note: If academic subjects are taught from a functional perspective, they will more likely stimulate student interest and improve life skills [see Volume III, *Functional Academics* (Valletutti, Bender, & Sims-Tucker, in press)].)

**Intermediate and Secondary Levels.**   Involve the student in planning functional academic activities and other functional activities that are based on leisure activities that can be pursued in the community, for example, planning a trip to a community playground or park. In your planning discussion, be sure to require the student to participate in making decisions about money requirements, time constraints, possible activities, materials to be taken, clothing to be worn, safety factors, and other key elements in the proposed leisure activity.

## Family Interventions

**Infant and Toddler/Preschool and Primary Levels.**   Encourage the parents to involve their child in planning family-oriented leisure activities that can be conducted in the home setting, such as planning a surprise party for a relative or close friend. Remind them to require the child to make suggestions relevant to such things as *whom* to invite; *how* to arrange the surprise; *what* decorations, refreshments, party games, and music will be required; *when* it should be scheduled; and *how much* money should be budgeted for the occasion.

**Intermediate and Secondary Levels.**  Ask the parents to involve their youngster in planning family-oriented leisure activities that can be pursued in the community, for example, planning a trip to a theme park.

Tell the parents that in their planning discussion, they should be sure to require the youngster to participate in making decisions about transportation needs, money and time requirements, possible activities, needed clothing and supplies, safety elements, and other key elements in the proposed leisure activity.

---

## ☎ Specific Objective I

The student communicates needs, thoughts, and feelings to pertinent members of the household.

---

## Teacher Interventions

**Infant and Toddler/Preschool and Primary Levels.**  Suggest to the student a preferred activity, and ask him or her what is needed to engage in it. In the beginning, emphasize tangible elements such as baseball bats, several softballs, and baseball gloves for a game of softball. As the student progresses, add less tangible elements such as a scorekeeper, an umpire, a safe playing field, the necessary time, and appropriate weather conditions.

**Intermediate Level.**  At this level, emphasize the communication of feelings. Describe different incidents and situations, and ask the student to respond to these situations or incidents by indicating how he or she feels, for example, "You opened your birthday present, and it was the game you have been wanting for a long time" (happiness), "Your pet turtle died" (sadness), "You watched a movie on television about creatures from outer space" (fear), "You walked in the house and everyone shouted, 'Happy Birthday'" (surprise), "Your friend called, and he can't come over to play with you" (disappointment), and "Someone stole your bicycle while you were in the grocery store" (anger).

**Secondary Level.** At this level, emphasize the communication of beliefs, opinions, values, and attitudes as well as feelings. Discuss current events, especially those of a local nature that affect the student and his or her family members directly, for example, "The County Department of Parks and Recreation is planning to close the nearby recreation center. How do we feel about that, and what, if anything, can and should we do about it?"

## Family Interventions

**Infant and Toddler/Preschool and Primary Levels.** Encourage the parents to suggest a possible activity that their youngster and other family members can engage in. Tell them to ask him or her what is needed for the activity to be a successful experience. In the beginning, urge them to emphasize tangible elements such as sandwiches, drinks, a cooler, bathing suits, towels, sun block, sandals, a float, a beach blanket, a beach umbrella, and a portable radio. As the student progresses, add less tangible elements such as money for the bridge toll and for the amusements on the boardwalk, safety and health factors, and appropriate weather conditions.

**Intermediate Level.** At this level, encourage the parents to emphasize the communication of feelings as they arise from the actual events in the life of the family. Remind the parents to demonstrate the healthy and suitable expression of feelings that arise naturally from these events.

**Secondary Level.** At this level, ask the parents to emphasize the communication of beliefs, opinions, values, and attitudes as well as feelings. Encourage them to discuss family matters and items of concern in the local environment, for example, "Grandma is no longer able to live by herself. I wonder what options we have to make sure that she lives as comfortably and as happily as possible, given her special needs at this time!" or "The state is considering raising the sales tax. Do you think it is a good idea? How do you think it might affect our family and you, personally?"

---

### ☏ Specific Objective J

The student shares information of importance obtained from the media and other sources with other members of the household.

---

## Teacher Interventions

**Primary Level.** Tell the student or read from a newspaper information that may have a direct effect on the student and his or her family, for example,

"There is a water shortage and restrictions are being placed on water use," "All pet owners are required to have their dogs and cats vaccinated against rabies," or "There may be a strike of local garbage collectors starting next Monday." Explain that the student's parents and other family members may not have heard this news and he or she should inform them, even if it is only to remind them of something they already know. Follow up with a role play in which the student tells you or a classmate (playing the role of a family member) the information.

**Intermediate Level.** Repeat the activity identified for the primary level. This time play a teacher-made videotape for the student that contains the same information, with you or another teacher acting as the newscaster.

**Secondary Level.** Repeat the activity identified for the primary level. This time play a teacher-made audiotape for the student that contains the same information, with you or another teacher acting as the newscaster. Design lessons that assist the student in differentiating between news items that may have a direct impact on the family and local community and those that do not.

## Family Interventions

**Primary Level.** Encourage the parents to tell their child information they have heard on news broadcasts for the purpose of telling it to a family member who is not present. In the beginning, remind the parents to monitor the child to make certain that he or she delivers the correct information with all the key details.

**Intermediate and Secondary Levels.** At these levels, ask the parents to give the youngster the responsibility of watching televised news programs, when they are too busy to watch them, and then sharing any important reports that directly affect the family and the local community. Remind the parents to assist their youngster in differentiating between stories that affect the family and community and those that do not.

---

☎ ## Specific Objective K

The student makes telephone calls requested by household members or that deal with factors and issues pertinent to the household.

---

| Serious Emergencies—<br>Outside Help Needed | Nonemergencies—<br>Outside Help Needed | Nonemergencies—<br>No Help Needed |
|---|---|---|
| Someone is bleeding and it is not stopping<br><br>Someone is unconscious<br><br>Someone is suddenly unable to move or walk<br><br>A fire can't be controlled even with the home fire extinguisher<br><br>Someone is attacking the home or its occupants | The commode keeps running—call a skilled neighbor or plumber<br><br>The television set won't work—call the repair shop<br><br>The new toaster doesn't work—call the store where it was purchased<br><br>A mistake was made by the supermarket cashier—call the manager<br><br>You need new bookcases built—call a carpenter | The electricity has gone off only in the house—check the fuse box<br><br>Someone has a small cut—get the first-aid kit<br><br>The baby is crying—the diaper needs changing<br><br>The milk container has dropped—clean up the mess<br><br>The jar won't open—use the jar opener |

**FIGURE 2.42.**  Emergency and nonemergency situations.

(Note: As early as possible, both Teacher Interventions and Family Interventions should concentrate on making telephone calls in emergency situations. Further, teachers and trainers should make certain to emphasize distinguishing between situations that are critical and those that are not emergencies, even when help is needed but can be provided through other than emergency sources. Thus, there are three types of situations: emergencies, nonemergencies where outside help is needed, and nonemergencies where no help is needed. See Figure 2.42.)

## Teacher Interventions

**Primary Level.**  Role-play situations in which you ask the student to make telephone calls for you. (If the school has an intercom system, either role-play its use or actually use it, at prearranged times, to have the student give information to another teacher who has agreed to participate.) At this level, ask the student to make telephone calls to transmit simple and short messages, such as calling the public library or a teacher supply store to ask for operating hours.

**Intermediate and Secondary Levels.** At these levels, increase the complexity of the message to be communicated as the student progresses. Once the student has demonstrated sufficient skill, arrange for him or her to make actual telephone calls, especially those that deal with giving important messages to parents and family members as well as those that involve making arrangements for trips in the community.

## Family Interventions

**Infant and Toddler/Preschool Level.** At this level, ask the parents to say to their child immediately before making an important telephone call (preferably as they pick up the receiver and are dialing the number), for example, "I am calling Uncle Oscar to ask if he will need a lift to Saturday's family reunion." Remind the parents that, at these levels, the purpose is simply to demonstrate using the telephone to communicate information to others who are not present.

**Primary Level.** Encourage the parents to give their child the responsibility of making telephone calls, in their presence, that involve delivering simple messages, for example, "My mother asked me to remind you to vote today" or "My sister is sick and won't be able to play with Sabine today."

**Intermediate and Secondary Levels.** Encourage the parents to give their youngster increasing responsibility for making calls to relatives, friends, and neighbors as well as to communicate with business entities, for example, to seek information about the cost of repair services, special sales, or whether a desired item is in stock.

---

☎ ## Specific Objective L

The student participates in simple conversations (small talk).

---

## Teacher Interventions

**Primary Level.** Involve the student in simple conversations that people typically engage in when they come together. The weather is always a good topic for small talk. Listen to the conversations of the student's age peers to determine topics that are of interest to that age group. Topics generally include the latest toys and games, actors and recording stars, and fashions. Be sure to stop the student if he or she brings up a topic that is not

| Small Talk Topics | Big or Too "Hot" Topics |
|---|---|
| The weather | Political parties and politics |
| Toys and games | Religion and religious practices |
| Clothing and fashions | Sex and sexual practices |
| Recording artists and songs | Ethnic and racial prejudices |
| Television programs | Personal financial matters |
| Sports and sport teams | Bodily functions |
| Motor vehicles | Family secrets |
| Movies and movie stars | Personal matters |
| Foods and beverages | |

**FIGURE 2.43.**   Conversational topics.

small talk, and explain that the topic is too "hot" for a simple, casual conversation.

**Intermediate Level.**   Prepare several videotapes of conversations, some of which are typical small talk exchanges and several that are too "hot." Assist the student in differentiating between the two types of conversations and in following up the small talk videos with small talk sessions of his or her own.

**Secondary Level.**   Schedule a daily conversation or discussion time. When the student is able to differentiate between small talk and talk that is apt to become too "hot," on some days schedule small talk conversations, and on some days schedule more provocative discussions, where there is likely to be more controversy and a more heated interchange of opinion. (See Figure 2.43.)

## Family Interventions

**Infant and Toddler/Preschool and Primary Levels.**   Ask the parents to set aside a time when all family members engage in small talk conversations. Encourage them to help their child differentiate between a casual conversation in which there are pleasant interchanges and a more serious discussion. Remind the parents that the seriousness of a discussion is communicated not only in words but also, and perhaps more importantly, in body language, vocal tone, and facial expressions. (See Unit 1, "Nonverbal Communication," Goals I–VI.)

**Intermediate and Secondary Levels.**  At these levels, ask the parents to give their youngster increasing responsibility for introducing small talk into family get-togethers. Also, at these levels, encourage them to monitor the youngster's conversations with peers and others who are visiting the home as well as when the youngster is participating in community-based activities, for example, when visiting the homes of relatives, neighbors, and friends.

---

☎  ## Specific Objective M

The student participates in important or serious discussions relative to the household, for example, making short- and long-range plans, budgeting, purchasing needed furniture and appliances, identifying home safety and security measures, and handling emergencies.

---

## Teacher Interventions

**Primary Level.**  Involve the student in serious discussions about school health and safety and the handling of emergencies. Make certain to point out the difference in your behavior (nonverbal as well as verbal) when you are having a serious talk.

**Intermediate and Secondary Levels.**  At these levels, discuss matters of general interest to the community as they relate to school and educational matters. Emphasize that, just like a family, the school system has to make plans, prepare budgets, and make needed purchases of equipment and services.

Talk about how you design lesson plans, and discuss the IEP and Individualized Treatment Plan (ITP) processes as a planning strategy that involves the school and the student's parents (and the student as appropriate). Whenever new equipment is purchased or repairs are made to the classroom, the school, or the school's exterior, comment on the planning that took place before the arrangements were made to purchase materials and services.

## Family Interventions

**Intermediate and Secondary Levels.**  At these levels, urge the parents to involve their youngster in family-oriented discussions involving budgeting and the setting of short- and long-range plans, including plans involving work and leisure activities.

Remind the parents to include their youngster in discussions that deal with plans that directly influence his or her school placement, education, and future life, including such serious topics as living arrangements, courtship and marriage, sexuality and family planning, health and safety, and matters that deal with spiritual as well as mental and physical well-being.

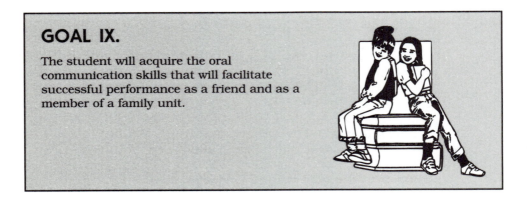

## GOAL IX.

The student will acquire the oral communication skills that will facilitate successful performance as a friend and as a member of a family unit.

# SPECIFIC OBJECTIVES

The student:

- ❒ A. Acquires and maintains friendships.

- ❒ B. Seeks the assistance of friends and family members, when needed, and responds appropriately to requests for assistance from friends and relatives.

- ❒ C. Communicates with friends and relatives on a regular basis by telephone or in person, as appropriate to the situation.

- ❒ D. Responds to the invitations of friends and relatives and invites friends and relatives to share in various social activities, including holiday meals, religious observances, parties, family celebrations, and diverse recreational activities.

- ❒ E. Provides emotional support and comfort to friends and family members during times of need and personal, family, and other crises.

- ❒ F. Responds appropriately to friends' and family members' requests for advice and counseling, when appropriate, and seeks advice and counseling from appropriate friends and family members.

❒ G. Communicates needs, feelings, and thoughts to friends and family members, including, when applicable, the student's spouse (e.g., family planning and specific needs relevant to affection and sexual practices) and children.

❒ H. Participates in simple conversations (small talk) with friends and family members.

❒ I. Participates in important discussions with friends concerning communication problems, dating and courtship, and recreational matters and with family members concerning family matters, for example, illness or death in the family, the financial needs of family members, family misunderstandings and quarrels, educational and employment concerns, and short- and long-term planning.

❒ J. Teaches family members, including any children of his or her own, specific skills and knowledge.

# SUGGESTED ACTIVITIES

---

☎ Specific Objective A

The student acquires and maintains friendships.

---

## Teacher Interventions

**Infant and Toddler/Preschool Level.**   Identify a peer of the student with a similar temperament and personality and similar interests and abilities. Assign them a task that requires two people (including cooperative tasks), and observe their behavior. Stop the student if he or she engages in any behaviors that disturb or annoy the peer and substitute a more constructive and friendly behavior.

Provide as many positive interactions as possible until the students begin to seek out each other's company independently of you. In this way, attempt to build two or three relationships with peers that are friendly ones.

**Primary Level.**   Share with the student the ways you and people you have known have acquired friends. Review these techniques, and ask the student to describe how he or she acquired a friend. (See Figure 2.44.)

They meet in neighborhood play areas.

They belong to the same group (e.g., Boy Scouts and Girl Scouts) or club.

They go to the same church or temple or meet at a social function held there.

They attend the same school or Sunday or Saturday school.

They meet at a community leisure site such as a bowling alley, shopping mall, movie theater, or skating rink.

They meet at a party or other social gathering at a friend's, neighbor's, or relative's home.

They are introduced by a friend or family member.

They go to the same gym or physical fitness center.

They take private lessons from the same teacher or at the same center.

They belong to the same sports team.

They meet because their parents are friends of each other.

They meet at a rehabilitation agency, hospital, clinic, or other service agency.

**FIGURE 2.44.**   Some of the ways people meet and acquire friends.

**Intermediate and Secondary Levels.**   Discuss with the student the behaviors that help to maintain friendships. Following these conversations, role-play these strategies. (See Figure 2.45.)

## Family Interventions

**Infant and Toddler/Preschool Level.**   Ask the parents to arrange situations in which their child has the opportunity to play with other children who live in the neighborhood or who are members of their social groups. Suggest that they invite these potential friends to their home to participate in interesting games and leisure activities.

**Primary Level.**   Encourage the parents to share with their child how they have acquired and maintained friends in their own life. Also, ask them to observe their child as he or she interacts with friends and to reward behaviors that help to maintain friendships (e.g., "I really like the way you gave your new truck to Audrey to play with first!"), to reprimand the child for not acting in a friendly way (e.g., "You should apologize to Bonnie for playing with her doll and getting it dirty"), and to provide the child with new strategies (e.g., "Why don't you ask Joe to go to the zoo with us?").

---

Invite them to your home to play, for meals, and for parties.

Invite them to join you in community-based recreational activities, like going shopping.

Share experiences, tell anecdotes, and otherwise engage in small talk and serious conversations.

Engage together in hobbies and projects.

Remember their special occasions; join them in celebrating events such as birthdays and remember to send greeting cards and give gifts.

Comfort them when they are sad, upset, or grieving.

Communicate with them on a regular basis, face-to-face, by telephone, and in writing.

Assist them when they need help.

Provide them with advice and counseling when appropriate.

Avoid exploiting them, acting immature, being selfish, or engaging in other behaviors that may result in quarrels and friction and may end the friendship.

---

**FIGURE 2.45.**    Some ways to maintain friendships with others.

**Intermediate and Secondary Levels.**    Encourage the parents to review with their youngster ways to acquire and maintain friendships, as presented in the Teacher Interventions. Tell them to develop those that are appropriate to the age of their youngster, for example, "I think it would be a good idea to go to the barn dance. You might meet someone new whom you might like for a friend" or "Audrey thinks you should invite your friend Pat over to stay the weekend. She needs to be in the company of a good friend to help her through this sad time since her father died."

---

☎ ## Specific Objective B

The student seeks the assistance of friends and family members, when needed, and responds appropriately to requests for assistance from friends and relatives.

---

## Teacher Interventions

**Infant and Toddler/Preschool Level.**    Assist the student in differentiating between situations in which he or she needs your help and those in which he or she does not, for example, "You don't need my help taking off your coat. Do it yourself!" or "While you buttoned the large buttons on your shirt (or blouse) all by yourself, you do need help to button the small buttons on your sleeve."

**Primary Level.** Model asking for help from others in a way that is likely to gain that help, for example, "I am having trouble opening this carton of supplies. Mark, please help me!" Reward the student for asking for *needed* help in a socially acceptable way. Correct the student when he or she seeks help in an inappropriate way, such as pulling the sleeve of a classmate or whining when asking for assistance.

**Intermediate and Secondary Levels.** Give the student projects or tasks that require the collaboration or cooperation of others, whether these tasks are recreational ones (e.g., "Please hold the other end of the rope so our friends can jump rope") or work-oriented (e.g., "Please mash the potatoes and open the cans of cranberries while I carve the turkey for our luncheon party").

## Family Interventions

**Infant and Toddler/Preschool Level.** Ask the parents to help their child differentiate between situations in which he or she needs their help and those in which he or she does not, for example, "You can drink from the cup. You *don't* need to use a baby bottle anymore" or "Yes, you *do* need help eating the soup by yourself even though you can use the spoon to eat the mashed potatoes without our help."

**Primary Level.** Encourage the parents to demonstrate asking family members for help in an acceptable way, for example, "It is hard for me to reach the top shelf of the closet. Mark, you've grown so tall that it is easy for you. Please bring me the package of rice from the pantry closet." Remind the parents to praise their child for asking for needed help in a socially acceptable way and to correct the child when he or she does so in an inappropriate way, for example, demanding the help of a family member who is occupied with an important task.

**Intermediate and Secondary Levels.** At these levels, encourage the parents to give their youngster household chores that he or she will need to do with someone else or will do more efficiently with the help of others, for example, "Please fold the sheets for the king-size bed and put them away" or "It is that time again—spring cleaning. You and your brothers and sister are responsible for doing it since Dad is working overtime and I have to visit and take care of Grandma, who just got home from the hospital and needs special care."

---

☎   ## Specific Objective C

The student communicates with friends and relatives on a regular basis by telephone or in person, as appropriate to the situation.

---

## Teacher Interventions

**Infant and Toddler/Preschool Level.**   Say to the student, while working with him or her on a one-to-one basis, for example, "Oh, I forgot to tell David (a classmate) that he has to go to see Ms. Travalino, the physical therapist, this morning at 10:00 instead of 11:00. Excuse me while I give him the message." When there is a need for the student to communicate with classmates on these occasions, point out the reason for the communication.

**Primary Level.**   Using real but unconnected telephones, role-play calling friends and relatives and making appointments to see or join them in an activity of interest, for example, "I need to go shopping for new shoes. Can you go with me to Southpark Mall this evening to help me pick them out?" Follow up by asking the student to role-play making similar telephone calls to friends and/or relatives.

**Intermediate and Secondary Levels.**   At these levels, role-play making telephone calls that deal with more serious matters, such as calling a friend or relative to ask about the status of someone who has been ill or, when appropriate, calling a special "friend" to ask for a date.

## Family Interventions

**Infant and Toddler/Preschool Level.**   Ask the parents to interrupt quiet activities with their child by announcing that they have to give a family member, who is nearby, a message, for example, "Oh, I forgot to tell LaToya that her friend, Karen, called and wanted her to call back as soon as possible. Excuse me while I give her the message."

Ask the parents also to interrupt quiet activities with the child by saying, "I must telephone Aunt Jessica to tell her that I need her help this evening in making the fried chicken for tomorrow's family reunion."

**Primary Level.**   Encourage the parents to call friends and relatives in the presence of their child. Suggest that after the telephone call has been made, they say such things as "I'm glad my friend, Alice, was home because I needed to speak to her about the fund drive for the school library." Remind the parents to encourage the child to use the telephone to communicate with relatives and friends.

**Intermediate and Secondary Levels.**   At these levels, ask the parents to give their youngster the task of making telephone calls to relatives and friends, for example, "My hands are dirty from housecleaning; please call Uncle Max and remind him to bring the folding chairs for the cookout" or "I'm busy writing the checks to pay the monthly bills; please call my friend, Bob, and explain that I'm running late and I'll meet him at the bowling alley instead of picking him up."

---

 ## Specific Objective D

The student responds to the invitations of friends and relatives and invites friends and relatives to share in various social activities, including holiday meals, religious observances, parties, family celebrations, and diverse recreational activities.

---

## Teacher Interventions

**Infant and Toddler/Preschool and Primary Levels.**   Ask a fellow teacher to invite your class to view a class play or other presentation or to join the class for a snack or lunch. Tell the student that he or she is invited and explain how much you would like to join the other class for the event. Comment on how nice it is to be invited to share pleasant experiences.

   Follow up by arranging for the student and his or her classmates to reciprocate, by inviting the other teacher's class to participate in an activity held in your classroom.

**Intermediate and Secondary Levels.**   Invite another class or classes to join your class in going on a field trip. Also, prepare an art exhibit, a choral reading, a musical presentation of dance and song, a play, a puppet show, or a pantomime, and invite other classes, school administrators, parents, and family members to the performance. Design written invitations and ask the student to deliver them and to formally invite the recipients.

## Family Interventions

**Infant and Toddler/Preschool and Primary Levels.**   Ask the parents to share invitations from friends and relatives for events to which their child is also invited.

Suggest that they say such things as "Our friend, Mrs. Hartman, has invited us to a pool party this Saturday. I know how you love to go swimming, so we were glad to accept the invitation." They should follow up by discussing the need to reciprocate by inviting the Hartman family to join their family on a trip to the zoo.

**Intermediate and Secondary Levels.**  Ask the parents to invite friends and relatives to join them for family celebrations such as holiday meals. Tell them to give their youngster the task of doing the inviting in person or by telephone. Encourage them to arrange for the youngster to have his or her own party or activity to which he or she will invite friends (e.g., a slumber party) and relatives (e.g., the child's confirmation, bar or bas mitzvah, or graduation).

---

 ## Specific Objective E

The student provides emotional support and comfort to friends and family members during times of need and personal, family, and other crises.

---

## Teacher Interventions

**Infant and Toddler/Preschool Level.**  Demonstrate the appropriate way to comfort someone who is in distress by role-playing comforting a doll or stuffed animal. Comfort the student when he or she is upset.

**Primary Level.**  Discuss and demonstrate the body language signs that indicate that a person needs to be comforted. Talk about the fact that talking to someone or hugging someone are not the only ways to comfort someone. Explain that holding another person's hand and just listening sympathetically are also ways of comforting others. Conduct several role plays in which the student uses different comforting behaviors.

**Intermediate and Secondary Levels.**  At these levels, discuss crises that people face and when friends and relatives need to comfort them during these crises. Discuss such crises as serious illness, injury, the death of a loved one, divorce, the loss of a job, and being the victim of a crime. Role-play some of these situations, and monitor the student to make certain that he or she is being a source of comfort in a suitable way.

## Family Interventions

**Infant and Toddler/Preschool and Primary Levels.** Encourage the parents to demonstrate the appropriate way to comfort someone whenever their child or another family member is in distress. Tell them to explain how being comforted helps to ease the "pain" of the person being comforted and also makes the person doing the comforting feel better. If they agree and believe it is appropriate, suggest that the parents and child comfort each other whenever the occasion presents itself.

**Intermediate and Secondary Levels.** At these levels, ask the parents to discuss actual crises that are being experienced by friends and relatives. Encourage them to discuss these crises and demonstrate how they give emotional support (e.g., making telephone calls and sending cards, flowers, and fruit baskets) and to provide direct comfort by visiting the person at his or her home, the hospital, or a place of mourning.

---

☎ ### Specific Objective F

The student responds appropriately to friends' and family members' requests for advice and counseling, when appropriate, and seeks advice and counseling from appropriate friends and family members.

---

## Teacher Interventions

**Intermediate Level.** Present the student with school-related decisions that need to be made (in a role play or in response to actual occurrences), for example, "I need your advice on where we should go on our walk in the community to see the spring flowers. Should we go to Byrd Park, the botanical gardens, or someplace else in the community? What do you suggest?"

**Secondary Level.** Involve the student in role plays in which he or she plays various family members (parent, child, spouse, younger sibling, older sibling, sibling of the same sex, sibling of the opposite sex, or grandparent). Provide experiences in which the student gives advice or counseling and others in which he or she seeks advice or counseling. (See Figures 2.46 and 2.47.)

## Family Interventions

**Intermediate Level.** Ask the parents to provide their youngster with family-oriented problems that require his or her advice, for example, "We need your

| Role | Sample Situation |
|---|---|
| Parent | Advising a child who believes he or she is being exploited by a friend |
| Child | Telling a parent his or her preference for an activity |
| Spouse | Advising a mate who is experiencing difficulties on his or her job |
| Younger sibling | Counseling the sibling on inappropriate behavior with strangers |
| Older sibling | Reporting on a sale for a clothing item that the older sibling would like to buy |
| Same-sex sibling | Advising the sibling on matters relevant to menstruation (female) and nocturnal emissions (male) |
| Opposite-sex sibling | Counseling the sibling on dating and courtship practices |
| Grandparent | Giving a son or daughter advice on household furnishings |

**FIGURE 2.46.** Giving advice and counseling.

| Role | Sample Situation |
|---|---|
| Parent | Asking a grandparent about recommended disciplinary practices |
| Child | Asking a parent how to deal with a peer who is physically aggressive |
| Spouse | Asking a mate for his or her advice about a physical condition and whether or not to go to a physician |
| Younger sibling | Asking an older sibling what to do about his or her poor report card |
| Older sibling | Asking a younger sibling which outfit looks best on him or her |
| Same-sex sibling | Asking a same-sex sibling about sexual matters |
| Opposite-sex sibling | Asking an opposite-sex sibling about the best way to attract someone of the opposite sex |
| Grandparent | Asking a son or daughter for advice on vacation plans |

**FIGURE 2.47.** Seeking advice and counseling.

advice on what should be done about the neighbor's dog who barks all night long and keeps us awake. Should we call the police or should we talk to the neighbors directly? What do you think?"

**Secondary Level.**   Encourage the parents to involve their youngster in actual family interactions in which he or she is asked for advice and to engage in role plays in which the youngster asks actual family members for advice or counseling.

Also, tell the parents that whenever the youngster needs advice, they should direct him or her to the most appropriate family member for that advice (e.g., an older sibling of the same sex for advice on courtship) and respond themselves when it is appropriate (e.g., in matters concerning birth control and family planning).

---

 ## Specific Objective G

The student communicates needs, feelings, and thoughts to friends and family members, including, when applicable, the student's spouse (e.g., family planning and specific needs relevant to affection and sexual practices) and children.

---

## Teacher Interventions

**Intermediate and Secondary Levels.**   Engage the student in role plays in which he or she expresses his or her needs, feelings, and thoughts to friends and family members; for example, in communicating with a friend, the student might say, "I am hurt that you didn't ask me to go with you to the mall when you were going with our other close friend, Juan!" and in communicating with a mate, the student might say, "We really need to discuss how we feel about having children and what size family we would like to have!"

## Family Interventions

**Infant and Toddler/Preschool and Primary Levels.**   Ask the parents to interact with their youngster, at the preschool and primary levels, on a one-to-one basis in which they share needs, feelings, and thoughts. For example, they might discuss personal hygiene and grooming; family routines, rules, regulations, and consequences; interpersonal relationships in the family; budgetary needs; discipline; recreational activity preferences; and all other pertinent matters that have a direct impact on the child's daily life in the home and the community.

**Intermediate and Secondary Levels.**  At the intermediate and secondary levels, tell the parents to schedule interactions with family groups. Make certain that they understand that the subjects to be discussed should be determined by the maturity of the student and should be age-appropriate and age-specific, when applicable.

---

 ## Specific Objective H

The student participates in simple conversations (small talk) with friends and family members.

---

## Teacher Interventions

**Infant and Toddler/Preschool Level.**  Schedule a sharing time ("Show and Tell") in which you engage in simple conversations with the student. Model sharing some "news" such as "I watched the Baltimore Orioles on television last night and they won the game" or "I got caught in the rain yesterday and got all wet. The weather report is for more rain today, and I wanted to work in my garden." Follow up by asking the student to share some "news" with you.

**Primary, Intermediate, and Secondary Levels.**  On a daily basis, schedule a class period to hold simple conversations about casual or nonserious topics such as the weather, sports events, toys and games, television programs and movies, personal recreational activities, clothing and clothing styles, performing artists, and foods and restaurants.

Explain that these topics are suitable for conversations with most people and in most places. If the student brings up a topic that is not small talk, tell him or her that the topic is one that should be discussed with only certain people and at certain times. (See Goal VIII, Specific Objective L.) Choose topics for each of the three levels based on the age of the student.

## Family Interventions

**Infant and Toddler/Preschool Level.**  Ask the parents to engage their child in simple conversations, especially during meals and playtimes. Tell them to talk about the toys and the food, even if they believe that the child does not comprehend all that is being said.

**Primary, Intermediate, and Secondary Levels.** Tell the parents to schedule a time of the day when the family gets together for the purpose of holding simple conversations about casual or nonserious topics (see Teacher Interventions). Remind them that if the child raises a topic that is not small talk, they should tell him or her that the topic is one that should be discussed privately or during a family discussion time when serious matters are examined. (See Goal VIII, Specific Objective L.) Choose topics for each of the three levels based on the age of the student.

---

### ☎ Specific Objective I

The student participates in important discussions with friends concerning communication problems, dating and courtship, and recreational matters and with family members concerning family matters, for example, illness or death in the family, the financial needs of family members, family misunderstandings and quarrels, educational and employment concerns, and short- and long-term planning.

---

## Teacher Interventions

**Intermediate and Secondary Levels.** Engage the student in role plays in which he or she participates in group discussions with either a group of peers or a family group. Discuss such topics as dating and courtship, sex and marriage, family planning, leisure-time pursuits, illness and death, financial and economic matters, misunderstandings and quarrels, educational and employment concerns, and short- and long-term planning.

(Note: Discuss these topics with the parents to determine whether some discussions may conflict with family values and beliefs.)

## Family Interventions

**Intermediate and Secondary Levels.** Ask the parents to set aside times for family discussions on serious topics and to discuss personal matters and issues (see Teacher Interventions). Encourage the parents also to deal with these matters whenever they arise, when they are apparently disturbing, or when the child seeks advice and counsel directly.

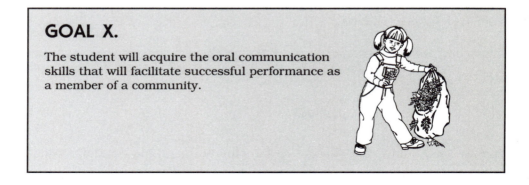

---

### ☎ Specific Objective J

The student teaches family members, including any children of his or her own, specific skills and knowledge.

---

## Teacher Interventions

**Primary, Intermediate, and Secondary Levels.** Identify a skill that the student possesses and is able to teach a peer. Assign him or her the task of teaching this skill to a classmate. Guide the student as he or she tutors the peer, providing assistance as needed. Give the student additional opportunities to teach someone a skill.

Explain that he or she may have children of his or her own someday and may have to teach them some things, such as how to eat by themselves; how to dress, undress, and groom themselves; and how to take care of their clothing and personal property. If feasible, practice child care activities with dolls.

## Family Interventions

**Intermediate and Secondary Levels.** Ask the parents to identify tasks that their youngster is able to teach another family member. Remind them to provide needed assistance when the child is actually carrying out the teaching assignment. Encourage them to give the youngster as many opportunities as possible to teach a skill to a family member.

Tell the parents that if there is a baby, toddler, or other young child in the family, they should show the youngster how to care for the child. Urge them to give the youngster a baby-sitting task with a younger sibling when the youngster demonstrates the skill to do so independently and in a responsible and safe manner.

## GOAL X.

The student will acquire the oral communication skills that will facilitate successful performance as a member of a community.

# SPECIFIC OBJECTIVES

The student:

☐ A. Plans, with neighbors and friends in the community, neighborhood clean-up campaigns and other efforts to conserve and beautify the environment.

☐ B. Comprehends, internalizes, and obeys the laws and regulations that have been established for the community.

☐ C. Comprehends, internalizes, and obeys the regulations of public and private agencies in the community.

☐ D. Uses a telephone to obtain help during an emergency.

☐ E. Seeks the help of police, special police, and security guards during a potentially dangerous or life-threatening situation or when a crime is taking place or has taken place.

☐ F. Comprehends and internalizes his or her rights as a citizen and special rights as a person with disabilities and makes certain that he or she is not denied those rights.

# SUGGESTED ACTIVITIES

---

☏ ## Specific Objective A

The student plans, with neighbors and friends in the community, neighborhood clean-up campaigns and other efforts to conserve and beautify the environment.

---

## Teacher Interventions

**Infant and Toddler/Preschool Level.** Involve the student in keeping the classroom neat, well ordered, and clean. Assign the student the task of keeping his or her desk and area around the desk clean and neat. Involve the student, also, in decorating the room and in changing bulletin boards and exhibit table displays.

**Primary Level.** Give the student responsibility for taking care of special classroom exhibits and furnishings, such as selecting and taking care of plants, terraria, and aquaria.

**Intermediate Level.** Engage the student in campaigns to clean up the school play area and the area around the school. If possible, plant a flower garden near the school building and assign the student the task of watering and tending the plants.

**Secondary Level.** Become part of the "Adopt a Street" or "Adopt a Highway" campaigns by adopting a street near the school, which you, the student, and his or her classmates share the responsibility for maintaining. Be sure to observe safety factors during clean-up times.

## Family Interventions

**Infant and Toddler/Preschool Level.** Encourage the parents to assign their child household cleaning and maintenance chores. Ask them to also involve the child in household decoration and furnishing activities, for example, asking the child to assist them in hanging up a new picture; taking him or her on a visit to a florist or floral section of the supermarket and saying, "Let's pick out some flowers to put on the kitchen table"; or saying, when buying furniture, "I think this is a beautiful couch. The color is right, and the price is right."

Remind the parents that their child does not need to understand all the words being said. The involvement in the functional behavior is the primary goal at this level.

**Primary Level.** Encourage the parents to assign their child the responsibility for cleaning and maintaining his or her own bedroom. Also, tell them to assist the child in keeping closets, drawers, and other storage areas neat and well ordered.

**Intermediate Level.** Ask the parents to involve their youngster in maintaining the appearance of the outside of the house, including the care of any lawn and garden areas. Also, at this level, encourage them to give the youngster increasing responsibility for selecting furniture and furnishings for his or her own bedroom.

**Secondary Level.** Ask the parents to volunteer for and involve their youngster in community clean-up campaigns and other citizen efforts to conserve and beautify the environment.

---

☎ **Specific Objective B**

The student comprehends, internalizes, and obeys the laws and regulations that have been established for the community.

---

## Teacher Interventions

**Infant and Toddler/Preschool Level.** Establish routines, rules, regulations, and consequences for classroom behavior. Be consistent in applying these rules and in dispensing consequences.

**Primary Level.** Ask the student to describe and explain the reasons for the rules and regulations that govern the class. Whenever the student fails to observe a rule or regulation, be sure to apply the consequence *and* expect the student to state the applicable rule or regulation.

When the student observes a rule or regulation, be sure to apply the positive consequence and to comment on the specific rule that was observed, for example, "You remembered to clean your desk and wash your hands before going to lunch. I didn't have to remind you. Wonderful!"

**Intermediate and Secondary Levels.** At these levels, concentrate on the rules and regulations established for the school itself. Also, review the rules and laws of the student's community, for example, "Our county has a local leash law. What does that mean we must do, and what may happen if someone doesn't obey this law?" "Our town prohibits burning of leaves before sundown. What does this mean we shouldn't do, and what may happen if we don't obey this law?" or "Our city, because of the current water shortage, forbids watering lawns on Mondays, Wednesdays, and Fridays. What does this mean we *can do* and *shouldn't do?*"

## Family Interventions

**Infant and Toddler/Preschool Level.** Urge the parents to establish household routines, rules, regulations, and consequences for all family members. Remind them to apply these rules and dispense the agreed-upon consequences to all family members, especially in the child's presence.

**Primary Level.** Encourage the parents to ask their child to periodically describe household rules and regulations, the reasons why they are necessary, and their identified consequences. Remind them that when they apply positive consequences, they should comment on the rule that was observed, for example, "You picked all your dirty clothes off the floor and placed them in the laundry basket, and I didn't have to remind you. Great!"

Also, remind the parents that when they apply negative consequences, they should comment on the rule that was disobeyed, for example, "You made yourself a snack but didn't clean up afterward. You left a mess and didn't put food away. You know what that means." (At this point the parents should seek a response from the child!) "Yes, that's right—you cannot watch television this evening!"

**Intermediate and Secondary Levels.** At these levels, ask the parents to concentrate on the rules and regulations established by the community in which they live, for example, "Our city has alternate-side-of-the-street parking regulations. What does that mean drivers must do, and what might happen if people fail to obey this regulation?" "Our county requires its residents to have smoke detectors in their homes. What does this mean that people who live in this county must do, and what are the possible things that might happen if a person doesn't obey this law?" or "Our town has laws against dumping trash except in the town dump. What does this mean we should do with trash if we don't have a trash pickup service?"

---

☎ **Specific Objective C**

The student comprehends, internalizes, and obeys the regulations of public and private agencies in the community.

---

## Teacher Interventions

**Primary, Intermediate, and Secondary Levels.** Take the student for a trip to a public library or a museum. Point out how the people there are behaving, and explain about situation-specific behavior, in other words, say that there are places where we should be very quiet (talking only in a whisper), places where we may talk at a normal level, and places where we may talk loudly or even shout. Follow up this explanation by taking the student to a place where he or she may talk above a whisper and a place where the student may talk loudly or even shout. (See Figure 2.48.)

## Family Interventions

**Primary, Intermediate, and Secondary Levels.** Review Figure 2.48 with the parents and ask them to provide their youngster with these different experiences,

| Quiet Places | Normal Talking | Loud Talking or Shouting |
|---|---|---|
| Hospitals | School (during conversations and discussions) | At a sports stadium |
| Libraries | | On the playground |
| School (during quiet activities) | Family discussions | During an outdoor game |
| Church, temple, mosque | Friends' homes | At a rock concert |
| | At a party | At a political rally |
| Funerals | At a group meeting | On the floor of the stock exchange |
| Movies | In one-on-one talks | At picnic games such as relay and sack races |
| Theaters | When answering a teacher's questions | |

**FIGURE 2.48.**   Appropriate talking and vocalization levels.

when possible. Remind them to demonstrate and explain the difference in talking levels at these places and in these situations.

Also, ask the parents to review the regulations of public and private agencies in the community with which they and the student come into contact and those with which they are likely to come into contact in the future, such as a clinic, a social service agency, a state employment office, diverse recreational sites (e.g., public and private swimming pools), and various business enterprises.

---

 ## Specific Objective D

The student uses a telephone to obtain help during an emergency.

---

## Teacher Interventions

**Primary Level.**   Demonstrate with an unconnected telephone how to call 911 or other emergency numbers pertinent to the community. Describe the difference between emergency situations and situations that require some degree of assistance but do not involve calling emergency numbers. (See Goal VIII, Specific Objective B.)

Visit fire, police, and first-aid stations as well as the ambulance sections of hospitals, if possible.

**Intermediate and Secondary Levels.**   Videotape a television program, such as "911," that dramatizes emergencies and depicts a person who uses a telephone to call for help. Follow up by role-playing different emergency situations. Make sure that the student provides the operator with the previously established details of the location and type of emergency. If possible (and with parental permission) visit a hospital emergency room.

## Family Interventions

**Primary Level.**   Ask the parents to demonstrate with an unconnected telephone how to call 911 or other emergency numbers pertinent to their community. Remind them to review the difference between emergency situations and situations that require some degree of assistance but do not involve calling emergency numbers. (See Goal IX, Specific Objective B.)

**Intermediate and Secondary Levels.**   Ask the parents to tell their youngster anecdotes about various types of emergencies from their own experiences, the experiences of people they know, and incidents they have read about or seen on television. Suggest that they point out emergency vehicles that they see on trips in the community.

---

### ☎ Specific Objective E

The student seeks the help of police, special police, and security guards during a potentially dangerous or life-threatening situation or when a crime is taking place or has taken place.

---

## Teacher Interventions

**Primary Level.**   Take the student to a community facility that has special police or security guards, such as a shopping mall, a bank, or a sports event. Explain their purpose, and role-play seeking their help when witnessing (or having witnessed) a crime or becoming a victim of a crime.

**Intermediate and Secondary Levels.**   Invite a police officer to class to discuss (a) what people can do to lessen the likelihood that they might be a crime victim, (b) what people should do if they witness a crime, and (c) what people should do if they see something that is highly suspicious, for example, if they return to their home and find the front door open and the lock broken. Follow up by engaging the student in role plays in which he or she seeks the assistance of a police officer, a security guard, or a special police officer.

## Family Interventions

**Primary Level.**   Encourage the parents to take their child to a public place that has security guards, such as an amusement park, a county fair, or a sports arena. Tell them to point out that these special community helpers are needed to control the crowds, to handle emergencies (e.g., accidents and illness), and to prevent crime. If possible, suggest that the parents engage one of the security guards in a brief discussion in the child's presence.

**Intermediate and Secondary Levels.**   Ask the parents to share anecdotes and news accounts about how security guards and special police have thwarted crimes and handled emergencies. Suggest that they engage their youngster in role plays in which the youngster seeks the help of the police, security guards, or special police in an emergency situation.

 ## Specific Objective F

The student comprehends and internalizes his or her rights as a citizen and special rights as a person with disabilities and makes certain that he or she is not denied those rights.

## Teacher Interventions

**Intermediate Level.**   At this level, review with the student the rights that all citizens have. Discuss what these rights are and what the student should do if someone or some agency has denied him or her these basic rights of citizenship. (See Figure 2.49.)

**Secondary Level.**   At this level, review with the student the rights that he or she has, based on his or her disability status. Review P.L. 94-142 and its several amendments (including P.L. 101-476, IDEA) and the Americans with Disabilities Act, P.L. 101-336. (See Figure 2.50.)

To receive eligible government-supported benefits, entitlements, and services

To choose a religion (if desired) and practice the religion of one's choice

To express oneself freely in speech and general behavior and appearance, with some limited restrictions

To obtain needed medical and other services of one's choice

To rent and purchase housing and personal property of one's choice

To travel freely within one's country and its possessions

To marry, have children, and raise them as desired (with some limitations resulting from child protection laws)

To have the right to legal counsel and to take legal action against others for grievances and the protection against self-incrimination

To have the right to vote

**FIGURE 2.49.** Some basic legal rights.

## Family Interventions

**Intermediate Level.** Ask the parents to point out to their youngster the behaviors in which they engage that are guaranteed by federal and state constitutions and legislation, for example, voting, attending and participating in a religion, giving an opinion at a town meeting, and obtaining legal counsel in a dispute with a neighbor.

**Secondary Level.** Ask the parents to point out to their youngster the rights they have as parents of a youngster with a disability, especially as they relate to federal and state special education laws and bylaws. (Note: Obtain

To obtain a free and appropriate public education and related services according to stipulated federal and state guidelines

To obtain due-process rights in educational evaluation, placement, program design, and program implementation

To participate, when appropriate, in the design of education and transition plans and rehabilitation and adult service plans

To obtain employment without being discriminated against because of a disability

To obtain access to the courts, public buildings, and public transportation

To obtain access to all personal, school, and medical records and to deny access to others

**FIGURE 2.50.** Special legal rights of persons with disabilities.

your State Department of Education's pamphlet on the rights of parents of students with disabilities under federal and state law. Review these pamphlets with the parents.)

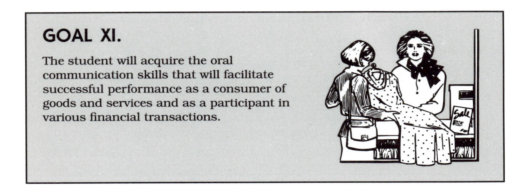

## GOAL XI.

The student will acquire the oral communication skills that will facilitate successful performance as a consumer of goods and services and as a participant in various financial transactions.

## SPECIFIC OBJECTIVES

The student:

❐ A. Makes needed purchases of food; clothing and household linens; medicines, medications, vitamins, and minerals; grooming and personal hygiene materials and equipment; educational, assistive, and prosthetic devices; household cleaning and maintenance products and equipment; furniture, accessories, and appliances; cooking, serving, and eating utensils; entertainment and other recreational materials and equipment; indoor and outdoor plants; and pets and pet supplies.

❐ B. Contacts and arranges for needed services, including medical and health services, non-health-related professional services (e.g., attorneys, counselors, and consumer advocates), repair persons, grooming and physical fitness services, and services from private and public agencies and companies.

❐ C. Engages in financial transactions with bank personnel.

❐ D. Rents or purchases suitable living quarters.

❐ E. Purchases needed insurance from insurance agents or agencies.

❐ F. Communicates with an appropriate individual for the purpose of completing relevant tax forms.

❏ G. Negotiates agreements and contractual relationships.

❏ H. Engages in an investment program with an appropriate investment adviser.

# SUGGESTED ACTIVITIES

---

☎ ## Specific Objective A

The student makes needed purchases of food; clothing and household linens; medicines, medications, vitamins, and minerals; grooming and personal hygiene materials and equipment; educational, assistive, and prosthetic devices; household cleaning and maintenance products and equipment; furniture, accessories, and appliances; cooking, serving, and eating utensils; entertainment and other recreational materials and equipment; indoor and outdoor plants; and pets and pet supplies.

---

## Teacher Interventions

**Primary Level.**  If you have a petty cash fund for small purchases, involve the student in decision-making discussions of how to spend this money for classroom supplies and materials. Take the student to a store to observe you as you make these purchases. Comment on the price of the item, the money used to make the purchase, and your verification of change received.

**Intermediate and Secondary Levels.**  Set up a class store, or encourage the school to establish a school store at which the student can purchase school and grooming supplies. Schedule a weekly visit to the school store. Pay particular attention to the way the student communicates with salespeople.

During leisure-time educational activities, play table games such as "Monopoly" and other real-life games that involve monetary transactions and negotiations.

## Family Interventions

**Infant and Toddler/Preschool Level.**  Ask the parents to take their child along on shopping trips. Encourage them to point out to the child that they are using money (or food stamps) to make *needed* purchases for the household and for personal use by family members.

**Primary Level.** At this level, encourage the parents to concentrate on making purchases of particular interest to their child. Suggest that they involve the child in decision-making discussions of what he or she needs or would like to purchase in terms of preferred food and clothing, required grooming and personal hygiene supplies, necessary assistive and prosthetic devices, furniture and accessories for his or her bedroom, and recreational materials and equipment for leisure-time interests. Suggest that the parents listen carefully to the child as he or she makes these purchases.

**Intermediate and Secondary Levels.** Encourage the parents to provide their youngster with an allowance and with opportunities to earn extra money for special chores. Ask them to assist him or her in establishing a personal budget, creating a personal shopping list, and making the needed purchases with his or her own money. Suggest that they no longer accompany the youngster on shopping trips when he or she has demonstrated sufficient competency in handling money and in the oral language elements of the task.

---

 ## Specific Objective B

The student contacts and arranges for needed services, including medical and health services, non-health-related professional services (e.g., attorneys, counselors, and consumer advocates), repair persons, grooming and physical fitness services, and services from private and public agencies and companies.

---

## Teacher Interventions

**Primary Level.** Whenever classroom repair and maintenance services are required, discuss them with the student, and explain that you need to contact the custodian or cleaning staff to obtain these needed services. Make sure the student is present when you discuss the needed repairs or service with the cleaning staff or the custodian.

Also, when taking field trips that require rental of a bus, make the arrangements in the presence of the student.

| Problem or Situation | Service Person or Agency |
|---|---|
| You have a fever of 102 degrees. | A physician |
| You have injured your leg and your physician wants you to get special exercises to strengthen it. | A physical therapist |
| You need to improve your eating skills and need special utensils made and instruction in their use. | An occupational therapist |
| You wish to improve your speech so that you will be more favorably viewed by members of the opposite sex. | A speech and language pathologist |
| You wish to have your artificial leg replaced since you've grown taller. | A prosthetist |
| You think your hearing has deteriorated and wish to be tested for a new hearing aid. | An audiologist |
| You were injured in an automobile accident that was not your fault. | An attorney |
| You have been very depressed lately. | A psychiatrist or a psychologist |
| The water pipe in your basement is leaking. | A plumber |
| You have discovered termites in your house's foundation. | An exterminator |
| You want to have your hair restyled. | A beautician |
| You are seeking food stamps, because you lost your job. | Social Services |
| You want to donate blood for the community blood drive. | The Red Cross |
| You left your umbrella on the bus. | The Transportation Department's lost-and-found |
| You wish to cancel a check. | The bank in which you have an account |

**FIGURE 2.51.** Problem situations and helping agents.

**Intermediate and Secondary Levels.** Engage the student in role plays in which he or she must seek needed services from a variety of service personnel or agencies, that is, give the student a hypothetical problem or situation and ask him or her to select the appropriate one to meet his or her needs. (See Figure 2.51.)

## Family Interventions

**Primary Level.**   Urge the parents to involve their child in any contacts they make with service personnel and service agencies, for example, "I am really suffering this spring with sinus problems; listen while I call my doctor," "The house hasn't been painted in 7 years and really needs to be painted; listen while I telephone the painter," or "I want to do some aerobic exercises; listen while I call the Chester Health and Fitness Center to get information about the cost and the times available."

**Intermediate and Secondary Levels.**   Suggest to the parents that they ask their youngster to indicate what person or agency to call whenever problem situations arise. Encourage them to expect the youngster, when he or she is able, to make the call and to negotiate times and costs, if applicable.

---

 ## Specific Objective C

The student engages in financial transactions with bank personnel.

---

## Teacher Interventions

**Primary Level.**   Engage the student in a role play in which you play the part of a teller and the student wishes to exchange coins for bills and vice versa.

**Intermediate Level.**   Set up a classroom bank in which the student can make deposits and withdrawals. If you employ a token reinforcement system, provide the opportunity for the student to deposit and withdraw tokens he or she has received.

Take a trip to a neighborhood bank. Obtain deposit and withdrawal slips and application forms for opening savings and checking accounts to use in relevant classroom activities.

**Secondary Level.**   Invite a bank officer to the class to discuss the various services available, including various types of savings accounts and loans. If this is not practical, pretend you are a "guest speaker" who works for a local bank. Use these forms for functional reading, writing, and arithmetic.

## Family Interventions

**Primary Level.**   Encourage the parents to take their child to their bank. Ask them to show him or her the various sections of the bank: the teller stations, the desks for the managers, the safe deposit box section, and the table or counter where the various forms are located.

**Intermediate Level.**  Ask the parents to assist their youngster in opening checking and savings accounts as appropriate to his or her level of functioning.

**Secondary Level.**  Suggest to the parents that they show their youngster how they balance their checkbook. Ask them to discuss the pros and cons of taking out personal loans.

   Also, tell the parents to demonstrate some of the other services offered by the bank, such as the sale of travelers' checks, certified checks, and insurance (if available in banks in their state).

---

 ## Specific Objective D

The student rents or purchases suitable living quarters.

---

## Teacher Interventions

**Intermediate Level.**  Discuss the various living quarters that you or relatives or friends have rented or purchased. Show the student how to locate houses and apartments for rent in an area newspaper.

   If business establishments in your community provide free booklets showing real estate, use these booklets to discuss the characteristics, location, and price of both rental property and houses that are for sale.

**Secondary Level.**  At this level, discuss the decisions that must be made when establishing one's own living quarters away from the family home. Invite a real estate agent to the class, or obtain forms used in your geographic area to obtain a lease and to apply for a mortgage.

## Family Interventions

**Primary Level.**  Tell the parents to discuss rental and mortgage payments with their child whenever they write and mail these checks or when they pay by cash and receive a signed receipt for the payment.

**Intermediate Level.**  Suggest to the parents that they take their youngster to Open House days to view houses that are for sale. Ask them to pick up the information sheets or pamphlets at these houses and to review the information located there in discussions of costs, architectural features, appliances, closeness to shopping areas and houses of worship, and other factors that are pertinent to the family's financial situation, housing needs, and style preferences.

**Secondary Level.** Encourage the parents to discuss any moving plans with their youngster and to talk about the elements that must be attended to in meeting these plans. Also, suggest that they involve their youngster when they negotiate arrangements with real estate agents, movers, and financial institutions.

---

☎ ## Specific Objective E

The student purchases needed insurance from insurance agents or agencies.

---

## Teacher Interventions

**Intermediate Level.** Discuss the various types of insurance that people need to function optimally in society. Include in your discussion household, health, automobile, disability, and life insurance. Discuss the special nature of each of these types of insurance, and give the student situations in which he or she must match specific events with the applicable type of policy. (See Figure 2.52.)

**Secondary Level.** Obtain application forms and specific costs for desired coverage for each type of insurance. If the student is able, ask him or her to figure the cost of insurance under different conditions, such as the age of the applicant, the amount of coverage, and the relationship of the coverage to the premiums.

## Family Interventions

**Intermediate Level.** Ask the parents to review their insurance policies with their youngster. Tell them to make sure that they explain why they need each type of insurance and what the coverage and premiums are.

**Secondary Level.** Encourage the parents to involve their youngster in making up a monthly and yearly budget in which insurance costs are listed. Suggest that they assist the youngster in making decisions about what insurance

| Specific Event | Applicable Insurance |
|---|---|
| You have had surgery and are unable to work for several months. | Disability |
| You have a wife and two young children and wish to protect them financially if you die. | Life |
| You need insurance to cover any large medical or hospital bills. | Health |
| You have bought new furniture for your home, and you want to protect yourself against any damages that might occur from a fire. | Household |
| Your brother has just bought a new car, so he must change his coverage on his insurance policy. | Automobile |

**FIGURE 2.52.**   Specific events and applicable insurance.

will be needed if and when the youngster has established a separate home, is working, or has a family of his or her own.

---

## Specific Objective F

The student communicates with an appropriate individual for the purpose of completing relevant tax forms.

---

## Teacher Interventions

**Intermediate Level.**   Discuss with the student the nature of local, state, and federal taxes, explaining why they must be paid. Locate advertisements for tax preparers in the Yellow Pages, in newspapers, and in mailed discount coupons. Ask the student to role-play calling for an appointment with one or more tax preparers and to ask pertinent information such as charges and available appointment times.

**Secondary Level.**   Show the student the short (simple) forms of federal, state, and any local income taxes. Review the information sought and discuss how to respond to each item located in these forms. Give the student hypothetical income and deduction figures to enter on these forms.

## Family Interventions

**Intermediate Level.** Ask the parents, if possible, to take their youngster along when they go to a tax preparer and to urge him or her to listen to the information they are giving the preparer. Tell them to explain that when they work and have income over a certain amount, they will have to pay taxes.

**Secondary Level.** Ask the parents to help their youngster identify potential individuals or businesses that prepare taxes. Tell them to assist him or her in setting up and keeping records of earnings and potential deductions (e.g., doctors' bills and contributions) and in compiling this information for a tax preparer.

---

☎ ## Specific Objective G

The student negotiates agreements and contractual relationships.

---

## Teacher Interventions

**Intermediate Level.** If a behavioral contract has been drawn up between you and the student, use this contract as the basis for discussing other contracts or agreements. Also, point out that order forms are a form of contract between the person filling out the form and the company that has promised to send selected items at a given price.

**Secondary Level.** Bring to class copies of contracts that you have entered into (while blacking out any items that invade your privacy) or ones that you have simulated. Review what both parties to the contract have promised. Explain that contracts are written promises between two people or between a person and a company. Indicate that many contracts are service contracts; that is, a company or a person promises to do something and the other party to the contract agrees to pay a designated amount at a designated time, if the services are provided in the way described in the contract.

## Family Interventions

**Intermediate Level.** Ask the parents to have their youngster present when they become parties to a contract. Remind them to follow up by showing the youngster a copy of the contract and by explaining its terms. Also, encourage them to point out to the youngster the reasons why they have decided not to enter into contractual agreements.

**Secondary Level.** Encourage the parents to assist their youngster whenever he or she must enter into a contractual agreement, whether it is merely to fill out an order form or to buy furniture for his or her new residence.

---

### ☏ Specific Objective H

The student engages in an investment program with an appropriate investment adviser.

---

## Teacher Interventions

**Secondary Level.** When appropriate, show the student the stock tables in a daily or Sunday newspaper. Introduce the concept underlying the term *investment.* Explain that some people invest money they do not need so that it can earn more money.

Discuss the various bank savings accounts (including IRAs, certificates of deposit, and money market accounts) as a form of investment before discussing mutual funds, stocks, bonds, real estate, and other investments. Be sure to discuss the term *risk* as it applies to uninsured investments and the need to find a financial adviser who can be trusted.

## Family Interventions

**Secondary Level.** Ask the parents, if appropriate, to share their investment strategies with the youngster, including any bank accounts. Remind them to assist their youngster in starting an investment plan, especially if he or she is working part-time or full-time.

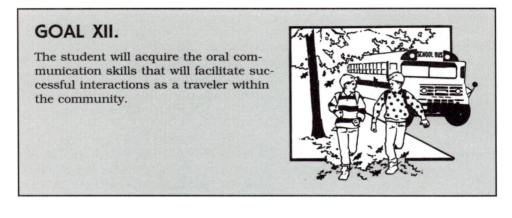

## GOAL XII.

The student will acquire the oral communication skills that will facilitate successful interactions as a traveler within the community.

# SPECIFIC OBJECTIVES

The student:

☐ A.  Asks for and follows directions, while traveling in the community, relevant to various places of interest, including work sites, and to businesses and agencies when conducting personal business, whether walking (with or without assistive devices) or using public or private transportation.

☐ B.  Asks for and follows directions to public restrooms, public telephones, drinking fountains, mailboxes, and other public conveniences.

☐ C.  Seeks the assistance, when needed, of transportation workers when using public and private transportation.

☐ D.  Asks for and follows directions to desired locations in various buildings (e.g., office buildings, museums, and flea markets), shopping centers and malls, and sports or entertainment arenas and stadiums.

☐ E.  Provides directions and assistance to other travelers when requested.

☐ F.  Plans with others for social, leisure, and vacation trips in the community and to other locations outside of his or her immediate community.

# SUGGESTED ACTIVITIES

☎ ## Specific Objective A

The student asks for and follows directions, while traveling in the community, relevant to various places of interest, including work sites, and to businesses and agencies when conducting personal business, whether walking (with or without assistive devices) or using public or private transportation.

## Teacher Interventions

**Infant and Toddler/Preschool Level.** Take the student for a walk around the classroom to locate various points of interest, including bulletin boards, work areas, learning stations, and storage areas for supplies and materials. Engage in a role play in which you pretend that you are a new student in the class and the student tells and/or shows you where the requested item is. Ask such questions as "Where are the pencils, pens, and scissors?" "Where do you keep the picture books?" and "Where is the clothes closet?"

**Primary Level.** Take the student for a walk around the school building and school grounds. Tell the student to pretend that he or she is new to the school and to ask you for directions to various points of interest, for example, "Where is the auditorium?" "the principal's office?" "the gymnasium" "the bathroom?"

**Intermediate Level.** Engage the student in a variation of a treasure hunt. Place various items around the classroom and, if practical, the school building. Name each hidden item, and say, "There is a hidden treasure, a toy truck, somewhere in the room. Before you look for it, you must ask me for the directions." Tell the student that he or she may then play with the hidden toys.

**Secondary Level.** Identify a place in the community with which the student is not familiar and that is likely to be of interest to him or her, for example, "A new shopping center has just opened. If you would like to go there with your friends, I will be happy to give you the directions."

# Family Interventions

**Infant and Toddler/Preschool Level.** Encourage the parents to give their child tasks for which he or she must find needed materials and equipment without knowing their location, for example, "Please get me the screwdriver so I can tighten this loose screw," "Please bring me the flashlight; I am having difficulty seeing which one is the correct switch," or "Please get the box of birdseed; the bird feeder is empty."

**Primary Level.** Encourage the parents to walk through the house to locate various articles and items found there, such as tools and equipment, furniture, and decorative items. Tell them to engage the child in a role play in which he or she must pretend to be a houseguest who asks where the various rooms are and where he or she can store clothing and personal grooming items.

**Intermediate Level.** Ask the parents to model asking a friend or relative the directions to a safe meeting place in the community. Encourage them to follow up by calling their youngster and asking him or her to meet them at a community site. Remind them not to provide the directions unless the youngster asks for them in an appropriate manner. Stress all aspects of safety in this activity.

**Secondary Level.** Ask the parents to identify a place in the community with which their youngster is not familiar and that is likely to be of interest to him or her, for example, "A new tennis court has been built in Druid Hill Park. If you would like to go there with your friend, Robert, who also likes to play, I will be happy to give you the directions."

---

☎ ## Specific Objective B

The student asks for and follows directions to public restrooms, public telephones, drinking fountains, mailboxes, and other public conveniences.

---

# Teacher Interventions

**Infant and Toddler/Preschool and Primary Levels.** Take the student for a walk through the school building to locate and use bathrooms, water fountains, and public telephones. Explain that these items are found in schools and other places in the community because people need (a) bathrooms or restrooms when they have to void or evacuate or need to wash their hands and face, (b) water fountains when they are thirsty, and (c) public telephones when they need to call someone while they are not at home.

**Intermediate Level.** Take the student for a walk in the community. On the walk, comment on public conveniences such as mailboxes and trash cans. While in a shopping mall or restaurant, model asking a salesperson or waiter where the restroom is. Then proceed to a new location, and ask the student whether he or she needs to go to the bathroom or restroom; if so, tell him or her to ask an appropriate person how to locate the appropriate bathroom.

**Secondary Level.** Take the student for a trip into the community to a department store or shopping mall. Tell the student that you need to call the school to speak to the secretary, and ask him or her to ask for the directions to a public telephone from a salesperson or security guard.

Also, take the student to a building in the community with public drinking fountains. Take the student to the information desk to ask the directions to the nearest water fountain.

## Family Interventions

**Infant and Toddler/Preschool Level.** Encourage the parents to take their child along with them when they mail letters at mailboxes in the community. Suggest that they purchase a toy mailbox that has slots for different-shaped blocks. Tell them to hide this toy so that the child needs to ask directions to find it.

**Primary Level.** Ask the parents to take their child on a trip to a neighborhood park or playground with working drinking fountains. Suggest that they play an active game in which all the participants are likely to become thirsty and ask the child to find directions to a water fountain.

**Intermediate Level.** Ask the parents to pack a lunch and take their youngster to a picnic area or a beach. Remind them to ask the youngster to find directions to a wastebasket so that paper plates, napkins, and other trash can be disposed of in a proper way.

**Secondary Level.** Encourage the parents to give their youngster the task of finding directions to public conveniences during trips in the community, for example, "I forgot to mail these letters. Please ask someone where the nearest mailbox is" or "We need to use the restroom. Please ask the person at the information desk where the restrooms are located."

---

☎ **Specific Objective C**

The student seeks the assistance, when needed, of transportation workers when using public and private transportation.

---

## Teacher Interventions

**Primary Level.** Ask the school bus driver to visit the class and to explain problems that he or she has experienced in transporting students to and from school. Ask this guest to concentrate on problems that passengers have had, such as wanting the window to be opened or closed, requesting that the heat or air conditioning be turned on, reporting that another student is bothering them, or informing the driver of illness.

**Intermediate Level.** Take the student to a bus depot, railroad and/or subway station, and airport, if they are available in your community. On your return to the school, role-play being a bus driver, a subway or railroad conductor, a flight attendant on an airplane, and a receptionist at an airport, as appropriate to the community.

In each of the role plays, arrange for the student to ask for assistance or information, for example, "You are a passenger on an airplane and are thirsty. What should you do? Show me!" or "You are not sure where you must get off the bus. Ask the driver to announce when you are approaching the stop where you should get off the bus to arrive at your destination." If there is a Traveler's Aid office at a bus or train station, visit it and explain the role and function of this agency.

**Secondary Level.** Show the student a videotape of the television show "Taxi" that demonstrates a passenger telling the driver his or her destination. Then role-play taking a taxi and responding to the driver's question, "Where to?" Follow up by taking the student by taxi (when it is the most efficient means of transportation and economically sensible to do so) to a place in the community. Ask the student to inform the driver of the desired destination.

## Family Interventions

**Primary Level.** Ask the parents to model seeking the assistance of appropriate people when using public and private transportation. Suggest that they point out information desks, ticket counters, schedule boards, and arrival and departure displays at terminals as well as the uniform and other clues that help to identify appropriate personnel to whom requests for needed assistance should be directed.

**Intermediate and Secondary Levels.** Ask the parents to take trips into the community during which their youngster will be expected to seek assistance and information from the appropriate personnel. Remind them to monitor the youngster to determine whether assistance is needed in identifying the appropriate personnel and in the youngster's oral language.

 ## Specific Objective D

The student asks for and follows directions to desired locations in various buildings (e.g., office buildings, museums, and flea markets), shopping centers and malls, and sports or entertainment arenas and stadiums.

## Teacher Interventions

**Primary Level.** Take the student to a shopping mall and demonstrate asking a receptionist at an information desk for the directions to a desired location in the mall. Proceed to the location and conduct the desired business. At the completion of the business, ask the student to ask a salesperson the directions to a new destination and to lead you there.

(Note: It would be helpful if you arranged this beforehand with the salesperson, who should give simple, precise, and clear directions.)

**Intermediate Level.** Take the student to an office building in the community that has a receptionist. Demonstrate asking the receptionist where a specific office may be found. Repeat the directions and follow them to the identified office.

Make sure to arrange this beforehand so that you can actually conduct some business there, for example, "You called to say my tax forms were ready. I am here to pick them up" or "I read your advertisement in the newspaper about the trip to Mexico. May I have a brochure to review?"

**Secondary Level.** At this level, arrange to go to a sports event or entertainment spectacle (e.g., an ice show, air show, or circus) in the community, and assign the student the task of getting the directions to the arena or stadium and then asking for and following the directions to the location of the seats when arriving at the arena or stadium.

## Family Interventions

**Primary Level.**  Ask the parents to take their child with them to places in the community such as libraries and hospital centers where they demonstrate asking for and following directions to a desired location, for example, "Where may I find the rental videos?" or "Where is the orthopedic clinic located?"

**Intermediate Level.**  Ask the parents to take their youngster to a department store with two or more floors. Suggest that they ask the youngster to find the location of specific departments and to lead them to the location to make a desired purchase.

**Secondary Level.**  At this level, encourage the parents to expect their youngster to obtain directions to various buildings in the community by using the telephone and then repeating the directions to them. Remind them to take this trip with the youngster at a later date, following the directions as he or she leads them to the facility and to the exact place within the facility where they wish to go.

---

### ☎ Specific Objective E

The student provides directions and assistance to other travelers when requested.

---

## Teacher Interventions

**Intermediate Level.**  With the school as the starting point, take a trip to a site in the community. On your return, review the directions to the site and role-play pretending to be a new teacher and asking the student to give you the directions to the site.

**Secondary Level.**  Arrange for a special event to take place in the classroom (e.g., a play, song and dance recital, or arts-and-crafts fair) or respond to a special event that is scheduled to take place in the school (e.g., graduation, a school concert, a basketball game) by suggesting that the student invite local and out-of-town guests. Ask the student to make real or simulated calls to the prospective guests and to give them the directions to the school.

## Family Interventions

**Intermediate Level.** Ask the parents to hold a party or other celebration for friends and relatives and to expect their youngster to give the guests the directions to the home via the telephone.

**Secondary Level.** Ask the parents to role-play being asked for directions or assistance by a fellow passenger on a bus, train, or airplane. Ask them to follow up by taking their youngster on trips where they assist other travelers, if the situation arises.

Encourage the parents to follow up any actual occurrences by engaging the youngster in a role play in which they reenact the event, with the youngster supplying the directions or assistance and the parents acting as the traveler who is in need of directions or assistance.

 ## Specific Objective F

The student plans with others for social, leisure, and vacation trips in the community and to other locations outside of his or her immediate community.

## Teacher Interventions

**Intermediate Level.** Involve the student in planning a social or leisure trip in the community. Discuss costs, means of transportation, a schedule of activities, times, clothing and other requirements, and other essential plans. Follow up by actually taking the trip.

**Secondary Level.** Obtain travel brochures from travel agents and travel clubs such as the American Automobile Association, and posters and other information from tourist agencies of nearby states and foreign countries. Use the photographs and pictures found there to identify possible vacation sites. Ask the student to join you in planning vacation trips to several possible vacation sites.

## Family Interventions

**Intermediate Level.** Encourage the parents to involve their youngster in planning family leisure-time activities that involve traveling into the community. Ask them to discuss preferences, financial and time requirements and constraints, means of transportation, and other essential elements. Remind them to follow up by actually engaging in the activity.

**Secondary Level.** If feasible, ask the parents to involve their youngster in family vacations that entail travel outside the local community. Tell them to show their youngster photographs and brochures of the proposed site and to explain why they have selected it as a possible family vacation site.

Tell them to assign the youngster, when feasible, several of the tasks involved in carrying out the plan, such as purchasing needed supplies, packing the luggage, and making the reservations.

# Sample Lesson Plan 1

**Topic Area:**  Oral Communication Skills: Preverbal

**Designed by:**  Anthony Salpino

**Time Recommended:**  20 minutes (11:40 A.M. to 12 noon)

**Student Involved:**  Mark (Infant/Toddler Program)

## Background Information:

Mark looks at my face whenever I call his name or say something that interests him. During play and at rest he makes cooing and vowel sounds. He has developed significant skill in imitating my gaze patterns when I point to, show, or move an object. However, he has not yet begun to engage in simple visual-motor rituals and routines.

## General Goal *(Oral Communication Skills I)*:

The student will develop the basic visual, motor, auditory, vocal, play, and interactive skills that facilitate the development of oral language during the Preverbal Stage (0–12 months).

## Specific Objective *(Oral Communication Skills I-B)*:

The student engages in simple visual-motor rituals and routines such as playing "Peek-a-Boo" and "Pat-a-Cake" (by 4 months).

## Lesson Objective:

When Mark is encouraged to join in the simple visual-motor ritual and routine of "Peek-a-Boo," he will join in and participate throughout the activity.

## Materials and Equipment:

A hand puppet

## Motivating Activity:

Play "Peek-a-Boo" and "Pat-a-Cake" with one of Mark's peers who is functioning at this level. Laugh and give other indications that you are having a fun time.

## Instructional Procedures:

**Initiation**—Go to Mark with a hand puppet that he enjoys playing with. Give the puppet several commands that it must follow. After playing with the puppet for several minutes, cover the puppet's eyes with its hands (which you have manipulated), and then play "Peek-a-Boo" using the puppet. Follow up by removing the puppet and covering your eyes to play "Peek-a-Boo."

**Guided Practice**—Show Mark how he can play the part of the person who is doing the peek-a-booing. Play in this way, taking turns doing the peek-a-booing. Provide encouragement and assistance as needed.

**Independent Practice**—Ask Mark to play "Peek-a-Boo" with a parent or other family member.

**Closure**—Engage Mark in the new visual-motor ritual or routine of "Pat-a-Cake" as a reward. (Note: This activity will be practiced in the follow-up lesson.)

## Assessment Strategy:

Observe Mark as he engages in the visual-motor routine of "Peek-a-Boo" to determine whether he initiates this ritual during play with you and with his parents or family members.

## Follow-Up Activity or Objective:

If Mark achieves the lesson objective, proceed to a lesson involving the visual-motor routine and ritual of "Pat-a-Cake."

## Observations and Their Instructional Insights:

# Sample Lesson Plan 2

**Topic Area:**   Oral Communication Skills: Stage I

**Designed by:**   Charles Yamaguchi

**Time Recommended:**   30 minutes (8:45–9:15 A.M.)

**Student Involved:**   Jonathan (Preschool Special Program)

## Background Information:

In his connected speech, Jonathan sometimes substitutes one sound for another, for example, /d/ for the voiced sound /th/ in words such as "there" or "that." Despite variation in his articulation, he produces the single words in his vocabulary in a consistent pattern. His one-word utterances usually express a whole idea (a holophrase); for example, he says, "Up!" to express, "Come over here and pick me up!" He says, "Car," for a car, motorcycle, bicycle, and even an airplane.

## General Goal *(Oral Communication Skills III)*:

The student will progress through Stages I–V of oral language development (18–48 months).

## Specific Objective *(Oral Communication Skills III-A)*:

The student uses two-word combinations (the beginning of syntax) of his or her first words to communicate intentions (18–27 months).

## Lesson Objective:

When placed in different situations in which he must indicate a choice, Jonathan will use a pivot word and add different words to the pivot word to indicate his or her intentions, for example, "No bed!" for "I don't want to go to bed," "No down!" for "I want you to continue holding me," "No fix!" for "It's still broken," and "No more!" for "Stop tickling me!"

## Materials and Equipment:

- two 4-ounce glasses
- a container of orange juice
- two toy cars

- assorted toys and games
- a nutritious snack
- tangible rewards

## Motivating Activity:

Place a half-full 4-ounce glass of orange juice in front of you and one in front of Jonathan, who really enjoys orange juice. Join him in drinking the juice. When you have finished drinking the juice, indicate your disappointment facially and vocally, and then say, "More juice!" Next, pour yourself another glass, and communicate in some way through gestures and other body language and speech (by saying "More juice?" with a rising inflection pattern) the question, "Would you like more juice?" If Jonathan indicates "Yes!" in some way, encourage him to say, "More juice!"

## Instructional Procedures:

**Initiation**—Give the student a favorite toy such as a toy car; you should have the same type of toy. Engage Jonathan in playing with the car, rolling it along a desktop, rolling the wheels with your hands, and having a race against your car. While he is still enjoying the game, take his car away and say, "More car?" If he says, "Yes," ask him to say, "More car!" After he does this successfully, ask him if he would like to have another race. Say to him, "If you want to have another race with me, you must tell me by saying, 'More car!'"

**Guided Practice**—Engage Jonathan in a variety of other fun or play activities that encourage him to use the pivot word "more" to indicate his intentions, for example, "More sing," when he wants you to sing a song again, and "More Rosy," when he wants to dance and sing to "Ring-Around-a-Rosy." Provide assistance and models as needed.

**Independent Practice**—Ask a classmate or instructional aide to repeat the motivating activity, initiation, and guided practice. Tell him or her not to provide a model and to require Jonathan to indicate his wants in response to the question, "Tell me what you want!"

**Closure**—Engage Jonathan and a classmate in a variety of play activities with toys. Remove the toys before they have grown tired of playing with them. Give the students a nutritious snack, and reward them for saying, "More ___!" when they want and can have more.

## Assessment Strategy:

Listen to Jonathan to determine whether he used the pivot words "More!" and "No!" to indicate his intentions.

## Follow-Up Activity or Objective:

If Jonathan achieves the lesson objective, proceed to a lesson involving the use of the pivot word "all," as, for example, in "All broke!" for "All the toys are broken!" "All clean!" for "My hands are clean!" "All gone!" for "Nothing is left!" and "All go!" for "Let's all go!"

## Observations and Their Instructional Insights:

# Sample Lesson Plan 3

**Topic Area:**    Oral Communication Skills: Stage II

**Designed by:**    Shirley Roberts

**Time Recommended:**    40 minutes (10:00–10:40 A.M.)

**Student Involved:**    Jacqueline (Primary Special Class)

## Background Information:

Jacqueline is putting two or more words together in her connected discourse. These word combinations consist primarily of nouns, verbs, and adjectives. She has just begun to occasionally use the preposition "on" when asking someone to put something on an object located near her. She is also occasionally using the preposition "in" when asking someone to get a toy or object that is out of her reach because it is in a drawer, a closet, or her toy box.

## General Goal *(Oral Communication Skills III):*

The student will progress through Stages I–V of oral language development (18–48 months).

## Specific Objective *(Oral Communication Skills III-E):*

The student comprehends prepositions that designate position in space or location of objects (21–34 months). (Note: Comprehension of "in" and "on" sometimes occurs as early as 18 months.)

## Lesson Objective:

When asked to tell where someone or something is, Jacqueline will use prepositions to indicate the position of that object or person.

## Materials and Equipment:

- a teddy bear (or other stuffed animal)
- a colorful toy
- pictures of people, animals, and objects in different positions
- a thermometer
- an empty medicine bottle
- a pillow
- assorted items as needed

## Motivating Activity:

Take various positions relative to your desk and say, "I am standing (behind) (beside) (next to) (in front of) (to the right of) (to the left of) (near) (away from) my desk." Then say to one of Jacqueline's classmates, "Let's pretend I am a puppet or a robot and you control my movements with your speech. Tell me where to stand in relation to my desk." Tell Jacqueline that she soon will also be able to describe where various objects and people are.

## Instructional Procedures:

**Initiation**—Take a colorful toy, such as a stuffed animal, and place it in various positions relative to a stationary point such as a classroom table. As you place the object, ask the question, "Where is the teddy bear?" and answer your own question, "The teddy bear is (under) (on) (over) (next to) (behind) (in front of) (to the left of) (to the right of) (in) the table." Then review each of the positions taken, ask the "where" question, and encourage Jacqueline to respond. Model each answer as needed.

**Guided Practice**—Ask Jacqueline to place a colorful toy in various positions relative to another object in the classroom. Once she has done so, ask her to tell you where the toy is. Provide assistance as needed. Then show her pictures that depict animals, people, and objects in various positions, and ask her to describe where each person, animal, or object is. Provide assistance as needed.

**Independent Practice**—Place various items around the classroom, and ask one of Jacqueline's classmates who already possesses this language skill to engage her in a role play in which the classmate pretends to be ill and in bed while asking Jacqueline where different items are, for example, "Where are my pills?" ("On the dresser"), "Where is the thermometer?" ("Next to your bed"), and "Where is the pillow?" ("In the closet").

**Closure**—Repeat the role play with different items, giving each student in the class an opportunity to play the part of the sick person with his or her "buddy."

## Assessment Strategy:

Listen to Jacqueline to make sure that she used the correct preposition to indicate the position of people and objects. Ask the parents to take Jacqueline on a tour of her home and to describe where various things are. For example, Jacqueline should be expected to say, "My toys are in the toy chest" and "My lamp is on my nightstand."

## Follow-Up Activity or Objective:

If Jacqueline achieves the lesson objective, proceed to a lesson in which prepositions are used to indicate other relationships such as direction and time.

## Observations and Their Instructional Insights:

# Sample Lesson Plan 4

**Topic Area:**   Oral Communication Skills: Stage III

**Designed by:**   Timothy McClean

**Time Recommended:**   40 minutes (10:00–10:40 A.M.)

**Student Involved:**   Ariel (Intermediate Special Class)

## Background Information:

Ariel uses the subject pronouns "I" and "you" appropriately in his conversational speech. He is also beginning to use the pronouns "he" and "she" correctly and consistently. When he wishes to indicate "we," however, he says to another person such things as "Me-you play blocks."

## General Goal (*Oral Communication Skills III*):

The student will progress through Stages I–V of oral language development (18–48 months).

## Specific Objective (*Oral Communication Skills III-O*):

The student continues to develop subject pronouns to indicate gender, plurality, and possession (23–37 months). (Note: "I" and "you" were established in earlier stages.)

## Lesson Objective:

When he is asked to tell you what he and another student are doing, Ariel will use "we" to indicate the plurality of the subject pronoun.

## Materials and Equipment:

- blocks, balls, and other toys of interest
- a delicious snack

## Motivating Activity:

Engage another student in a cooperative activity and say, "*We* are having a good time. *We* are helping each other, and when *we* finish *we* will have a delicious snack. Would you like to join us?" If the student joins you, ask Ariel and his classmate to hold each other's hand and your hand as well. Say, "*We* are going to have a good time. After *we* work together, *we* will have a delicious snack." Then stop holding hands, point to yourself, and say, "I." Next, point to each of the students, and say, "You." Then resume holding hands, and say, "We."

## Instructional Procedures:

Initiation—Begin playing with an interesting toy, such as large blocks, and say, "I want to play ball. Do you want to play, too?" If the student indicates, "Yes," say, "*We* are going to build a castle. *We* should have a lot of fun." After you have invited Ariel to join you in various play activities, ask him to invite you to join him. When you join him, ask the question, "What are *we* doing?" Encourage him to say, "*We* are ___."

**Guided Practice**—Ask Ariel to invite one or more classmates to join him in playing a game. After he and his classmates have been involved for a while, ask him what he and his classmates are doing. (Note: Ariel is likely to omit the auxiliary verb. Ignore this. Concentrate on the use of the subject pronoun "we.") Provide assistance and reinforcement as appropriate.

**Independent Practice**—Involve Ariel in a game in which the students do things first as individuals and then as part of a group or pair. (The game requires them to use the subject pronoun "I" when performing alone and "we" when joining others in the activity.)

**Closure**—Review the subject pronouns "I" and "you." Give the students a task that they must do alone and then one that they must do with others. When the two tasks are completed, ask the students to describe what they did. (Do not be concerned with the correct usage of the past tense. Concentrate on the correct usage of "I" and "we.")

## Assessment Strategy:

Listen to Ariel to determine whether he used the subject pronoun "we" correctly when referring to an activity in which he participated with others.

## Follow-Up Activity or Objective:

If Ariel achieves the lesson objective, proceed to a lesson in which he uses the subject possessive pronouns "your" and "yours."

## Observations and Their Instructional Insights:

# Sample Lesson Plan 5

**Topic Area:**  Oral Communication Skills: Stage IV

**Designed by:**  Michelle Garlitz

**Time Recommended:**  40 minutes (11:00–11:40 A.M.)

**Student Involved:**  Lynda (Intermediate Special Class)

## Background Information:

Lynda has begun to use both regular and irregular action verbs in their present and past tenses in her connected speech. She has only just begun to use copula verbs such as "feel," "smell," and "appear." As of yet, she is not producing sentences containing predicate adjectives and predicate nouns with the cupola verb "to be." She does say, on occasion, such things as "I happy," while leaving out the cupola.

## General Goal (Oral Communication Skills III):

The student will progress through Stages I–V of oral language development (18–48 months).

## Specific Objective (Oral Communication Skills III-T):

The student uses the copula verb "to be" (35–40 months).

## Lesson Objective:

When asked to describe herself, both in actuality and as part of pantomimes and role plays, Lynda will use appropriate predicate adjectives and nouns without omitting the copula "am."

## Materials and Equipment:

- a large-sized photograph of yourself
- a large-sized photograph of Lynda

## Motivating Activity:

Pantomime various states of being (e.g., happiness, sadness, anger, and fear), and then say, "I am ___." Repeat, and this time ask Lynda to identify the emotion. If Lynda identifies the emotion from the facial expression and body language demonstrated, praise her. Continue by asking what possible reasons there might be for your emotional state.

## Instructional Procedures:

**Initiation**—Repeat the pantomimes demonstrated in the motivating activity. Ask Lynda to imitate both what you do and what you say. Then name an emotion, and tell her to pantomime it and answer the question, "How do you feel?" (If she answers, "I feel ___," ask her to say it in another way.)

**Guided Practice**—Show Lynda a large-sized photograph of yourself and describe your characteristics, using the copula "am." For example, say, "I am tall." Then show her a large photograph of herself, and ask her to tell you whether she is tall or short. Tell her that there are other things you can say about yourself, such as "I am strong," "I am cold," "I am tired," "I am a teacher," "I am a mother," and "I am an American." Ask her to tell you something about herself. Provide guidance, if necessary, by giving her hypothetical situations such as "It is a very hot day. Tell me something about yourself," "You worked very hard just now. Tell me something about yourself," and "You belong to the Girl Scouts. Pretend that I don't know that and you are proud of being a Girl Scout and want me to know it."

**Independent Practice**—Assign Lynda to a buddy to play the "Pantomime Game," in which each student acts out an emotion or state of being, says, "I am ___," and then gives a possible reason for the identified state of being.

**Closure**—Ask each of the students in the class to act out the emotion or state of being that you whisper in his or her ear. Ask the students to follow up by stating the emotion or feeling while the class evaluates whether they were good "actors" or not.

## Assessment Strategy:

Listen to Lynda to determine whether she used the copula verb "am" along with predicate adjectives and predicate nouns to describe various states of being, personal qualities, and personal characteristics. Ask her parents and other family members to tell Lynda about themselves using the "I am ___" sentence structure.

## Follow-Up Activity or Objective:

If Lynda achieves the lesson objective, proceed to a lesson on using the copula "is" with the subject pronouns "he" and "she."

## Observations and Their Instructional Insights:

# Sample Lesson Plan 6

**Topic Area:**  Oral Communication Skills: Stage V

**Designed by:**  Brandon Scott

**Time Recommended:**  40 minutes (11:00–11:40 A.M.)

**Student Involved:**  Alberto (Intermediate Special Class)

## Background Information:

Alberto is now using the modals "can" and "will" in his everyday speech with a high degree of consistency. He is also beginning to use the negative "can't" as well as the modal "could" to seek permission to do things and go places and its negative form "couldn't" to indicate a lack of success in completing a task, as in "I couldn't do it."

## General Goal (Oral Communication Skills III):

The student will progress through Stages I–V of oral language development (18–48 months).

## Specific Objective (Oral Communication Skills III-FF):

The student uses the modal auxiliary verbs "could," "would," "may," "might," "should," and "must" (41–46 months).

## Lesson Objective:

When asked to do something that he does not wish to do, Alberto will refuse by saying, "I won't ___."

## Materials and Equipment:

- a newspaper or magazine article or a videotaped segment of a television news program
- a video camera and videotape
- a VCR
- a television set

## Motivating Activity:

Read or relate an incident that is currently being highlighted in the media about someone who was asked to do something against his or her will, for example, someone who was sexually exploited. Discuss how the victim, in spite of his or her wishes, failed to indicate a desire *not* to participate.

## Instructional Procedures:

**Initiation**—Relate incidents that have occurred in your life and the lives of family members, friends, and acquaintances in which the individual appropriately refused to do something by saying, "I won't ___!" Discuss refusing to smoke an offered cigarette, refusing an alcoholic drink, and rejecting the offer of illicit drugs or licit drugs prescribed for someone else. Follow up by role-playing the scenarios discussed, with one of the student's classmates acting the part of the intended victim and you playing the part of the villain.

**Guided Practice**—Repeat these vignettes. This time assign the student the part of the intended victim and the classmate the part of the villain. Tell Alberto that this is only a rehearsal because you plan to make a video later of the various scenes to show to other classes. (Check beforehand with the parents or guardian for permission and for a signed release.)

**Independent Practice**—Assign Alberto the part of the intended victim in the role plays while you videotape the performance. For one of the scenes, assign Alberto the part of the villain, for the sake of variety.

**Closure**—Ask Alberto to join you in showing the video to another class.

## Assessment Strategy:

Listen to Alberto to determine if he used the modal "won't" to indicate his refusal to do something that he did not wish to do, is against the law, or is harmful. Ask his parents and other family members to check to see whether Alberto is beginning to use the modal "won't" in his conversational speech.

## Follow-Up Activity or Objective:

If Alberto achieves the lesson objective, proceed to a lesson on using the modal "wouldn't."

## Observations and Their Instructional Insights:

# Sample Lesson Plan 7

**Topic Area:**   Functional Oral Communication Skills

**Designed by:**   Patrick Hightower

**Time Recommended:**   50 minutes (10:00–10:50 A.M.)

**Student Involved:**   Pearl (Intermediate Special Class)

## Background Information:

Pearl is beginning to use language courtesies in her communicative speech patterns. She often says, "Please," when she wants something and will repeat, "Please," when reminded to do so. She also is beginning to say, "Thank you," when receiving a desired toy or other object. She does not as yet use any other language courtesies in her speech, although she will move out of the way when an adult says, "Excuse me!"

## General Goal *(Oral Communication Skills V)*:

The student will acquire the oral communication skills that will facilitate successful performance in diverse interpersonal and social interactions.

## Specific Objective *(Oral Communication Skills V-A)*:

The student uses language courtesies.

## Lesson Objective:

When confronted with a situation that requires saying, "Excuse me!" (when interrupting someone doing something or speaking to someone or when wishing to pass in front of someone), Pearl will use this language courtesy.

## Materials and Equipment:

- tables and chairs
- books and newspapers
- a puzzle
- closed envelopes
- a storybook or newspaper article

## Motivating Activity:

Read a story to Pearl and, while reading the story, pretend to cough, sneeze, hiccup, yawn, and burp. Then say, "Excuse me!" Explain that we say, "Excuse me," when we make body noises such as burping. Ask Pearl what else she should do when she coughs, sneezes, hiccups, yawns, or burps. Praise her if she indicates that she should also cover her mouth. Proceed by encouraging her to tell about experiences she may have had when others had to excuse themselves. Tell Pearl that she is going to practice saying, "Excuse me!"

## Instructional Procedures:

Initiation—Set up pretend bus seats, using classroom chairs. Place Pearl in the aisle seat and role-play moving in front of her to get to the window seat. Remember to say, "Excuse me!"

**Guided Practice**—Repeat the initiation step, setting up pretend bus seats. This time, however, you take a seat and tell Pearl that her seat is a window seat and she must pass in front of you. If Pearl says, "Excuse me," praise her for remembering to be courteous when she has to pass directly in front of a person who is seated or standing. If Pearl fails to say, "Excuse me," tell her that she has forgotten something, and encourage her to excuse herself. Follow up with a role play of a new scene in which you have to interrupt someone who is engaged in a conversation in order to deliver a message to him or her.

**Independent Practice**—Continue the role, but this time use two tables to simulate store counters and place sample merchandise on these counters. Ask two of Pearl's classmates to stand in the aisle and talk about a purchase. Tell Pearl that she must pass between her classmates through this very narrow store aisle.

**Closure**—Review with Pearl, joining several classmates who use the language courtesy "Excuse me" consistently in different contexts. Then engage them in several different role plays, for example, interrupting someone doing a puzzle or interrupting someone reading a book or newspaper.

## Assessment Strategy:

Listen to Pearl to make certain that she says, "Excuse me!" when appropriate. Next, ask Pearl to tell what she worked on today. Encourage her to describe life situations when she should say, "Excuse me!"

## Follow-Up Activity or Objective:

If Pearl achieves the lesson objective, proceed to a lesson on using the language courtesy "I beg your pardon."

## Observations and Their Instructional Insights:

# References

Anisfeld, M. (1984). *Language development from birth to three.* Hillsdale, NJ: Erlbaum.

Bates, E. (1976). *Language and context: The acquisition of pragmatics.* New York: Academic Press.

Bates, E., Benigni, L., Bretherton, I., Camioni, L., & Volterra, V. (1979). *The emergence of symbols: Cognition and communication in infancy.* San Diego, CA: Academic Press.

Bellugi, U. (1965). The development of interrogative structures in children's speech. In K. F. Riegel (Ed.), *The development of language functions* (Report No. 8, pp. 103–137). Ann Arbor: University of Michigan Press.

Bender, M., Valletutti, P. J., & Baglin, C. A. (in press). *A functional curriculum for teaching students with disabilities: Self-care, motor skills, household management, and living skills.* (Vol I, 3rd ed.). Austin, TX: PRO-ED.

Benedict, H. (1979). Early lexical development: Comprehension and production. *Journal of Child Language, 15,* 183–200.

Bloom, L. (1970). *Language development: Form and function of emerging grammars.* Cambridge, MA: MIT Press.

Bloom, L., & Lahey, M. (1978). *Language development and language disorders.* New York: Wiley.

Braine, M. (1963). The ontogeny of English phrase structure: The first phase. *Language, 39,* 1–13.

Bretherton, I. (Ed.). (1984). *Symbolic play: The development of social understanding.* San Diego, CA: Academic Press.

Brown, R. (1973). *A first language. The first stages.* Cambridge, MA: Harvard University Press.

Clark, E. (1973). What's in a word? On the child's acquisition of semantics in his first language. In T. Moore (Ed.), *Cognitive development and the acquisition of language* (pp. 65–110). San Diego, CA: Academic Press.

Condon, W., & Sanders, L. (1974). Neonate movement is synchronized with adult speech: Interactional participation and language acquisition. *Science, 183,* 99–101.

Dore, J. (1975). Holophrases, speech acts and language universals. *Journal of Child Language, 2,* 21–40.

Dore, J., Franklin, M., & Ramer, A. (1976). Transitional phenomena in early language acquisition. *Journal of Child Language, 3,* 13–28.

Fein, G. (1981). Pretend play in childhood: An integrative view. *Child Development, 52,* 1095–1118.

Fillmore, C. (1968). The case for case. In E. Bach & R. Harmas (Eds.), *Universals in linguistic theory* (pp. 1–88). Troy, MO: Holt, Rinehart & Winston.

Finch-Williams, A. (1984). The developmental relationship between cognition and communication: Implications for assessment. *Topics in Language Disorders, 5,* 1–13.

Furuno, S., O'Reilly, K., Kosaka, C., Inatsuka, T., Allman, T., & Zeisloft, B. (1979). *HELP Chart.* Palo Alto, CA: VORT Corporation.

Gleason, H. A. (1961). *An introduction to descriptive linguistics* (rev. ed.). Troy, MO: Holt, Rinehart & Winston.

Halliday, M. A. (1975). *Learning how to mean: Explorations in the development of language.* New York: Elsevier North-Holland.

Hill, P., & McCune-Nicolich, L. (1981). Pretend play and patterns of cognition in Down's syndrome children. *Child Development, 52,* 611–617.

Kamhi, A., & Nelson, L. (1988). Early syntactic development: Simple clauses and grammatical morphology. *Topics in Language Disorders, 8,* 26–43.

Kelly, C., & Dale, P. (1989). Cognitive skills associated with the onset of multiword utterances. *Journal of Speech and Hearing Research, 32,* 645–686.

Khan, J. (1984). Cognitive training and initial use of referential speech. *Topics in Language Disorders, 5,* 14–28.

Klima, E., & Bellugi, U. (1973). Syntactic regularities in the speech of children. In C. Ferguson & D. I. Slobin (Eds.), *Studies of child language development* (pp. 333–350). Troy, MO: Holt, Rinehart & Winston.

Leonard, L., & Fey, M. (1991). Facilitating grammatical development: The contribution of pragmatics. In T. Gallagher (Ed.), *Pragmatics of language* (pp. 333–355). San Diego, CA: Singular.

Lewis, M. M. (1951). *Infant speech: A study of the beginnings of language* (2nd ed.). New York: Routledge Kegan Paul.

Lund, N., & Duchan, J. (1993). *Assessing children's language in naturalistic contexts.* Englewood Cliffs, NJ: Prentice-Hall.

Meltzoff, A., & Moore, M. (1977). Imitation of facial and manual gestures by human neonates. *Science, 198,* 75–78.

Miller, J. (1981). *Assessing language production in children.* Baltimore: University Park Press.

Morehead, D., & Ingram, D. (1973). The development of base syntax in normal and linguistically deviant children. *Journal of Speech and Hearing Research, 16,* 330–352.

Nicolich, L. (1977). Beyond sensorimotor intelligence: Assessment of symbolic maturity through analysis of pretend play. *Merrill Palmer Quarterly, 23,* 89–99.

Norris, J. (1994). Early sentence transformations and the development of complex syntactic structures. In W. Haynes & B. Shulman (Eds.), *Communication development* (pp. 295–340). Englewood Cliffs, NJ: Prentice-Hall.

Owens, R. E., Jr. (1992). *Language development: An introduction* (3rd ed.). New York: Merrill/Macmillan.

Patterson, J., & Westby, C. (1994). The development of play. In W. Haynes & B. Shulman (Eds.), *Communication development* (pp. 136–161). Englewood Cliffs, NJ: Prentice-Hall.

Quirk, R., Greenbaum, S., Leech, G., & Sartvik, J. (1989). *A comprehensive grammar of the English language.* White Plains, NY: Longman.

Reed, V. (1994). *An introduction to children with language disorders.* New York: Macmillan.

Reich, P. (1976). The early acquisition of meaning. *Journal of Child Language, 7,* 117–123.

Reich, P. (1986). *Language development.* Englewood Cliffs, NJ: Prentice-Hall.

Rescorla, L. (1980). Overextension in early language development. *Journal of Child Language, 7,* 321–335.

Rossetti, L. M. (1990). *Infant-toddler assessment: An interdisciplinary approach.* Austin, TX: PRO-ED.

Scott, C. (1988). Producing complex sentences. *Topics in Language Disorders, 8,* 44–62.

Slobin, D. (1978). Cognitive prerequisites for the development of grammar. In L. Bloom & M. Lahey (Eds.), *Readings in language development* (pp. 407–432). New York: Wiley.

Stern, W. (1924). *Psychology of early childhood up to the sixth year of age.* New York: Cambridge University Press.

Sugarman, S. (1984). The development of preverbal communication. In R. Schiefelbusch & J. Pikar (Eds.), *The acquisition of communicative competence.* Baltimore: University Park Press.

Uzgiris, I., & McVee Hunt, J. (1975). *Assessment in infancy.* Urbana: University of Illinois Press.

Valletutti, P. J., Bender, M., & Sims-Tucker, B. (in press). *A functional curriculum for teaching students with disabilities: Functional academics* (Vol. III, 3rd ed.). Austin, TX: PRO-ED.

Waterman, P., & Schatz, M. (1982). The acquisition of personal pronouns and proper names by an identical twin pair. *Journal of Speech and Hearing Research, 35,* 149–154.

Westby, C. (1980). Assessment of cognitive and language abilities through play. *Language, Speech and Hearing Services in the Schools, 11,* 154–168.

Westby, C. (1988). Children's play: Reflections of social competence. *Seminars in Speech and Language, 9,* 1–14.

Westby, C. (1991). A scale for assessing children's pretend play. In C. Schaefer, K. Gitlin, & A. Sangrund (Eds.), *Play diagnosis and assessment* (pp. 131–161). New York: Wiley.

Wilcox, S., & Palermo, D. (1974–1975). "In," "on," "under" revisited. *Cognition, 3,* 245–254.

Abbeduto, L. (1991). Development of verbal communication in persons with moderate to mild mental retardation. In N. Bray (Ed.), *International review of research in mental retardation* (Vol. 17, pp. 91–151). San Diego, CA: Academic Press.

Abbeduto, L., & Nuccio, J. B. (1991). Relation between receptive language and cognitive maturity in persons with mental retardation. *American Journal of Mental Retardation, 96,* 143–149.

Adams, C. (1990). Syntactic comprehension in children with expressive language impairment. *British Journal of Communication, 25,* 149–171.

Allen, D. A. (1989). Developmental language disorders in preschool children: Clinical subtypes and syndromes. *School Psychology Review, 18,* 442–451.

Anastasiow, N. J., Hanes, M., & Hanes, M. (1982). *Language patterns in poverty children.* Austin, TX: PRO-ED.

Andrews, M. (1991). *Voice therapy for children.* San Diego, CA: Singular.

Au, K. (1990). Children's use of information in word learning. *Journal of Child Language, 17,* 393–416.

Bashir, A. S. (1989). Language intervention and the curriculum. *Seminars in Speech and Language, 10,* 181–191.

Bates, E. (1976). Pragmatics and sociolinguistics in child language. In D. Morehead & A. Morehead (Eds.), *Normal and deficient child language* (pp. 411–436). Baltimore: University Park Press.

Beirne-Smith, M., Patton, J. R., & Ittenbach, R. (1994). *Mental retardation* (4th ed.). New York: Merrill/Macmillan.

Beitchman, J. H., & Peterson, M. (1986). Disorders of language, communication, and behavior in mentally retarded children: Some ideas on their co-occurrence. *Psychiatric Clinics of North America, 9,* 689–698.

Bernstein, D., & Tiegerman, E. (1989). *Language and communication disorders in children.* Columbus, OH: Merrill.

Biklen, D., & Schubert, A. (1991). New words: The communication of students with autism. *Remedial and Special Education, 12,* 46–57.

Blachowicz, C.L.Z. (1987). Vocabulary instruction: What goes on in the classroom? *Reading Teacher, 41,* 132–137.

Bloom, L. (1973). *One word at a time: The use of single-word utterances before syntax.* The Hague, The Netherlands: Mouton.

Bohannon, J. N., & Warren-Leubecker, A. (1989). Theoretical approaches to language acquisition. In J. B. Gleason (Ed.), *The development of language* (pp. 167–224). Columbus, OH: Merrill.

Boone, D. R. (1987). *Human communication and its disorders.* Englewood Cliffs, NJ: Prentice-Hall.

Booth, D., & Thornley-Hall, C. (Eds.). (1992). *Classroom talk: Speaking and listening activities from classroom-based teacher research.* Portsmouth, NH: Heinemann.

Booth, D., & Thornley-Hall, C. (Eds.). (1992). *The talk curriculum.* Portsmouth, NH: Heinemann.

Bricker, D., & Carlson, L. (1981). Issues in early language intervention. In R. L. Schiefelbusch & D. Bricker (Eds.), *Early language acquisition* (pp. 477–510). Baltimore: University Park Press.

Brinton, B., & Fujiki, M. (1982). A comparison of request-response sequences in the discourse of normal and language-disordered children. *Journal of Speech and Hearing Disorders, 47,* 57–62.

Brinton, B., & Fujiki, M. (1989). *Conversational management with language-impaired children.* Gaithersburg, MD: Aspen.

Britten, J. (1993). *Language and learning: The importance of speech in children's development* (2nd ed.). Portsmouth, NH: Heinemann.

Brown, R. (1968). The development of WH questions in child speech. *Journal of Verbal Learning and Verbal Behavior, 7,* 279–290.

Bruner, J. (1981). The social context of language acquisition. *Language and Communication, 1,* 155–178.

Bryen, D., & Joyce, D. (1985). Language intervention with the severely handicapped: A decade of research. *Journal of Special Education, 19,* 7–36.

Calculator, S. N. (1988). Promoting the acquisition and generalization of conversational skills by individuals with severe disabilities. *Augmentative and Alternative Communication, 4,* 94–103.

Caro, P., & Snell, M. E. (1989). Characteristics of teaching communication to people with moderate and severe disabilities. *Education and Training in Mental Retardation, 24,* 63–77.

Carter, A. (1975). The transfer of sensory motor morphemes into words. *Papers and Reports on Child Language Development, 10,* 31–47.

Casby, M. W., & Ruder, K. F. (1983). Symbolic play and early language development in normal and mentally retarded children. *Journal of Speech and Hearing Research, 26,* 404–411.

Catts, H. W. (1991). Facilitating phonological awareness: Role of speech-language pathologists. *Language, Speech and Hearing Services in Schools, 22,* 196–203.

Cavallaro, C. C. (1983). Language interventions in natural settings. *Teaching Exceptional Children, 16,* 65–70.

Cavallaro, C. C., & Bambra, L. M. (1982). Two strategies for teaching language during free play. *Journal of the Association for the Severely Handicapped, 7,* 80–92.

Chadsey-Rusch, J., Karlan, G. R., Riva, M., & Rusch, F. R. (1984). Competitive employment: Teaching conversation skills to adults who are mentally retarded. *Mental Retardation, 22,* 218–222.

Charlop, M. H., & Walsh, M. E. (1986). Increasing autistic children's spontaneous verbalizations of affection: An assessment of time delay and peer modeling procedures. *Journal of Applied Behavior Analysis, 19*, 307–314.

Chomsky, N. (1965). *Syntactic structures.* The Hague, The Netherlands: Mouton.

Chomsky, N. (1969). *The acquisition of syntax in children from five to ten.* Cambridge, MA: MIT Press.

Chomsky, N. (1972). *Studies on semantics in generative grammar.* The Hague, The Netherlands: Mouton.

Cipani, E. C., & Spooner, F. (Eds.). (1994). *Curricular and instructional approaches for persons with severe disabilities.* Des Moines, IA: Longwood.

Clark, E., & Hecht, R. (1984). Comprehension and production in language acquisition. *Annual Review of Psychology, 34*, 325–332.

Coggins, T., & Sandall, S. (1983). The communicative handicapped infant: Application of normal language and communication development. In S. G. Garwood & R. R. Fewell (Eds.), *Educating handicapped infants: Issues in development and intervention* (pp. 165–214). Gaithersburg, MD: Aspen.

Collins Block, C. D. (1993). *Teaching the language arts: Expanding thinking through student-centered instruction.* Needham Heights, MA: Allyn & Bacon.

Craig, H. (1983). Applications of pragmatic language models for intervention. In T. Gallagher & C. Prutting (Eds.), *Pragmatic assessment and language intervention issues in language* (pp. 101–127). Austin, TX: PRO-ED.

Craig, H., & Evans, J. (1989). Turn exchange characteristics of SLIO children's simultaneous and nonsimultaneous speech. *Journal of Speech and Hearing Disorders, 54*, 334–347.

Culatta, B., & Horn, D. (1982). A program for achieving generalization of grammatical rules to spontaneous discourse. *Journal of Speech and Hearing Disorders, 47*, 178–180.

Dever, R. B. (1988). Community living skills: A taxonomy of community living skills. *Exceptional Children, 55*, 395–404.

Dore, J. (1974). A description of early language development. *Journal of Psycholinguistic Research, 4*, 423–430.

Dore, J. (1986). The development of conversational competence. In R. L. Schiefelbusch (Ed.), *Language competence: Assessment and intervention* (pp. 85–96). Austin, TX: PRO-ED.

Dudley-Marling, C., & Searle, D. (1991). *When students have time to talk: Creating contexts for learning language.* Portsmouth, NH: Heinemann.

Dunst, G., & Dunst, C. (1988). Communication competence: From research to practice. *Topics in Early Childhood Special Education, 6*, 1–22.

Ervin-Tripp, S., & Gordon, D. (1986). The development of requests. In R. Schiefelbusch (Ed.), *Language competence: Assessment and intervention* (pp. 61–95). Austin, TX: PRO-ED.

Ezell, H. K., & Goldstein, H. (1991). Comparison of idioms of normal children and children with mental retardation. *Journal of Speech and Hearing Research, 34,* 812–819.

Ferguson, C. A., & Farwell, C. (1975). Words and sounds in early language acquisition: English initial consonants in the first words. *Language, 51,* 419–439.

Ferguson, C. A., Menn, L., & Stoel-Gammon, C. (Eds.). *Phonological development: Models, research, implications.* Parkton, MD: York Press.

Fey, M. E. (1986). *Language intervention with young children.* New York: Macmillan.

Fey, M. E. (1988). Generalization issues facing language interventionists: An introduction. *Language, Speech and Hearing Services in Schools, 19,* 272–281.

Fey, M. E., Warr-Leper, G., Webber, S., & Disher, L. (1988). Repairing children's repairs: Evaluation and facilitation of children's clarification requests and responses. *Topics in Language Disorders, 8,* 63–64.

Field, T. (1984). Affective and interactive disturbances in infants. In J. D. Osofsky (Ed.), *Handbook of infant development* (pp. 972–1005). New York: Wiley.

French, L., & Brown, A. (1977). Comprehension of "before" and "after" in logical and arbitrary sequences. *Journal of Child Language, 4,* 247–256.

Gallagher, T. M., & Prutting, C. (1983). *Pragmatic assessment and intervention issues in language.* Austin, TX: College-Hill.

Gallagher, T. M., & Rees, N. (1991). *Pragmatics of language.* San Diego, CA: Singular.

Gleason, J. B. (Ed.). (1993). *The development of language* (3rd ed.). New York: Merrill/Macmillan.

Goetz, L., Gee, K., & Sailor, W. (1985). Using a behavior chain interruption strategy to teach communication skills to students with severe handicaps. *Journal of the Association for Persons with Severe Handicaps, 10,* 21–38.

Goldstein, H., Wickstrom, S., Hoyson, M., Jamieson, B., & Odom, S. (1988). Effects of sociodrama script training on social and communication interaction. *Education and Treatment of Children, 11,* 97–117.

Gruenewald, L. J., & Pollak, S. A. (1990). *Language interaction in curriculum and instruction: What the classroom teacher needs to know* (2nd ed.). Austin, TX: PRO-ED.

Guess, D., Sailor, W., & Baer, D. (1978). *Functional speech and language training for the severely handicapped.* Austin, TX: PRO-ED.

Hamre-Nietupski, S., Nietupski, J., & Strathe, M. (1992). Functional life skills, academic skills, and friendship/social relationship development: What do parents of students with moderate/severe/profound disabilities value? *Journal of the Association for Persons with Severe Handicaps, 17,* 53–58.

Hargrove, P. M., & McGarr, N. S. (1993). *Prosody management of communication disorders.* San Diego, CA: Singular.

Haring, T. G., Kennedy, C. H., Adams, M. J., & Pitts-Conway, V. (1987). Teaching generalization of purchasing skills across community settings to autistic youth using videotape modeling. *Journal of Applied Behavior Analysis, 20,* 89–96.

Haring, T. G., & Lovinger, L. (1989). Promoting social interaction through teaching generalized play initiation responses to children with autism. *Journal of the Association for Persons with Severe Handicaps, 14,* 58–67.

Haring, T. G., Neetz, J. A., Lovinger, L., Peck, C. A., & Semmel, M. I. (1987). Effects of four modified incidental teaching procedures to create opportunities for communication. *Journal of the Association for Persons with Severe Handicaps, 12,* 218–226.

Hartley, L. L. (1994). *Functional approaches to cognitive-communicative deficits following traumatic brain injury.* San Diego, CA: Singular.

Hedrick, D. L., & Kemp, J. C. (1984). Guidelines for communicative intervention with younger retarded children. *Topics in Language Disorders, 4,* 58–65.

Higginbotham, D., & Yoder, D. (1982). Communication within natural conversational interaction: Implications for severely communicatively impaired persons. *Topics in Language Disorders, 2,* 1–19.

Hoffnung, A. S. (1989). The development of oral language. In P. J. Valletutti, M. McKnight-Taylor, & A. S. Hoffnung, *Facilitating communication in young children with handicapping conditions: A guide for special educators* (pp. 63–113). Austin, TX: PRO-ED.

Hoffnung, A. S. (1989). Speech and language problems and their remediation. In P. J. Valletutti, M. McKnight-Taylor, & A. S. Hoffnung, *Facilitating communication in young children with handicapping conditions: A guide for special educators* (pp. 190–225). Austin, TX: PRO-ED.

Hughes, D. (1989). Generalization from language therapy to classroom academics. *Seminars in Speech and Language, 10,* 218–230.

Hughes, F. P. (1991). *Children, play, and development.* Needham Heights, MA: Allyn & Bacon.

Hulit, L. M., & Howard, M. R. (1993). *Born to talk: An introduction to speech and language development.* New York: Merrill/Macmillan.

Hunt, N., & Marshall, K. (1994). *Exceptional children and youth: An introduction to special education.* Boston: Houghton Mifflin.

Hunt, P., Alwell, M., & Goetz, L. (1991). Establishing conversational exchanges with family and friends: Moving from training to meaningful communications. *Journal of Special Education, 25,* 305–319.

Hunt, P., Goetz, L., Alwell, M., & Sailor, W. (1986). Using an interrupted behavior chain strategy to teach generalized communication responses to students with severe disabilities. *Journal of the Association for Persons with Severe Handicaps, 11,* 196–204.

Hurtig, R., Enrud, S., & Tomblin, J. B. (1982). The communicative function of question production in autistic children. *Journal of Autism and Developmental Disorders, 12,* 57–69.

Hurvitz, J. A., Pickert, S. M., & Rilla, D. C. (1987). Promoting children's language interaction. *Teaching Exceptional Children, 19,* 12–15.

Ingram, D. (1989). *First language acquisition.* New York: Cambridge University Press.

Isenberg, J. P., & Jalongo, M. R. (1993). *Creative expression and play in the early childhood curriculum.* New York: Macmillan.

Israel, L. (1984). Word knowledge and word retrieval: Phonological and semantic strategies. In G. Wallace & K. Butler (Eds.), *Language learning disabilities in school-age children* (pp. 230–250). Baltimore: Williams & Wilkins.

James, S. L. (1990). *Normal language acquisition.* New York: Macmillan.

James, S. L., & Seebach, M. A. (1982). The pragmatic function of children's questions. *Journal of Speech and Hearing Research, 25,* 2–11.

Kaczmarek, L. (1990). Teaching spontaneous language to individuals with severe handicaps: A matrix mode. *Journal of the Association for Persons with Severe Handicaps, 15,* 160–169.

Kennedy, M. D., Sheridan, M. K., Radlinski, S. H., & Beeghly, M. (1991). Play-language relationships in young children with developmental delays: Implications for assessment. *Journal of Speech and Hearing Research, 34,* 112–122.

Kent, R., & Bauer, H. (1985). Vocalizations of one-year-olds. *Journal of Child Language, 12,* 491–526.

Kernan, K. T., & Sabsay, S. (1993). Discourse and conversational skills of mentally retarded adults. In A. M. Bauer (Ed.), *Children who challenge the system* (pp. 145–184). Norwood, NJ: Ablex.

Klein, M. D., & Briggs, M. H. (1987). Facilitating mother-infant communicative interaction in mothers of high-risk infants. *Journal of Childhood Communication Disorders, 10,* 91–106.

Koetting, J. B., & Rice, M. L. (1991). Influence of the social context on pragmatic skills of adults with mental retardation. *American Journal on Mental Retardation, 95,* 435–443.

Kysela, G., Holdgrafer, G., McCarthy, C., & Stewart, T. (1990). Turntaking and pragmatic language skills of developmentally delayed children: A research note. *Journal of Communication Disorders, 23,* 135–149.

Lahey, M. (1988). *Language disorders and language development.* New York: Merrill/Macmillan.

Lasky, E., & Katz, J. (Eds.). (1983). *Central auditory processing disorders: Problems of speech, language, and learning.* Austin, TX: PRO-ED.

Leonard, L. B. (1986). Early language development and language disorders. In G. H. Shames & E. H. Wiig (Eds.), *Human communication disorders* (2nd ed., pp. 291–330). Columbus, OH: Merrill.

Lindbloom, B., & Zetterstrom, R. (Eds.). (1986). *Precursors of early speech.* New York: Stockton Press.

Locke, J. (1983). Speech perception in the emergent lexicon: An ethological approach. In P. Fletcher & M. Garman (Eds.), *Language acquisition* (2nd ed., pp. 240–250). New York: Cambridge University Press.

Lucas, E. V. (1980). *Semantic and pragmatic language disorders.* Gaithersburg, MD: Aspen.

MacNamara, J. (1982). *Names for things: A study of human learning.* Cambridge, MA: MIT Press.

Masterson, J. J. (1993). Classroom-based phonological intervention. *Language, Speech and Hearing Services in Schools, 2,* 5–9.

McCormick, L. (1987). Comparison of the effects of a microcomputer activity and toy play on social and communication behaviors of young children. *Journal of the Division for Early Childhood, 11,* 195–205.

McCormick, L. (1990). Sequence of language and communication development. In L. McCormick & R. L. Schiefelbusch (Eds.), *Early language intervention: An introduction* (2nd ed., pp. 71–105). New York: Merrill/Macmillan.

McKeown, M. C., & Curtis, M. E. (1987). *The nature of vocabulary acquisition.* Hillsdale, NJ: Erlbaum.

McShane, J. (1980). *Learning to talk.* New York: Cambridge University Press.

McTear, M. F., & Conti-Ramsden, G. (1992). *Pragmatic disability in children.* San Diego, CA: Singular.

Messick, C. (1988). Ins and outs of the acquisition of spatial terms. *Topics in Language Disorders, 8,* 14–25.

Meyer, L. H., Peck, C. A., & Brown, L. (1991). *Critical issues in the lives of people with severe disabilities.* Baltimore: Paul H. Brookes.

Miller, G. A., & Gildea, P. M. (1987). How children learn words. *Scientific American, 257,* 94–99.

Miller, J., & Chapman, R. (1981). The relation between age and mean length of utterance in morphemes. *Journal of Speech and Hearing Research, 24,* 154–161.

Miller, L. (1989). Classroom-based language intervention. *Language, Speech and Hearing Services in the Schools, 2,* 153–169.

Mire, S. P., & Chisholm, R. W. (1990). Functional communication goals for adolescents and adults who are severely and moderately mentally handicapped. *Language, Speech and Hearing Services in Schools, 21,* 57–58.

Musselwhite, C. R. (1986). *Adaptive play for special needs children: Strategies to enhance communication and learning.* Austin, TX: PRO-ED.

Musselwhite, C. R., & St. Louis, K. W. (1988). *Communication programming for the severely handicapped* (2nd ed.). Boston: Little, Brown.

Naigles, L. (1990). Children use syntax to learn verb meanings. *Journal of Child Language, 17,* 357–374.

Nelson, N. W. (1989). Curriculum-based language assessment and intervention. *Language, Speech and Hearing Services in the Schools, 2,* 170–184.

Nelson, N. W. (1993). *Childhood language disorders in context: Infancy through adolescence.* New York: Merrill/Macmillan.

Nippold, M. A. (1985). Comprehension of figurative language in youth. *Topics in Language Disorders, 5,* 1–20.

Odom, S., & Karnes, M. (Eds.). (1988). *Early intervention for infants and children with handicaps.* Baltimore: Paul H. Brookes.

Oller, D. K. (1985). Infant vocalizations. In N. J. Anastasiow & S. Harel (Eds.), *The at-risk infant* (pp. 323–332). Baltimore: Paul H. Brookes.

Oller, D. K., Wieman, L., Doyle, W., & Ross, C. (1976). Infant babbling and speech. *Journal of Child Language, 3,* 1–12.

Olswang, L., Stoel-Gammon, C., Coggins, T., & Carpenter, R. (1987). *Assessing linguistic behaviors.* Seattle: University of Washington Press.

Orelove, F., & Sobsey, D. (1987). *Educating children with multiple disabilities: A transdisciplinary approach.* Baltimore: Paul H. Brookes.

Ostrosky, M. M., & Kaiser, A. (1991). Preschool classroom environments that promote communication. *Teaching Exceptional Children, 23,* 6–10.

Owens, R. E., Jr. (1991). *Language disorders: A functional approach to assessment and intervention.* New York: Merrill/Macmillan.

Pearl, R., Donahue, M., & Bryant, T. (1981). Learning disabled and normal children's responses to non-explicit requests for clarification. *Perceptual and Motor Skills, 53,* 919–925.

Pinker, S. (1984). *Language learnability and language development.* Cambridge MA: Harvard University Press.

Polloway, E. A., & Smith, T.E.C. (1992). *Language instruction for students with disabilities.* Denver, CO: Love.

Prizant, B., & Bailey, D. B. (1992). Facilitating the acquisition and use of communication skills. In D. B. Bailey & M. Wolery (Eds.), *Teaching infants and preschoolers with disabilities* (2nd ed., pp. 299–361). New York: Merrill/Macmillan.

Prutting, C. A., & Kirchner, D. M. (1983). Applied pragmatics. In T. M. Gallagher & C. A. Prutting (Eds.), *Pragmatic assessment and intervention issues in language* (pp. 29–64). Austin. TX: PRO-ED.

Prutting, C. A., & Kirchner, D. M. (1987). A clinical appraisal of the pragmatic aspects of language. *Journal of Speech and Hearing Disorders, 52,* 105–119.

Rieke, J. A., & Lewis, J. (1984). Preschool intervention strategies: The communication base. *Topics in Language Disorders, 5,* 41–57.

Rippich, D. N., & Spinelli, F. M. (1985). *School discourse problems.* Austin, TX: PRO-ED.

Robinson, S. M. (1989). Oral language: Developing pragmatic skills and communicative competence. In G. Robinson, J. R. Patton, E. A. Polloway, & L. Sargent (Eds.), *Best practices in mental disabilities* (pp. 133–153). Reston, VA: Council for Exceptional Children, Division on Mental Retardation.

Rogers-Warren, A., & Warren, S. (1980). Mands for verbalization: Facilitating the generalization of newly trained language in children. *Behavior Modification, 4,* 230–245.

Romer, L. T., & Schoenberg, B. (1991). Requests made by people with developmental disabilities through the use of behavior interruption strategies. *Education and Training in Mental Retardation, 26,* 70–78.

Roth, F., & Clark, D. (1987). Symbolic play and social participation abilities of language-impaired and normally developing children. *Journal of Speech and Hearing Disorders, 52,* 17–29.

Schiefelbusch, R. L. (1980). Synthesis of trends in language intervention. In R. L. Schiefelbusch & D. Bricker (Eds.), *Language intervention with children* (New Directions for Exceptional Children, No. 2, pp. 277–284). San Francisco: Jossey-Bass.

Schober-Peterson, D., & Johnson, C. (1989). Conversational topics of 4-year-olds. *Journal of Speech and Hearing Research, 32,* 857–870.

Schwartz, I. S., Anderson, S. R., & Halle, J. W. (1989). Training teachers to use naturalistic time delay. Effects of teacher behavior on the language use of students. *Journal of the Association for Persons with Severe Handicaps, 14,* 48–57.

Schwartz, S., & Miller, J. E. (1988). *The language of toys: Teaching communication skills to special needs children.* Rockville, MD: Woodbine House.

Shames, G. H., Wiig, E. H., & Secord, W. A. (1994). *Human communication disorders* (4th ed.). New York: Merrill/Macmillan.

Shea, T. M., & Bauer, A. M. (1994). *Learners with disabilities: A social systems perspective of special education.* Madison, WI: WCB Brown & Benchmark.

Shuy, R. W., & Griffin, P. (Eds.). (1978). *The study of children's functional language and education in the early years.* Washington, DC: Center for Applied Linguistics.

Simon, C. S. (Ed.). (1985). *Communication skills and classroom success.* San Diego: College-Hill.

Smith, M., & Meyers, A. (1979). Telephone skills training for retarded adults: Group and individual demonstrations with and without verbal instruction. *American Journal of Mental Deficiency, 83,* 581–587.

Snyder, L. (1984). Developmental language disorders: Elementary school age. In A. Holland (Ed.), *Language disorders in children* (pp. 129–158). Austin, TX: PRO-ED.

Squires, E. L., & Reetz, L. J. (1989). Vocabulary acquisition activities. *Academic Therapy, 24,* 589–592.

Stephens, L. (1983). *Developing thinking skills through real-life activities.* Needham Heights, MA: Allyn & Bacon.

Stern, W. (1924). *Psychology of early childhood up to the sixth year of age.* New York: Cambridge University Press.

Sternberg, L., & McNerney, C. D. (1988). Prelanguage communication instruction. In L. Sternberg (Ed.), *Educating students with severe or profound handicaps* (2nd ed., pp. 311–363). Austin, TX: PRO-ED.

Stubbs, M. (1983). *Discourse analysis: The sociolinguistic analysis of natural language.* Chicago: University of Chicago Press.

Upsur, C. (1990). Early intervention as preventive intervention. In S. Meisels & J. Shonkoff (Eds.), *Handbook of early childhood intervention* (pp. 633–650). New York: Cambridge University Press.

Van Horn, J., Monighan, P., Sales, B., & Alward, K. R. (1993). *Play at the center of the curriculum.* New York: Macmillan.

Verriour, P. (1984). The reflective power of drama. *Language Arts, 61,* 125–130.

Vihman, M., Macken, M., Miller, R., Simmons, H., & Miller, J. (1985). From babbling to speech: A reassessment of the continuity issue. *Language, 61,* 397–445.

Wald, P. M. (1976). Personal and civil rights of mentally retarded citizens. In M. Kindred, J. Cohen, D. Penrod, & T. Shaffer (Eds.), *The mentally retarded citizen and the law* (pp. 20–30). New York: Free Press.

Wallace, G., Cohen, S. B., & Polloway, E. A. (1987). *Language arts: Teaching exceptional students.* Austin, TX: PRO-ED.

Warren, S. F., & Gazdag, G. (1990). Facilitating early language development with milieu procedures. *Journal of Early Intervention, 14,* 62–83.

Warren, S. F., & Kaiser, A. P. (1988). Research in early language intervention. In S. L. Odom & M. B. Karnes (Eds.), *Early intervention for infants and children with handicaps: An empirical base* (pp. 89–108). Baltimore: Paul H. Brookes.

Warren, S. F., & Reichle, J. (Eds.). (1992). *Causes and effects in communication and language intervention.* Baltimore: Paul H. Brookes.

Warren, S. F., & Rogers-Warren, A. (Eds.). (1985). *Teaching functional language: Generalization and maintenance for adults with developmental skills.* Baltimore: University Park Press.

Waterman, P., & Schatz, M. (1982). The acquisition of personal pronouns and proper names by an identical twin pair. *Journal of Speech and Hearing Research, 35,* 149–154.

Webber, M. S. (1981). *Communication skills for exceptional learners.* Gaithersburg, MD: Aspen.

Werker, J. F., & Tees, R. C. (1992). The organization and reorganization of human speech perception. *Annual Review of Neuroscience, 15,* 377–402.

Wiig, E. H. (1982). Communication disorders. In N. G. Haring (Ed.), *Exceptional children and youth* (3rd ed., pp. 81–109). New York: Merrill/Macmillan.

Wiig, E. H. (1990). Language disabilities in school-age children and youth. In G. H. Shames & E. H. Wiig (Eds.), *Human communication disorders* (3rd ed., pp. 193–222). New York: Merrill/Macmillan.

Wiig, E. H., & Freedman, E. (1993). *The word book: Developing words-by-concepts.* Columbus, OH: Macmillan/Science Research Associates.

Wiig, E. H., Freedman, E., & Secord, W. A. (1992). Developing words and concepts in the classroom: A holistic-thematic approach. *Intervention in School and Clinic, 27,* 275–285.

Winitz, H. (1969). *Articulatory acquisition and behavior.* New York: Appleton-Century-Crofts.

Wolery, M., & Bailey, D. B. (1989). Assessing play skills. In D. B. Bailey & M. Wolery (Eds.), *Assessing infants and preschoolers with handicaps* (pp. 428–446). Columbus, OH: Merrill.

Wood, B. S. (1976). *Children and communication.* Englewood Cliffs, NJ: Prentice-Hall.

Dever, R. B. (1988). *A taxonomy of community living skills.* Washington, DC: American Association on Mental Retardation.

Dinkmeyer, D. D. (1972). *Developing Understanding of Self and Others (DUSO).* Circle Pines, MN: American Guidance Service.

Doyle, E. (1980). *Skills for Daily Living Series.* Baltimore: Media Materials.

Dunn, L. M., Horton, K. B., & Smith, J. O. (1982). *Peabody Language Development Kits.* Circle Pines, MN: American Guidance Service.

Engelmann, S., & Osborn, J. (1976). *Direct Instruction for Teaching and Remediation (DISTAR).* Chicago: Science Research Associates.

Falvey, M. (1989). *Community-based curriculum: Instructional strategies for students with severe handicaps.* Baltimore: Paul H. Brookes.

Ford, A., Schnoor, R., Meyer, L., Davern, L., Black, J., & Dempsey, P. (1989). *The Syracuse community-referenced curriculum guide for students with moderate and severe disabilities.* Baltimore: Paul H. Brookes.

Hanna, R. P., Lippert, E. A., & Harris, A. B. (1982). *Developmental communication curriculum.* San Antonio, TX: The Psychological Corporation.

Hannon, K. E., & Thompson, M. A. (1992). *Life skills workshop: An active program for real-life problem solving.* East Moline, IL: LinguiSystems.

Hoskins, B. (1987). *Conversations: Language intervention program for adolescents.* Allen, TX: Developmental Learning Materials.

Johnston, E. B., Weinrich, B. D., & Johnson, A. R. (1984). *A sourcebook of pragmatic activities.* Tucson, AZ: Communication Skill Builders.

Kelner, L. B. (1993). *The creative classroom: A guide for using creative drama in the classroom, PreK–6.* Portsmouth, NH: Heinemann.

MacDonald, J. D., & Horstmeier, D. S. (1978). *Environmental Language Intervention Program (ELIP).* San Antonio, TX: The Psychological Corporation.

Marquis, M. A. (1988). *Pragmatic language trivia.* Tucson, AZ: Communication Skill Builders.

Nurss, J. R., & McGauvran, M. E. (1987). *Handbook of skill development activities for young children.* San Antonio, TX: The Psychological Corporation.

Owens, R. E., Jr. (1982). *Program for the Acquisition of Language (PALS).* San Antonio, TX: The Psychological Corporation.

Richey, J. (1978). *Drugstore language: A survival vocabulary.* Hayward, CA: Janus Books.

Richey, J. (1979). *Clothing language: A survival vocabulary.* Hayward, CA: Janus Books.

Richey, J. (1980). *Banking language: A survival vocabulary.* Hayward, CA: Janus Books.

Richey, J. (1980). *Credit language: A survival vocabulary.* Hayward, CA: Janus Books.

Richey, J. (1980). *Job application language: A survival vocabulary.* Hayward, CA: Janus Books.

Richey, J. (1980). *Restaurant language: A survival vocabulary.* Hayward, CA: Janus Books.

Richey, J. (1980). *Supermarket language: A survival vocabulary.* Hayward, CA: Janus Books.

Ritter, J. (1993). *The world is a wild place: When you share life experiences.* North Billerica, MA: Curriculum Associates.

Semel, E., & Wiig, E. H. (1982). *Clinical Language Intervention Program (CLIP).* San Antonio, TX: The Psychological Corporation.

Simon, C. (1980). *Communication competence: A functional-pragmatic language program.* Tucson, AZ: Communication Skill Builders.

Stiefel, B. (1987). *On my own with language.* East Moline, IL: LinguiSystems.

Tiedt, S., & Tiedt, I. (1978). *Language arts activities for the classroom.* Needham Heights, MA: Allyn & Bacon.

Wiig, E. H. (1982). *Let's Talk: Developing prosocial communication skills.* Columbus, OH: Merrill.

Wiig, E. H., & Bray, C. (1983). *Let's Talk for Children (LTC).* San Antonio, TX: The Psychological Corporation.

Wilcox, B., & Bellamy, G. T. (1987). *The Activities Catalog: An alternative curriculum for youth and adults with severe disabilities.* Baltimore: Paul H. Brookes.

Wilcox, B., & Bellamy, G. T. (1987). *A comprehensive guide to the Activities Catalog: An alternative curriculum for youth and adults with severe disabilities.* Baltimore: Paul H. Brookes.

Willoughby-Herb, S. J., & Neisworth, J. T. (1983). *HICOMP preschool curriculum.* San Antonio, TX: The Psychological Corporation.

# SOURCES OF TOYS, GAMES, BOOKS, AND OTHER HANDS-ON MATERIALS

American Guidance Service
4201 Woodland Road
P.O. Box 99
Circle Pines, MN 55014

Communication Skill Builders
3830 East Bellevue
P.O. Box 42050-CS4
Tucson, AZ 85733

Curriculum Associates, Inc.
5 Esquire Road
North Billerica, MA 01862

EBSCO Curriculum Materials
P.O. Box 11542
Birmingham, AL 35202

Educational Activities, Inc.
1937 Grand Avenue
Baldwin, NY 11520

EMC Corporation
300 York Avenue
St. Paul, MN 55101

Gryphon House
P.O. Box 275
Mt. Rainier, MD 20712

Guidance Associates
Communications Park, Box 3000
Mount Kisco, NY 10549

Lakeshore Learning Materials
2695 East Dominguez Street
Carson, CA 90749

LinguiSystems, Inc.
3100 Fourth Avenue
P.O. Box 747
East Moline, IL 61244

Milton Bradley Company
433 Shaker Road, East
Longmeadow, MA 01028

NASCO
901 Janesville Avenue
P.O. Box 901
Fort Atkinson, WI 53538

The Psychological Corporation
555 Academic Court
San Antonio, TX 78204

Puffin Books
375 Hudson Street
New York, NY 10014

S&S Company
P.O. Box 513
Colchester, CT 06415

Skylight Publishing, Inc.
200 East Wood Street, Suite 274
Palatine, IL 60067

Story House Corporation
Bindery Lane
Charlotteville, NY 12036

Teacher Book Club
P.O. Box 6009
Duran, NJ 08370

Teacher Ideas Press
Department F943
P.O. Box 6633
Englewood, CO 80155

Therapy Skill Builders
3830 East Bellevue
P.O. Box 42050-TS4
Tucson, AZ 85733

Triarco Arts and Crafts, Inc.
14650 28th Avenue
Plymouth, MN 55447

# Notes

# Notes

# Notes

# Notes

# Notes